ION
MAN
AGE
MENT

FASH ION MAN AGE MENT

Annick Schramme

Trui Moerkerke

Karinna Nobbs

LANNOO
CAMPUS

PREFACE

FASHION MANAGEMENT IN THE AGE OF GLOBALIZATION

Jennifer Craik

"Fashion is something so ugly that we have to change it every six months" Oscar Wilde

If fashion is so transient and trend based, why do we bother to check out next season's styles or update our wardrobes when we already have a closet full of clothes? Despite the over supply of clothes we have, individual expenditure on clothes continues to grow – as does the quantity of clothes that goes into land fill. The speed of the fashion industry has increased as it becomes more globalized and this poses major challenges for fashion management – the theme of this important book. How best can an aspiring fashion designer establish a viable career and business in this scenario?

The field of fashion management has always been regarded as much less sexy than the fields of fashion design and fashion merchandising (as noted by authors such as Atkinson 2012; Brunot and Posner 2011; San Martin 2009; Shaw & Koumbis 2014). The most common lament of teachers of fashion is that students resist lectures and courses on fashion business and fashion management because they just want to design "nice" clothes. It is not until a few years after graduation that they fully comprehend the complexity and toughness of the industry they have entered. Indeed, as the number of students studying fashion increases globally so does the need for educators to alert students to the realities of issues concerning fashion management as every aspect of the industry becomes increasingly global.

The phenomenon of globalization is exemplified by fashion perhaps more so than by any other industry. And yet, fashion studies have largely concentrated on the "art" rather than "science" side of fashion (Choi 2012). According to Xiao-Ming Tao from Hong Kong Polytechnic University, the scope of fashion management is "broad, complex, mathematical and highly technical" (Tao 2012: xv).

Fashion is one of the three most important global industries and is characterised by its long supply chain, the management of which is vital to the success of industry players (Tao 2012: xv). World trade in textiles and clothing is around US $350 billion. Textile and clothing industries worldwide represented 7 per cent of total world exports in 2004. Fashion management has become even more complex with successive relocation to low-cost supply sources, free trade policies, and the spike in the number of global fashion businesses. In addition, a number of new challenges have arisen in the form of "environmental sustainability, fast fashion models, use of advanced Information Technologies, social responsibility, and product innovations and development" (Tao 2012: xv).

The challenges for teaching and researching the subject of fashion management are substantial, especially balancing the inclination of students to focus on the stylistic and trend aspects of fashion with their need to grasp the fundamentals of business practice, supply chain management, and realities of fashion merchandising and retailing. Fashion Management makes a major contribution to that end, bringing together expertise in national and independent fashion design; financial planning; setting up and developing a business; developing collections on a seasonal timetable; meeting new techniques of merchandising and marketing; ensuring appropriate legal and intellectual property measures; and choosing viable promotional and distribution channels in an increasingly competitive and internationalized context. These issues have been explored in an important comparative analysis of recent transformations in the fashion industries of France, Italy and the United States of America (Djelic & Ainamo 1999).

A hardnosed approach is required to achieve a successful fashion business. This involves a number of compelling issues: conducting realistic risk analysis; attracting backers and investors to ensure cash flow; managing quality control at all stages of design and production; handling supply chain contractors and sub-contractors; conducting or commissioning trend analysis and forecasting; determining schedules of forward planning; monitoring stock and distribution processes and levels; adopting multiple approaches to retailing; and researching trends in consumer behaviour and attitudes (Brun & Castelli 2008; Caniato et al. 2011).

A particular strength of this book is its focus on Belgian fashion and its place in the global fashion industry. In the past few decades, Belgian fashion has received international acclaim as a niche and as a highly successful incubator for new fashion design and future-oriented designers (Gimeno Martinez 2007; de Bruyn & Ramiol 2007). It has gained an enviable reputation as a hub for independent designers who offer something genuinely distinctive and different from mainstream fashion. Synonymous with the so-called Antwerp Six, the Belgian fashion industry has attracted subsequent generations of young designers and today attracts applicants from around the world to study fashion design.

Complementing the rigorous and experimental approach to fashion design pedagogy is the emphasis on understanding the realities of the fashion industry and developing guidelines and schemes to assist the entry of graduates into the industry. While many young designers have their hearts set on making it as an independent designer catering for a niche clientele and market, they are competing in a highly commercial environment of fast fashion, global brands and flagship domination of the marketplace (Bhardwaj & Fairhurst 2010; Toktli 2008). Moreover, the emergence of "omni-channel" retailing (also called "e-tailing" or "seamless retailing") involves multiple forms of connecting with and selling to consumers including individual customers and niche client groups. These changes are transforming the foundations of fashion marketing and customer experiences and expectations (Posner 2011). These new competitors are savvy operators who may commit to the discourse of sustainability in principle but are constrained by the realities of bottom line turnover and profit margins. And although an increasing number of designers and labels are adopting Corporate Social Responsibility (CSR) charters, Free Trade practices, and transparent supply chains, the nature of this fast-paced industry mitigates against a comprehensive overhaul of mainstream fashion practices (Minney 2012).

These developments – at one level – might be read as the death knell for independent designers, however the advent of mass customisation (MC) puts consumers at the centre of fashion and offers opportunities for small- to medium-sized fashion businesses (SMEs) to target specific niche markets (demographics and lifestyles) and offer products and services that are increasingly customised to – and requested by – particular consumer groups.

New models for fashion designers include: the promotion of "micro-preneurs" who focus on exclusive products for a connected niche clientele; funding new ventures through crowdsourcing/crowdfunding; pop-up stores and fashion performance events; developing brand, online and store personalities that appeal to target consumer groups; and working in design teams that offer a variety of skills and products (Brabham 2008; Brengman 2009; McRobbie 2004; Radder 1996).

But how realistic are these scenarios in global fashion culture? The concept of globalization replaced the concept of modernization to refer to the connectivity between cultures, places and peoples increased and appeared to dilute national, ethnic, ideological and other differences. Yet it also raised the spectre of global cultural homogeneity, which, in the case of fashion, meant that we would all be wearing the same thing in the future. As a counterpoint, the idea of "glocalization" developed to describe the production of goods and styles that suit local taste preferences and are designed to compete with global brands and products. "Local" high-end couture is an example of glocalization (Ritzer 2003).

Glocalization and its companions – localisation and hybridity – are intended to "subvert, resist, and dissolve... global cultural asymmetry" (Chew 2010: 569). The positive spin put on the promise of glocalization is that it will result in "unique outcomes in different geographic areas" that will allow diverse cultural products and symbolism to flourish (Chew 2010: 193).

Two other terms have been coined to describe subsets of this phenomenon, namely, the "grobalization of something", that is, "the diffusion of local products across the globe" and the "glocalization of nothing", that is, the application of the practices of global corporations to produce inauthentic local products for "uninformed global consumers" (Chew 2010: 568; cf. Ritzer 2003). Examples of "grobalization" are the global reach of Hong Kong originated fashion brand, Shanghai Tang, or the global popularity of versions of the cheong sam; while examples of "glocalization of nothing" include global products that are localized in predictable ways (e.g. souvenir T-shirts and tourist ephemera).

Chew has contrasted these with the concept of "lobalization" (fakes, pass-offs and inspired products) that are approximate versions of products whose appearance confuses the consumer (a Versuce as opposed to a Versace labelled product or KLDY brand confused with DKNY) (Chew 2010: 560). Such products are produced locally for local markets though may appear to have foreign (Designed in Italy) or trans-national (marketed through Paris) referents. Menswear made in China and sold to mid-range consumers is an example of the pass-off phenomenon.

Yet, while this may seem to open up a "hybrid culture to facilitate an alternative in-between space that avoids the dangers of both indigenous chauvinism and global homogenization" (Chew 2010: 564), it arguably perpetuates global cultural asymmetry and undermines the opportunities for local creative industries such as fashion, which remain "undeveloped" (Chew 2010: 570).

In this account, the impact of globalizing trends in fashion management are pervasive and limit the potential for anti-global, micro, niche and place-specific fashion businesses. Should this be so, the need for infusing fashion education with a robust grasp of the practices and relevance of fashion management is stronger than ever. The present book, *Fashion Management*, is a vital contribution to this new approach to the business of fashion.

REFERENCES

Atkinson, M. (2012) *How to Create Your Final Collection*. London: Laurence King.

Bhardwaj, V. & Fairhurst, A. (2010) Fast Fashion; Response to Changes in the Fashion Industry. *The International Review of Retail, Distribution and Consumer Research*, 20 (1), 165-173.

Brabham, D. (2008) Crowdsourcing as a Model for Problem Solving: An Introduction and Cases. *Convergence: The International Journal of Research into New Media Technologies*, 14 (1), 75-90.

Brengman, M. (2009) Determinants of Fashion Store Personality: A Consumer Perspective. *Journal of Product and Brand Management*, 18 (5), 346-355.

Brun, A. & Castelli, C. (2008) Supply Chain Strategy in the Fashion Industry: Developing a Portfolio Model Depending on Product, Retail Channel and Brand. *International Journal of Production Economics*, 116, 169-181.

Brunot, T. nd. What Challenges Do Fashion Merchandisers Face? Demand Media, http://smallbusiness.chron.com/challenges-fashion-merchandisers-face-77698.html.

Caniato, F., Caridi, M., Castelli, C. & Golini, R. (2011) Supply Chain Management in the Luxury Industry: A First Classification of Companies and Their Strategies. *International Journal of Production Economics*, 133, 622-633.

Chew, M. (2010) Delineating the Emergent Global Cultural Dynamic of "Lobalization": The Case of Pass-off Menswear in China. *Continuum: Journal of Media and Cultural Studies*. 24 (4), 559-571.

Choi, T.-M. (2012) (ed.) *Fashion Supply Chain Management: Industry and Business Analysis*, Hershey. Pennsylvania: IGI Global, http://www.igi-global.com/book/fashion-supply-chain-management/49569.

De Bruyn, T. & Ramiol, M. (2007) *"Wonderwear". Organisational Case Study on Design in the Clothing Industry – Belgium*. WORKS project, CIT3-CT-2005-006193, Leuven, BE.

Djelic, M.-L., Ainamo, A. (1999) The Coevolution of New Organizational Forms in the Fashion Industry: A Historical and Comparative Study of France, Italy, and the United States. *Organization Science*, 10 (5), 622-637.

Gimeno Martinez, J. (2007) Selling Avant-garde: How Antwerp Became a Fashion Capital (1990-2002). *Urban Studies*, 44 (12), 2449-2464.

McRobbie, A. (2004) *British Fashion Design: Rag Trade or Image Industry?* London: Taylor & Francis.

Minney, S. (2012) *Naked Fashion. The New Sustainable Fashion Revolution*. London: New Internationalist Publications.

Posner, H. (2011) *Marketing Fashion*. London: Laurence King.

Radder, L. (1996) The Marketing Practices of Independent Fashion Retailers: Evidence from South Africa. *Journal of Small Business Management*, 34 (1), 78-84.

Ritzer, G. (2003) Rethinking Globalization: Glocalization/Grobalization and Something/Nothing. *Sociological Theory*, 21 (3), 193-209.

San Martin, M. (2009) *How to Be a Fashion Designer*. Singapore: Page One.

Shaw, D. & Koumbis, D. (2014) *Fashion Buying. From Trend Analysis to Shop Floor*. London: Bloomsbury.

Tao, X.-M. (2012) Preface. In T.-M. Choi (2012) (ed.) *Fashion Supply Chain Management: Industry and Business Analysis*, Hershey, Pennsylvania: IGI Global, http://www.igi-global.com/book/fashion-supply-chain-management/49569. Toktli, N. (2008) Global Sourcing: Insights from the Global Clothing Industry – The Case of Zara, a Fast Fashion Retailer. *Journal of Economic Geography*, 8, 21-38.

Ann Demeulemeester
FW 13-14

INTRODUCTION

Annick Schramme

Both from a societal and economic perspective, fashion is important. It is a critical part of the so-called creative industries. Fashion plays also a significant role in the European economy. Louis Vuitton, Dolce & Gabbana, Stella McCartney, H&M and Zara are just a few of the well-known fashion labels created in Europe. On average, consumers spend €700 per year on fashion. In the past three years, the clothing and textile industry represented a turnover of €562 billion with 870,000 companies involved in the process of wholesale, retail and manufacturing (Eurostat 2012). Despite the financial crisis, the European Union clothing market will exceed €300 billion in 2016 (Verdict Research 2012). Within the thousands of companies involved in the European fashion industry, 5.4 million people are employed. According to a country ranking of clothing expenditure in the 27 members of the EU, Belgium comes in at the 8th place (Verdict Research 2012). Across the globe this picture grows considerably larger – fashion becomes a multi-trillion dollar industry employing an estimated 26 million people globally (Hines & Bruce 2007). Textile and clothing industries worldwide represented 7 per cent of total world export in 2004. These numbers suggest that it is a successful industry too and one of the most dynamic and internationally competitive creative industries.

Also in Flanders the fashion industry represents an important part of the creative industries. If we look at the overall numbers of the creative industries in Flanders (Demol et al. 2013), the creative industries represent 3% of the GDP; 13,2% of self-employed persons are working in the creative industries and they represent 3% of the total employees in Flanders.

Fashion industry in Flanders	Self-employed persons (#)	Employers (#)	Employees (FTE)	Turnover (€)	Added Value (€)
Creation and production	1.753	332	3.540	1.734.336.830	311.878.870
Distribution	2.276	604	4.993	2.284.515.758	454.195.059
Retail	3.243	3.022	19.394	4.540.558.811	1.169.386.187
TOTAL	7.272	3.958	27.927	8.559.411.399	1.935.460.116

Figure 1. | Value chain of the Flemish fashion industry 2010 (Schrauwen, Demol, Van Andel, Schramme 2013).

	Self-employed persons (#)	Employers (#)	Employees (FTE)	Turnover (€)	Added Value (€)
Fashion	7.272	3.958	27.927	8.559.411.399	1.935.460.116
Creative Industries	52.882	8.586	73.862	22.602.952.389	6.902.263.728

Figure 2. | Employment, turnover and added value in 2010 of Flemish fashion industry compared to that of creative industries as a whole (Schrauwen, Demol, Van Andel, Schramme 2013).

When we look at the share of fashion in the creative industries, we can ascertain that the fashion industry contributes 30% of the total turnover of the creative industries in Flanders, and 35% of the value added. The fashion industry is therefore one of the most important creative industries in Flanders.

Yet a closer look reveals a number of concerns – not least of which is a move towards globalization, homogenization and vertical and horizontal integration, without much thought to the consequences – economic and creative – for the local industry.

In this book we look ahead and critically explore the impact of globalization on the fashion industry. More specifically, we focus on the local (Belgian) fashion industry and the situation of the independent designer. How can he/she survive in this globalized fashion industry, where luxury labels and global retailers dominate? While most publications focus on the luxury companies, this book aims to concentrate on the business situation of the *independent creative designer*. The main question is whether there is still a future for young independent designers in this globalized world. What are the critical success factors – and the potential pitfalls – that designers must take into account when they have their own label? A career in the fashion industry can be tough. When we, as consumers, buy a shirt or a dress, we often don't realize how much effort it has cost and how many actors are involved in this complex industry.

Belgium is renowned for its independent high-end designers, particularly since the rise of the "Antwerp Six" in the eighties. The Textile Plan of the Flemish government in 1981 gave new life to the ailing textile industry. Together with the marketing campaign "Fashion, this is Belgium" and the creation of the "Golden Spindle" award, the Flemish fashion industry experienced a boost. Thanks to the very personal and stubborn style of some Belgian fashion designers, and to the strong artistic reputation of the Fashion Department of the Royal Academy of Fine Arts in Antwerp, Belgian fashion continues to have a strong presence on the global scene. This was proved once more in 2013 when the Royal Academy celebrated its 350th anniversary, while the fashion department has existed for 50 years.

With this book we look ahead at the business reality behind independent creative designers like Walter Van Beirendonck, Dries van Noten, Ann Demeulemeester and Raf Simons. How did they develop their business in a globalizing fashion world and how do they operate today? Trui Moerkerke (from the governmental organization Flanders District of Creativity) tells their stories – and others – by means of short interviews woven through the book.
The attentive reader will notice that the concept of "Belgium" or "Flemish" fashion will be alternated. When we use the term "Belgian", we are mostly referring to the way the designers communicate about themselves. Abroad, they mostly present themselves as "Belgian designers". The concept of "Flemish fashion" refers to where the designers originate. When we speak of "Antwerp fashion", we refer to the educational background of a designer at the fashion department of the Royal Academy in Antwerp. Some of these designers still live in Antwerp.

In this book you will distinguish TWO PARTS. One part focuses on global tendencies in the fashion industry with contributions of different young academics, like Karinna Nobbs, Francesca Rinaldi, and others. As Jennifer Craik describes in the foreword, the context of the fashion industry has changed fundamentally since the eighties. Tendencies towards globalization, digitization and technical innovation have had a huge impact on all the actors within the fashion industry and the value chain (creation, production, distribution, retail and consumption).

The second part of this book is written from the perspective of the locally based, independent designer with contributions from fashion professionals who have a lot of experience on the ground. These fashion experts are familiar with the challenges faced by independent designers and here, for the first time, a compilation of their expertise and insights is available to both aspiring designers and a broader public. It also hopes to offer a hand up to young designers seeking to find their way in the turbulent, tough and highly competitive world of fashion.

CHAPTER ONE of part one offers an overview of the structural segments of the fashion industry. When talking about fashion, people mostly think of "the fashion industry" as a whole. In reality the fashion industry contains a number of different industries or "segments". To position your label within the fashion industry, it is important to understand the particular environment in which your firm operates. Schrauwen & Schramme identify four main segments. At one end of the spectrum, you have the highly globalized luxury companies and concerns. These companies have a huge turnover and generate money primarily from the merchandising of perfumes, cosmetics and accessories linked to their labels. This segment is of course present in the Flemish market, but luxury labels of Belgian origin are rare. Labels from Belgium tend to be more present in the other segments, namely the middle market and retailers. However, at the other end of the spectrum, is the independent creative designer – the most typical expression of the Belgian Fashion industry. In CHAPTER ONE, the value chain and business model of each segment is clarified. The authors also emphasize that the differences between the segments of the fashion industry are not always strict. Companies are increasingly making use of innovative strategies to break out of their segment and to reach new client groups.

In CHAPTER TWO Karinna Nobbs outlines the impact of globalization on the retail industry and on the rise of new retail formats. In particular, she reflects on two types of specialty retail format: the phenomenon of the "flagship store" and, more recently, the "pop up store". The chapter begins by outlining and defining the retail format concept and explaining its wider purpose for a fashion brand. Then the history and characteristics of both the flagship and the pop up are discussed and interesting examples of each are presented. Because of the impact of digitization on the organisation of the retail industry (Hines & Bruce 2007), brands need to give consumers a reason to visit a brick-and-mortar store (Nobbs et al 2012). This shift has forced change and innovation within the fashion retail sector. Retail organizations are obliged to constantly renew and revitalize themselves and their identities (Hines & Bruce 2007).

In the past decade fashion companies have been experiencing a dramatic transition in their relationship with consumers. In order to maintain a point of differentiation, fashion brands increasingly have to seek new and innovative methods of capturing the hearts, minds and wallets of savvy consumers.

In CHAPTER THREE Francesca Rinaldi explores the impact of social media on these relationships. The emergence of "click and mortar" retailers – traditional retailers offering Internet sites – has stimulated Internet shopping. The new consumers increasingly trust online recommendations and feel comfortable sharing their choices and ideas. Boundaries between retailers, manufacturers and dotcom companies are becoming blurred. Alongside this re-organization of the industry, consumers seem to be less loyal (Hines & Bruce 2007). Consumers do "shop around" for the best deal, based on price, quality, convenience or brand awareness, but how they conduct online fashion shopping is not predictable. The "old" paradigms of management thinking in the fashion industry are therefore being challenged. Quick response, flexible approaches and the constant drive to offer innovative products to consumers have to be managed effectively (Hines & Bruce 2007).

Consumers want also to be more informed about the origin of the product, manufacturing process and the labour used. In a second section Rinaldi focuses on environmental and social sustainability as an emerging topic in the communication strategy of the fashion companies. The new consumer is increasingly willing to participate in direct communication and dialogue with the company. Social media galvanised this revolution in business-to-client communication. Communicating fashion in this new era requires that companies develop new competences, exhibit greater transparency of their supply chain and increasingly invest in the online channel.

There are often press reports about exploitation in the industry. For example, clothing manufactured in the underdeveloped parts of the world is exported to markets in the developed world to be sold at very high prices. Workers in these factories often exist on subsistence wages. Their employers are a part of a global supply network to satisfy demand in markets in the developed world. Media attention surrounding these kinds of issues has increased. A company that operates in the fashion industry should be prepared to answer a series of questions: How does it reduce environmental impact? How does it contribute to the economic development of the area (district, region, country) in which it operates? How should it interact with stakeholders through new media? What can be given back to the territory of origin, local art and culture that have been sources of inspiration for the stylistic identity of the brand? Given the current process of globalization and outsourcing, how does the company ensure that the rights of workers in all countries in which it operates (produces) are respected and that their skills are developed? Does it respect consumers? Rinaldi presents the logics around the opportunities of managing and communicating sustainability in fashion. Rinaldi also focuses on the opportunities for brands to be more sustainable and develops some basic principles to help fashion brands become more sustainable.

In CHAPTER FOUR Van Andel, Demol and Schramme discuss internationalization strategies of fashion brands. Dicken (1998) makes a distinction between the processes of internationalization and globalization. In his view, globalization is a complex system of inter-related processes rather than an end-state. Internationalization processes involve the extension of economic activities across national boundaries. Internationalization is, essentially, a quantitative process which leads to a more extensive geographical pattern of economic activity. The internationalization of fashion brands is apparent on multiple levels, foreign market expansion being one aspect and the *internationalization of the value chain*. From creation to sourcing and manufacturing to distribution and marketing is a second and more fundamental evolution. During the past two decades, the international expansion of fashion brands has been unprecedented, facilitated by several factors and driven by push and pull factors. Several theories have been developed to explain the manner in which fashion companies internationalize their operations and sales. The *Uppsala model* suggests that companies, after a period of operating in the domestic market only, increase their commitment to new, relatively similar, markets, as they gain more knowledge of that market through experience. The more recent *Born Global model* states that firms operate in a different context and in a fast-paced competitive environment and must therefore find quick ways of internationalizing. The latter theory arguably relates more to high-end independent designers, who tend to quickly face limitations in their domestic market and perceive value in fast expansion abroad, both in terms of production and sales. The (Flemish) fashion industry includes many small and medium-sized enterprises (SMEs) with limited resources in terms of capital, management and time, yet they succeed in internationalizing their activities. CHAPTER FOUR describes the current state of internationalization in the independent and high-end fashion industry and includes an overview of the key locations for both international production and sales. Furthermore, this chapter provides insight into the process of internationalization, as well as its drivers and barriers. Finally the operational management of internationalization is discussed by zooming in on business models and the effect internationalization has on them.

In CHAPTER FIVE Dieter Geernaert, the former lawyer of the famous designer Dirk Bikkembergs, explores a number of legal issues that a fashion designer or a fashion business (the brand) may have to deal with at some point in the course of business. Although legal matters may be the last thing on a designer's mind, each designer should reflect on how his *intellectual property*, i.e. the manifestation of creative efforts (a name, an image, a design...), can be protected optimally. If he does not provide for any legal protection for his original creation, name, logo or invention, the story will come to an abrupt end sooner rather than later. The next step is to exploit his intellectual property, by entering into agreements with third parties who are given the right to use it, preferably in return for a financial consideration. In this chapter several agreements – such as *license agreements*, *manufacturing agreements* and *commercial agency agreements* – are briefly discussed and key provisions highlighted. Finally Geernaert offers some copyright-related tips and tricks for developing a fashion label.

In THE SECOND PART of the book, we will exchange the academic, global perspective for a more practical and individual approach: that of the independent designer.

After graduating most creative designers dream of bringing out their own label/collection. But there is one major problem: nobody is waiting for a new fashion label to emerge. The Western fashion market has been saturated for a long time. Contrary to other industries, the fashion industry does not work solely according to the laws of supply and demand. The need for fashion items is created by the suppliers. Due to globalization there has also been an incredible acceleration of the fashion system (Gielen 2012), with pre-fall and pre-summer collections, or capsule collections that follow each other very quickly. It is almost impossible for an independent designer to keep up with this hectic rhythm.

Paradoxically, most young creative designers are not interested in consumer preferences. They start from their own creative universe and often are not even interested if there is a public for their creations. Disillusionment often follows quickly after graduation. One reason for this disillusionment is that the designers are not prepared to the business reality and market of fashion. They may have learned to be creative, but know little about the fashion system and the management competencies that are needed to start a label. Career paths of fashion designers are therefore diverse, unpredictable and hybrid (Keysers 2012; Harlange 2012). Many give up after a few years, leaving the industry or are going to work in a bigger fashion company to learn the business on the floor. Most of them combine different jobs.

This book aims to fill this knowledge gap and to share the key insights into management and entrepreneurship in the fashion industry.

In CHAPTER SIX Raf Vermeiren explains how the independent designer has to finance his fashion business. He is a former project manager of Cultuurinvest (the Flemish investment fund for the creative industries). In this capacity he has been supervising fashion companies for several years. In this chapter he shares his experience and expertise with aspiring designers in a comprehensive and accessible way. According to him, most creative people prefer (by nature) to focus their energies on their creative endeavours rather than on finance and figures. Nonetheless, in the complex fashion business, finance should be high on the agenda. *Cash flow planning* is key to the success of the business and there is no industry in which the problem of pre-financing is as prominent as in the fashion industry. This is due to the pace of the industry, in which collections quickly follow one after another. Thus a designer will simultaneously be at different stages of different collections. A comprehensive overview of the cash flow of his/her business, particularly in relation to his/her production flow, is therefore crucial. The secret to successful financial management lies in understanding each aspect of the business and in comprehending the impact of specific fashion-related deadlines on an organisational level and thereby on a financial level. The hands-on tools presented in this chapter will give designers the knowledge to steer their business; they will be a guide to a better-structured company. "Don't be afraid but eager", is the motto of Raf Vermeiren.

In CHAPTER SEVEN of the book, Marie Delbeke, former project manager of the Flemish Fashion Institute (the Flemish governmental organization that needs to give support and guidance to the fashion industry in Flanders and abroad) and now working for Cultuurinvest, wants to share her ground experience with starting fashion designers. She assumes the role of the creative person and gives an overview of all the steps that must be taken into account to develop an own fashion label in a sustainable manner. She emphasizes the importance of being well prepared starting an own fashion label. The designer needs to know in which industry he is working, who are his main competitors and who are his consumers. He also needs to develop a vision, keeping track of the forces that are influencing the sector, and a plan to enter the market the following years. She ends the chapter with some tips and wise advices for those who want to launch a fashion business.

No book about the Flemish fashion industry is complete without discussing the "Antwerp Six". No one is better placed than veteran fashion journalist Veerle Windels to tell their story. For more than 20 years she has been passionately following and critiquing the fashion scene, even witnessing the rise of the Antwerp Six at the end of the eighties. In the last chapter – CHAPTER EIGHT – Windels reveals never before published anecdotes about the Antwerp Six. For example, she puts an end for once and for all to the myth of the "Antwerp Six", including Martin Margiela in the canon of the "magnificent Antwerp Seven".

Windels also looks at the critical success factors of their career paths and emphasizes that – contrary to the perception – not all of the seven designers remained successful. She is showing how different their career paths – and *levels* of success – were. Finally she looks at the upcoming high-end Belgian designers and both the opportunities and threats they face. The Antwerp Seven may have paved the way for these new generations, but they will still have to find their position or place in a fashion industry that has become much more globalized and thus competitive.

REFERENCES

Guiette, A., Jacobs, S., Schramme, A., Vandenbempt, K. (2011a) *Creatieve industrieën in Vlaanderen: mapping en bedrijfseconomische analyse [Creative industries in Flanders: Mapping and business-management analysis]*. Antwerp Management School/Flanders District of Creativity.

Guiette, A., Jacobs, S., Schramme, A., Vandenbempt, K. (2011b) *De creatieve industrieën in Vlaanderen en hun drivers en drempels [The creative industries in Flanders, and their drivers and barriers]*. Antwerp Management School/Flanders DC.

Schrauwen, J., Schramme, A. (2013a). *De Modesector in Vlaanderen gesegmenteerd [The fashion industry in Flanders, by segment]*. Study commissioned by Flanders Fashion Institute, University of Antwerp/the Antwerp Management School.

Schrauwen, J., Schramme A. (2013b). *Annex: een gesegmenteerde bedrijfseconomische impactmeting [Annex: A segmented business-management impact measurement]*. Unpublished study commissioned by Flanders Fashion Institute, University of Antwerp and the Antwerp Management School.

Schrauwen, J., Demol, M., Van Andel, W., Schramme, A. (2013c). *Creatieve Industrieën in Vlaanderen in 2010, Mapping en Bedrijfseconomische Analyse [Creative industries in Flanders in 2010: Mapping and business-management analysis]*. Antwerp Management School/Flanders District of Creativity.

Verdict Research Ltd. (2012) *European Clothing retailing*.

De Voldere, I., Maenhout, T., Debruyne, M. (2007) *Fashionate about Creativity*. Vlerick Management School/ Flanders District of Creativity.

RECOMMENDED

Corbellini, E., Saviolo, S. (2012) *Managing Fashion and Luxury companies*. Milano: Rizzoli Etas.

Craik, J. (1993; 2013) *The Face of Fashion: Cultural Studies in Fashion*. London: Routledge.

Craik, J. (2009) Fashion. *The key concepts*. Oxford: Berg publishers.

Derycke, L., Van De Veire, S., (ed.) (1999) *Belgian Fashion Design*. Gent: Ludion.

Dicken, P. (1998) *The Global Shift: Transforming the World Economy*. 3rd Ed. London: Paul Chapman.

Gielen, P.J.D. (2012) Artistic Praxis and the Neoliberalization of the Educational Space. In: Pascal Gielen and Paul de Bruyne (2012), eds. *Teaching Arts in the Neoliberal Realm. Realism versus Cynism*, pp.15-31, Amsterdam, Valiz.(isbn 978-90-78088-57-8)

Gimeno Martinez, J. (2008) Fashion, country and city: the fashion industry and the construction of collective identities (1981-2001). In: *Modus Operandi State of Affairs in current research on Belgian Fashion*. Momu – Fashion Museum Province of Antwerp, 51-67.

Hines, T. & Bruce M. (2007) *Fashion Marketing. Contemporary issues*. the Hague: Elsevier Ltd.

Keysers, A. (2011-2012) *Van naald tot draad: knelpunten en succesfactoren van alumni van de Mode Academie 1988-2013. (From needle to thread: undressing the factors of success in the careers of fashion graduates 1988-2013)*. Unpublished masterthesis, Master Cultural Management, University of Antwerp.

Harlange, S. (2011-2012) *Succesfactoren ont(k)leed: kwantitatief en kwalitatief onderzoek naar de loopbanen van de alumni van de opleiding Mode aan de Koninklijke Academie voor Schone Kunsten Antwerpen, 1963-1987. (undressing the factors of success: quantitative and qualitative research on the carreer paths of graduates from the Royal Academy of Fine Arts Antwerp, 1963-1987)*. Unpublshed masterthesis, Master Cultural Management, University of Antwerp.

Menkes, S. (2013) De identiteit van de Antwerpse mode. In: *Mode Antwerpen Academie 50*, Tielt: Lannoo, 41-49.

Van Godtsenhoven, K. (2013) De wonderjaren van de Antwerpse 6+1. In: *Mode Antwerpen Academie 50*, Tielt: Lannoo, 65-125.

Jean-Paul Knott
SS 11

1

UNRAVELING THE FASHION INDUSTRY

Joke Schrauwen

Annick Schramme

Why do we admire the spectacular fashion shows of Dries Van Noten and Louis Vuitton every January and September, but do we buy most of our clothes in retail chains like Zara or H&M? When we talk about the fashion industry, it is important to realize that it involves several "businesses".

In nearly every industry there are distinct product varieties, multiple distribution channels and several types of consumers. The fashion system is made up of many industries (textiles, clothing, knitwear, leather, accessories, etc.). These industries in turn can be further subdivided into different competitive segments. Each firm has to decide how to compete, or position itself, within each industry segment. In this chapter we will describe the structural segmentation of the clothing industry.

Investigating the Flemish fashion industry, we identified four main segments: the independent designers and the luxury fashion concerns, the middle market segment, the retail chains. Particularly, the independent designers and the middle market segment are very present in Flanders.

In this chapter we will identify the differences between these various fashion segments and we also want to gain deeper insight in the dynamics of these fashion businesses. Afterwards we shall describe the various fashion segments according to their business model. Erica Corbellini and Stefania Saviolo (2012) define a business model in the fashion industry as consisting of four building blocks: 1. The value proposition of what is offered to the market 2. The segment(s) of clients that are targeted by the value proposition 3. The communication and distribution channels to reach clients and offer them the value proposition 4. The way the value chain is organized (degree of vertical or horizontal integration). We will focus on the composition of their collections, the interpretation of their value networks and the outlines of their general strategic, financial and marketing management.

CRITERIA FOR SEGMENTATION

What are the main criteria for our segmentation? Corbellini and Saviolo (2012) segment the clothing industry according to 3 macro-criteria: product end-uses, groups of clients and price. First, we will discuss price and product orientation. The groups of clients are integrated in the business model that we will discuss afterwards.

So, a primary difference between these basic segments is that each operates in a different price segment. Examining the price category for basic ready-to-wear pieces, we can make the following rudimentary classification:

Figure 1.
Segmentation of the fashion industry according to prices (in €) of basic ready-to-wear pieces.

The segments also differ according to the relative importance of the creativity or individuality of their collections.

At one extreme is the perception of creative goods as *positional goods*. The fashion designer is in the centre of the business and he is more product- than market-oriented. As defined by Jacobs et al. (2012) the symbolic value and market value of positional goods depend largely upon the opinion of peers and experts. This description emphasizes the creativity, the scarcity and uniqueness of the collection. In contrast, and at the other extreme, is the perception of creative products as *private consumer goods*. In this perspective, symbolic value and market value are derived from the satisfaction of individual consumers. Fashion labels are more likely to be motivated by extrinsic elements coming from the market. They have a more business-like structure, often with diversified business activities.

Figure 2.
The four fashion segments along the continuum between positional goods and private consumption goods.

The price category and conception of creativity also generate different structures for the value chain or value network. Before discussing the segments in greater detail, we will briefly consider the overall value chain or value network of the fashion industry.

THE VALUE CHAIN

The value chain represents all of the various actors involved in the process of value creation in a product or service; i.e. it shows how a drawing becomes a garment. A sketch for a new handbag does not become a product automatically, and it will not necessarily become the new it-bag. Many actors contribute to this process. In general, we can depict the value chain around a creative good or service as follows:

Figure 3.
The creative value chain
(Guiette et al. 2011a).

This circuit resembles a linear process. In reality, however, it involves an entire ecosystem with complex interactions between various actors. Presenting the value chain as a *network* is therefore more appropriate. The value network for a fashion company can be summarised as follows: The designer or design team prepares sketches, which they convert into patterns and prototypes, in consultation with pattern makers. This information is transferred to manufacturers, who produce the full collections. At the same time, a sales and marketing process is established. The prototypes are thus also used in the business-to-business (B2B) sales process, through fashion trade shows, sales agents, fashion shows and showrooms. A business-to-consumer (B2C) marketing campaign is also established, in which PR agencies, the media and bloggers all have roles to play. The sales and marketing processes also involve important roles for other creative businesses, including modelling agencies, make-up artists, fashion-show producers, photographers, designers and event planners. Finally, the collection pieces find their way to consumers through various retail channels, ranging from upscale department stores, self-contained multi-brand stores, proprietary flagship stores and branded chain stores to various "e-tail" channels.

It should be obvious that no single company performs all of these tasks. Most fashion brands are "head-tail" companies, meaning that they outsource their production entirely to contractors, most of which are situated in low-wage countries. Only the design (the "head") and the distribution or sale – or even just the marketing (the "tail") – remain in their hands. The head-tail company takes the position of the *chain director*: It controls the entire value chain, from design and manufacturing to distribution, without performing all of the associated activities in-house.

FASHION   MANAGEMENT   CHAPTER   ONE

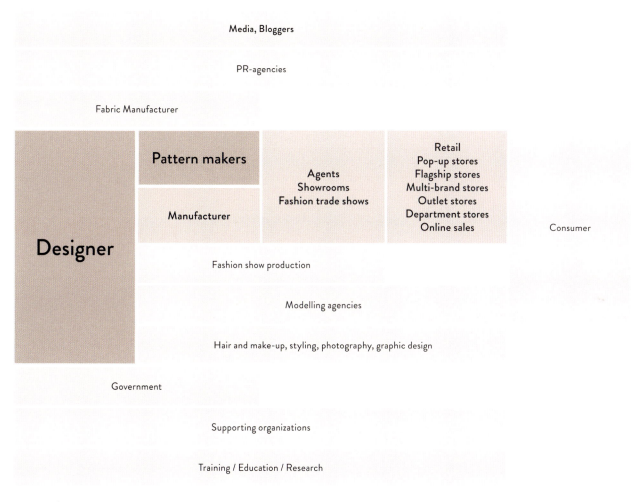

Figure 4. | The value network in the Flemish fashion industry (Schrauwen et al. 2013c).

Core creative links
Supporting creative links
Other sector / facilitator

As mentioned before we can observe several "businesses" or segments within the fashion industry based on different criteria,, like the criterium of *price* and/or the *conception of creativity*. Companies within each segment are likely to set different priorities in their general strategic, financial or marketing management.

In general we can distinguish four main segments: *independent designers*, *luxury fashion concerns*, *the middle market segment* and *retail chains*.

INDEPENDENT DESIGNERS

THE COLLECTIONS

For independent designers, the creative talent of the designer is the engine of the business. In most cases, designers establish labels and associate their names with them. The creative collections are identified by their particular styles or signatures. Independent designers often feel less tied to trends, still, they must also consider some basic rules regarding the composition of a collection. This general pyramid of collection composition provides a helpful overview:

5% – 10% Image-defining pieces (e.g. the couture or catwalk collection)

Ready-to-wear pieces for completing an entire wardrobe (derived from the core idea of the image-defining pieces) 60% – 80%

10% – 30% Best-sellers and basic pieces, often at introductory prices (small share of collection, large share of sales)

Many independent designers follow the traditional rhythm of fashion, bringing out collections twice each year: one for autumn/winter and one for spring/summer. The number of collections obviously doubles for companies that design lines for both men and women. The presentation of these collections usually coincides with an international fashion week (e.g. in London, New York, Paris or Milan). Some designers experiment with interim collections or capsule collections.

Figure 5.
Collection-composition pyramid.

THE VALUE NETWORK

The value network in this segment is fully dedicated to the creative input of individual designers and their teams. It is highly conceptual, focusing on the central idea of the collection. Designs are often more complex than those in the less expensive fashion segments, and considerable energy is invested in pre-production activities. The pattern makers and garment makers who produce the samples are important partners for the designer. For this reason, many designers also choose to keep their pre-production activities relatively close, whether in-house or in specialised studios in the same area.

The result is that the designer's company uses the production preparation – the samples – to set the B2B sales process in motion. The success of these B2B sales will determine the success of the collection.

Not all independent designers have their own stores. Even top designers may have their flagship stores in only one global city (or sometimes in just a few cities). In addition, a collection does not simply land in any multi-brand company. The style and image of the independent designer and that of the multi-brand store must be mutually reinforcing. Moreover, the collections are sold in mostly one, or sometimes just a few places in a city. The distribution network is thus very small and selective. Independent designers therefore feel obliged to distribute their collections abroad almost immediately. Therefore they are also called "born globals". (see CHAPTER FOUR: Internationalization Strategies of the Fashion Industry).

A similar story can be observed in contemporary online sales. Only a few independent designers manage their own online stores, because this requires them to build and maintain stock. Most independent designers operate through curated sites under their own labels or through the sub-pages of brick-and-mortar stores.

The B2B sales process, starts with a lot of exposure. Grand fashion shows and/or showrooms are staged during the international fashion weeks in Paris, London, Milan and New York. All of these activities are dedicated to creating the best possible symbolic value; the show and the showroom are the translation of the central idea behind the collection. Everything must therefore be perfect: the choice of fashion week, city and show location, as well as the models, make-up, lighting, music, set design, catering, photography and other aspects. In addition to the show and showrooms, independent designers work with representatives and agents during the fashion weeks. These parties maintain contact with stores within specific markets. A few designers invite their regular buyers to their headquarters or showrooms, either before or after the fashion weeks. This practice extends the sales process, and it allows designers the possibility of adjusting their collections before the fashion week, based on the feedback from these buyers.

After the order book has been filled and the designer has received an overview of orders from multi-brand stores, the entire collection goes into production. Unlike the pre-production process, the production of these collections is often outsourced to various producers in low-wage countries (e.g. the Mediterranean or Eastern Europe). Only very technical pieces are prepared or finished in Western European studios (see CHAPTER FOUR: Internationalization Strategies of the Fashion Industry).

THE CHAIN DIRECTOR

In this process, the company surrounding the independent designer is thus the chain director. Depending on the life phase of these organizations, they could be micro-companies (less than five employees) or small and medium enterprises (SMEs). The shares are usually in the hands of the designer, possibly supplemented by an investor. The company is linked to the career of the designer, thereby posing a risk in terms of continuity or succession if something should happen to the designer. Unlike other fashion segments (to be discussed later), horizontal or vertical integration rarely takes place with independent designers. *Horizontal integration* refers to the distribution of various similar brands by a parent company. *Vertical integration* refers to a situation in which the parent company purchases or controls several small companies within the value chain. The latter sometimes takes place in the form of a production licence. In these cases, the designer cedes the intellectual property rights to specific designs and patterns to the producer. The producer makes the prototypes and handles the production. Some licensees also manage the distribution. This situation is a case of vertical integration proceeding from the producer.

The competitive position of independent designers is weak (see also **CHAPTER SEVEN**: The nuts and bolts of starting an independent fashion label). Revenues from the collection are not always sufficient, particularly for small or emerging designers, making it necessary to seek other sources of income, including design contracts for other fashion companies, teaching assignments, and/or collaboration with artists. Artistic projects are often more important, given their potential to generate additional symbolic value or credibility. These aspects are also essential in the communication and promotion of the brand. For this reason, independent designers rarely use traditional promotional tools (e.g. adverts or billboard campaigns). In contrast, earned media attention enhances symbolic value and credibility. The reputations of independent designers and their collections are made through press attention and critical acclaim. The brand's representation at the fashion weeks constitutes the start of a communication campaign. In addition to buyers from multi-brand stores, members of the press are invited to shows and showrooms. In many cases, PR agencies are also engaged to ensure continued attention from the press by lending out collection pieces and reporting special events, collaborations and other notable developments.

The entire process thus focuses on the creative talent and aesthetic vision of the independent designer. The value network in this segment is fully dedicated to the creative input of individual designers and their teams. The chain director is usually a micro-company or SME surrounding the designer.

The luxury segment of the fashion market is aimed at the upper end of the consumer market. This segment has long been dominated by fashion houses operating more or less according to a dated version of the value network described above. In recent decades, however, this market has become increasingly dominated by multinational luxury groups, including LVMH, Kering (until March 2013, PPR), Richemont, Prada and Puig. These conglomerates have gradually bought many old fashion and luxury houses, changing the business models behind them in the process.

THE COLLECTION

In reductionist terms, we could say that the luxury fashion concerns now revolve around a "dream world" of couture, which has been created to sell licensed products. In many cases, the brands of a concern have an extensive product range. The least accessible luxury goods are the collections of hand-made and custom-made couture.[1] In addition, there is the ready-to-wear[2] line, which is more accessible than the luxury product. For many luxury labels, however, perfume, cosmetics, glasses (or sunglasses) and other derivative licensed products generate the largest profits. A decade ago, most luxury brands also added a separate collection of basics or a line of jeans, in order to reach an even wider group of consumers. This strategy is increasingly being phased out, however, in an effort to guarantee the exclusive character of the label. Moreover, the couture collections seem to be increasingly expensive. The dream world of couture is brought into production for a (very limited) niche within the consumer market. In the marketing of luxury labels, however, these catwalk collections must attract a broader group of consumers for the basic pieces and lines of accessories and cosmetics. The image of the label is thus created by a small part of the product range (the couture collection or the catwalk collection of the ready-to-wear), while its major profits are generated by derivative products (e.g. collection basics, accessories, cosmetics).

Most houses present their couture and ready-to-wear collections twice a year, during the fashion weeks. Between these periods, they regularly introduce pre-fall and pre-spring collections, cruise collections and other offerings. On the one hand, the collections are determined by the brand's identity and "heritage value". This brand identity consists of recognisable characters and iconic pieces that have made the brand famous. The brand identity is most strongly manifested in the catwalk collections of couture and ready-to-wear pieces. On the other hand, the artistry of the current chief designers affects both the couture and the ready-to-wear line. Multinational luxury brands often recruit famous designers to be their artistic directors. Finally, trends are also important in this segment.

The quality and aesthetics of the collection serve as criteria for playing in this top-level segment. For couture collections, the quality of the material, the customisation and the handwork (most of which is performed by proprietary or European studios) account for the greater expense in production costs. The production price for ready-to-wear lines and basic pieces is much lower, as these products are less complex and less labour-intensive. Despite the lower production costs, exclusivity is created in other ways. For example, international luxury brands often create an artificial scarcity around their products, in which the potential market exceeds actual production. *Objective scarcity* (limited production) and *subjective scarcity* (an exclusive network of distribution points) are essential for luxury products. All of these features together ensure that a luxury product is, by definition, an expensive product. For this reason, iconic pieces from these collections often fall victim to counterfeiting, despite the many measures that have been taken at the international level in recent years.

THE VALUE NETWORK

The value network of the luxury fashion concerns centres on exclusivity. A famous designer is usually recruited to design the basic concept for the collections. The designers then elaborate on these concepts, together with their design teams (who usually remain anonymous). In this fashion segment, special consideration is given to the projections of trend agencies and information from detailed sales figures. The influence of the company's marketing and merchandising services (see below) is apparent even in the design process.

The pre-production and production processes are carried out in proprietary or external studios. In many cases, the couture is still produced in proprietary studios, as prescribed by the *Chambre Syndicale de la Couture Parisienne* (see footnote I). Technically complex pieces in the ready-to-wear collections are usually produced locally as well. These artisan studios nevertheless produce only a fraction of the total product range. Serial production is usually outsourced to low-wage countries in Eastern Europe or Asia.

The distribution of luxury goods depends upon its intended accessibility. Couture collections are available only on order from the main house. Selective or exclusive distribution is nevertheless important, even for the less inaccessible luxury goods. The company focuses itself exclusively on flagship stores in major world cities, in prime locations. In these stores, the collection is often shown in its entirety in a luxurious atmosphere that fully coincides with the identity of the brand (see also **CHAPTER TWO**: The Evolving Nature of Specialty Retail Formats within the Fashion Sector: Flagships and Pop Ups). In addition, parts of the collections are sold worldwide in corners of a highly

FASHION MANAGEMENT

selective group of multi-brand shops and department stores. China and other BRICS countries continue to be growth markets for luxury concerns. For many luxury brands, the Asian market is even more important than the European market. As is the case with independent designers, the shows are of major importance in the B2B sales process for luxury fashion of concerns, given that such press attention helps to construct the dream world of luxury. The accessible luxury goods – the licensed products – are distributed more widely, making them available to a larger group of consumers. One final remark is the considerable bargaining power that these luxury concerns have with the multi-brand stores. In addition to controlling a large number of brands (thus representing a major potential source of sales for multi-brand stores), they also own and manage many more multi-brand retail channels (see below).

THE CHAIN DIRECTOR

The chain director in this fashion segment is the concern, with its fashion houses. The conglomerate contains only consolidated companies, often involving fashion companies that have long been independent and that had attained some level of maturity before their shares (or a portion thereof) were acquired by the group. In the 1990s, many concerns focused on historic, somewhat dormant luxury brands. In recent years, they have exhibited a preference for acquiring independent designers who are still quite active. In this regard, the concerns obviously prefer the established names and avoid young starters. At the head of the concern is a parent company or holding company, whose shares are held by investment companies (in many cases, belonging to the same family). A few of these holding companies are listed on the stock market.

The concerns are integrated both vertically and horizontally, and sometimes even diagonally. Horizontally integrated concerns have portfolios of brands with similar activities. Vertically integrated companies incorporate multiple companies within a single value chain. For example, in addition to their fashion labels, some concerns have acquired production studios and department stores. By controlling the design, the production channels and the key players in the distribution network, a conglomerate can become very powerful with respect to smaller players. In this context, diagonal integration refers to the acquisition of several companies in the value chains of related industries. For example, in addition to its clothing brands, a luxury concern might have brands of historical weapons, yachts, hotels, champagne or other items.

In addition to the various strategies for integration, licensing strategies are common in this segment. For example, companies sell licences to create other product groups under the same brand name: consider the lipstick and sunglasses sold under the Chanel brand. Another licensing strategy involves trading licences to open stores under a specific brand name. The high level of integration combined with great financial strength and global reach makes these concerns extremely powerful within the value chain, and thus gives them a strong competitive position.

The communication and promotion strategies of luxury fashion vary according to the product group. The dream world of inaccessible luxury products must generate earned media attention in order to sell the accessible luxury products as well. Advertising campaigns are created for the accessible luxury products. These massive advertising budgets also exert influence on earned media attention. In some cases, journalists are pressured by their marketing departments, and in other cases, informal barter deals may be made. The influence of fashion houses on bloggers is even clearer. Well-known bloggers with hundreds of thousands of followers and millions of hits per month are able to reach lucrative deals with fashion houses (even though some bloggers cling to their editorial freedom in order to maintain their credibility). Finally, for communication and promotion, it is essential to build a consistent brand image to cover all of these different product groups, as observed in the privately owned media and social media channels (see **CHAPTER THREE:** Communicating Fashion in the New Era: Understanding Social Media and Corporate Social Responsibility). Such an image might centre on the brand's history or heritage value. The combination of a consistent image and a plurality of communication channels generates added visibility.

We could say that the luxury fashion concerns deploy a dream world of couture in order to sell licensed products. The value network in this segment revolves around exclusivity. The chain director in this context is a powerful group of consolidated companies.

THE COLLECTIONS

The middle market segment consists of brands that bring fashion to a clearly defined target audience within the middle class. To please this target group as best as possible, collections are often based on the identity of the brand (ranging from very creative to sophisticated-conservative), as well as on projections made after analysing sales figures and trends. In this fashion segment, it is more common to experiment with different collections each season, although these tend to be derivatives of the main idea behind the collection. Production volumes are generally higher than in the previously discussed segments, but the technical complexity is somewhat lower. Both of these aspects have an impact on consumer prices.

THE VALUE NETWORK

Companies in this segment therefore aim to create maximum added value for the client. This philosophy extends into the value network. An anonymous team of designers, sometimes supplemented by freelancers, designs with a clear customer profile in mind. The design teams of several labels coordinate the collections with their merchandising and marketing departments. They analyse the sales figures in the proprietary stores and with key accounts, and follow the trends closely. These departments help to determine which type of collection pieces will be designed and how they will be put on the market. At the start of the design, the label is thus already considering such matters as the channels in which the pieces will be distributed, the niche for which the pieces are intended, the price at which the collection pieces will be sold and the image that will be dominant in the promotion.

During the pre-production phase – from design to prototype – the design team gives instructions to the manufacturer (in many cases, through technical design sheets) about various characteristics, including style, fabric, type and position of stitches, the kind of seam and placement of the zipper. Based on these instructions, the manufacturer produces prototypes and sales samples. The head-tail company surrounding the label outsources the entire production to several manufacturers. Production is outsourced almost entirely to low-wage countries in regions such as Eastern Europe, the Mediterranean or Eastern Asia. Some companies in this segment have developed out of production companies. In these businesses, some of the pre-production (i.e. collection development) and retouches are still performed in-house.

Distribution takes place through a network of proprietary and multi-brand stores. The proprietary boutiques, which are sometimes known as pilot stores or flagship stores, carry the name of the label and are usually located in larger cities. These stores embody the full image of the brand, thus serving as an important marketing tool in addition to being a point-of-sale. Efforts are also invested in retail through multi-brand stores. Some regions still have a relatively strong culture of independent boutiques in rural regions, as is the case in Belgium. In other countries, these independent retailers are increasingly surrendering to chains of multi-brand or proprietary stores. Several brands also set up corners in department stores. In this type of arrangement, department stores allocate a defined area to the brand. The department stores still select the pieces that they wish to offer, but the label has more opportunity to adapt the sales area to suit its image. The label also uses various other B2B channels to sell its pieces to B2B customers. The most important channels are the national and international fashion trade shows. In view of the high number of such trade shows, it is important for a label to select one that suits its image and that displays labels from its niche. In addition, a label may use its own permanent showrooms or self-organized fashion shows (usually for buyers on the local market), in addition to its own representatives or agents who represent multiple labels. Only rarely do labels in this segment make use of fashion shows during the fashion weeks.

The e-tail strategies of these brands follow the logic of click-and-mortar commerce: while each label has its own webshop, most also offer pieces to "multi-brand e-shops". Curated sites, however, appear to be less prominent in this segment. In many cases, the likelihood that a brand will venture into online sales also depends on the familiarity of the target audience with online clothing sales, as well as on the distribution of physical points of sale. Brands that focus primarily on older women, the domestic market or well-branched distribution networks with personal boutiques have been more reluctant to venture into online sales.

THE CHAIN DIRECTOR

In the middle market segment, the chain director is usually a company with one fashion label or a limited number in its portfolio. Although several listed companies exist within this segment on the international market, most of the companies on the local market are SMEs that have existed for at least a decade and demonstrated a certain level of robustness. The founder of the company is often a business owner or family of entrepreneurs with experience in the sector. The companies tend to grow slowly, internationalizing only after they have established a firm foothold in the market at home (see CHAP-TER FOUR: Internationalization Strategies of the Fashion Industry). As stated before, horizontal integration is common. Vertical integration took place in some companies several decades ago. In the past, they operated primarily as manufacturers, but they re-oriented themselves toward running a label.

Competition in this segment is high, given the large number of labels (i.e. direct competitors), as well as in response to the pressure of the retail chains (i.e. alternatives or substitutes) existing within the same market segment. Consumers therefore have many (and often less expensive) alternatives to these labels. In this segment, therefore, marketing management receives considerable attention. Companies engage in a wide range of efforts to transform their labels into "love brands" in the minds of their target audiences. The labels make much greater use of promotion and communication tools than independent designers do in order to reach their target groups. Earned media attention is essential for these labels too, and adverts, posters, product placement and a consistent image (as visualised through the label's own stores and corners) constitute major promotion tools. Finally, the labels in this segment invest in good customer relationships with B2B customers, as well as with the end-consumers who know the brand through its network of stores.

The middle market segment can thus be summarised as fashion for a defined middle-class target audience. The value network revolves around added value for the end-consumer. The chain director is usually an SME owned by a genuine fashion entrepreneur, and is usually anchored locally.

RETAIL CHAINS

THE COLLECTIONS

The slogan of the retail chains is "fashion for the masses at very competitive prices". These companies reason from within a market-pull strategy. The collections are adjusted according to projections on what the market will demand. Trend forecasting, market research and sales figures from previous collections define the appearance and composition of the collection. In order to reach as many different types of consumers as possible, chains carry a variety of proprietary brands under one roof. To stimulate as many consumers as possible, new stock is also placed in store throughout each season. This new stock can range from bestsellers of the current (or previous) season to pieces derived from the core collection to new, separate capsule collections. The industry average for collection exchanges is around six weeks, although some retail chains are speed demons, refreshing the range of products in their stores every two weeks. Speed to market is thus vital in this fast-fashion business. Retail chains also try to keep the cost price as low as possible. This is reflected in the material used and the simplicity of the design, but it also affects the core philosophy of the value network.

THE VALUE NETWORK

In this segment, money can be earned only by reaching a very large group of consumers. In order to avoid "fashion failures" as much as possible, the anonymous design teams often work in close consultation with the merchandising team. They jointly determine what type of collection pieces will be designed for which target audiences, sub-segments and points of sale. The merchandising team provides feedback on the collection based on data about trends, market research and sales figures. Even in the development of the prototype, the merchandising team estimates how many pieces will be sold in which stores (*quantity per stock-keeping unit*, or *SKU*), and a marketing strategy is conceived around sub-collections. The collection might be supplemented by *white products*: garments with no label, which are designed completely in-house by the manufacturer and which the producer offers to multiple retail chains or other channels (e.g. market vendors and supermarkets).

As noted before, the extension of the value network revolves around cost-price reduction and speed. The pre-production is performed in-house or by the manufacturer, not according to vague sketches, extensive descriptions and complex patterns, but according to technical design sheets. The production is fully outsourced to low-wage countries. The exact location depends on the speed to market that the supplier can guarantee. For basic pieces, a delivery time of four to six months is often sufficient, making producers in Asia (e.g. Bangladesh, China, India, Cambodia) and boat transport viable options. For product lines with a shorter delivery time (four to eight weeks), European chains often prefer countries such as Turkey, Tunisia, Morocco, Poland, Romania, Bulgaria or Ukraine. Some chains (such as the Inditex group) bring the production back to the country of the parent company in an effort to respond even more quickly to the needs of the customer. For the production of its stock, a clothing chain often calls on about 60 to 150 suppliers, including about 40 core producers with whom a long-lasting relationship is built.

Although not applicable to this segment alone, retail chains are often criticised for the working conditions at their producers in low-wage countries, including excessively low minimum wages, long working hours, child labour, use of hazardous materials, and unsafe working conditions. Monitoring by independent agencies and quality certificates are becoming increasingly important, and the industry is trying to regulate itself through a global code of conduct (see **CHAPTER THREE**: Communicating Fashion in the New Era: Understanding Social Media and Corporate Social Responsibility). Nevertheless, the extensive internationalization and complexity of the supply chain make monitoring difficult.

For the classic retail chains, the B2B sales process is not active, as companies sell their pieces only within a network of their own stores and webshops. A few retail chains combine their own network of stores with B2B sales to multi-brand stores (e.g. the brands of the Bestseller group). Brands that engage in retail through multi-brand retail stores are often distributed through multi-brand websites (e.g. asos.com or zalando.com). By eliminating the middle layer of agents, representatives, trade shows and wholesalers, retail chains are able to operate more quickly and more cost-efficiently. On the other hand, the company's logistics branch is often much more elaborated, with its own distribution centre and transport network, as well as an extensive system of stock automation.

Within the store network, all sales units have a recognisable style and a uniform store concept. To reach as many buyers as possible, companies tend to adopt one of two real estate strategies. Some chains focus on shopping centres and the major shopping districts of central cities. Properties in these streets are expensive, but sought after, as they are frequented by large crowds and many recreational shoppers. Other retail chains design themselves as discounters or target their efforts towards family purchases. These chains tend to focus on retail areas in the periphery, the out-of-town retail parks. It is important for the store to be easily accessible by car, for sufficient parking to be available at the door. The price per square metre for property at out-of-town retail parks amounts to only a tenth of those for prime locations in city centres. In many cases, this makes it possible also to furnish large buildings. In both cases, sales and expansion strategies are determined in part by the availability of properties and prices on the real estate market.

THE CHAIN DIRECTOR

Chain management proceeds from the distributor, who has usually acquired a core creative link. Because the chain director has many stores and its own distribution network, many SME chains are driven out by larger companies or groups of companies with several hundred employees. The founder, a true fashion entrepreneur (or the family of one), controls the majority of the shares. His/Her capital and the profits of the company or large corporation are thus also used to finance expansions. Horizontal integration is becoming increasingly common at the international level. We already mentioned the Bestsellers group (which owns labels such as Only, Vero Moda and Selected). Other examples include the Inditexgroup (which owns Zara, Massimo Dutti, Bershka and others) and the H&M group. Because of their size, business structure and capital structure, such companies are able to play the market more aggressively. Vertical integration from the point-of-sale occurs in this segment as well, thereby increasing control over the value network and allowing reductions in cost and increases in speed to market. The inexpensive fashion segment is characterised by strong market concentration in favour of chains, to the detriment of independent retailers. Licences are less common in this segment, with the exception of licences for the image rights of popular figures. Another important point in the strategic management of these companies involves the organizational and operational implications of their high rate of speed to market. For example, many chains have adopted relatively flat decision-making structures. Moreover, there is considerable consultation between divisions (e.g. designers, buyers, retailers, marketing and merchandising department) in order to keep as close an eye as possible on what the customer wants.

The communication and promotion strategies involve a plethora of measures and channels, ranging from advertising in all media (not only the specialized press), poster campaigns, direct mail and sales promotions to earned media attention. It is interesting to note that, although various sub-brands in the chain stores often have their own images, communication and promotions tend to be based on the brand name of the store. Recurrent purchases and customer loyalty are often promoted through customer loyalty cards and personal discounts through direct mail. While it is less important in this segment to gain positive critiques from the specialised press and bloggers, these brands often engage PR agencies to make their collections available for fashion reports and to generate press attention for special collaborations or capsule collections. In addition, several chains enter into media deals (e.g. for product placement on television) or work through celebrity endorsements.

Retail chains thus offer fashion for the masses at competitive prices. The design is therefore highly market driven and inspired by trends and sales figures. The value network revolves around cost-price reduction and speed. Given their retail structure, retail chains are often large companies or groups of consolidated companies.

The four basic segments or fashion businesses can be summarised as follows:

Independent designers	Luxury fashion / concerns	Middle market segment	Retail chains	
Focus on the creative talent of the designer; designer push	"Dream world" couture sells licensed products	Fashion for a defined target group in the middle class	Fashion for the masses at competitive prices; market pull	PRODUCT
Value network dedicated to creative input	Value network dedicated to exclusivity	Value network dedicated to added value for the customer	Value network dedicated to cost-price reduction and speed	VALUE NETWORK
Micro-business or SME around the designer	Powerful group of consolidated companies	SME owned by a fashion entrepreneur	Large company or group of consolidated companies developed around the distributor	CHAIN DIRECTOR

Figure 6.
Overview of fashion businesses.

The four segments described above should not be interpreted as laws set in stone. The descriptions are better seen as dominant thinking and acting (or "logic") within a given segment. Moreover, some actors are sometimes breaking through the dominant logic of their own segments, thereby gaining a strategic advantage or arriving at their own *Unique Selling Propositions* (USP).

We distinguish three strategies for innovation:

··· The first category consists of **segment switchers**: labels that have switched from one segment to another throughout their histories. For example, the first achievement of the Swedish label Acne was a collection of jeans for the middle market segment. Because of its *avant-garde*, creative image, however, the brand increasingly acquired the allure of the independent designer and luxury segments. The brand currently presents its collections during London and Paris fashion weeks, and it has become highly selective in choosing its points of sale.

··· A second strategy is that of the **segment stretchers**: companies that expand by moving into other segments, while striving to maintain their positions in their original segment. The segment-stretching strategy can often be observed in the concerns of fashion companies. In the past, many luxury brands (e.g. Armani or Versace) attempted to increase sales by offering a line of jeans with very basic garments for the middle market segment, alongside the couture and ready-to-wear lines that they presented during the fashion weeks. Several luxury houses have recently been dialing back this strategy, because it has been eroding the symbolic value (which is based on exclusivity) of their creative core collections. At the level of concerns, portfolios continue to be differentiated according to a segment-stretch strategy. In 2002, OTB (the concern that grew out of the middle-market Diesel) bought shares of the company behind independent designer Martin Margiela (NEUF SARL). OTB also controls Staff International, a production company for the luxury segment, with licences to produce the collections of Vivienne Westwood, Marc Jacobs Men and Just Cavalli.

··· The final category consists of **segment combiners**: companies that combine segmentation criteria (price/product) from one segment with the interpretation of the value network or management of another segment, or those that combine the segmentation criteria of two segments. For example, many independent multi-brand stores attempt to differentiate themselves within their own regions by combining brands from two segments. In this way, the portfolio can consist largely of brands from the middle market segment, supplemented by brands from retail chains. The brands COS and &Other Stories have established their USP by combining the production and distribution logic of retail chains (through the value chain of their parent holding company H&M) with a level of creativity and quality resembling that of the middle market segment.

SUMMARY

As demonstrated in this chapter, there is no single "fashion industry". Instead, there are four major segments, each exhibiting its own dynamics: independent designers, luxury fashion concerns, the middle market segment and retail chains. Their collection and the value chains are arranged in different ways, and the chain directors must address different issues in carrying out their general, strategic, financial and marketing management. Nevertheless, these four main segments should not be interpreted too rigidly. A company can break through the dominant logic of a segment, thus innovating, by stretching, combining or switching between segments. A company can use these strategies to develop its USP within the fashion scene.

REFERENCES

Schrauwen, J., Schramme, A. (2013a) *De Modesector in Vlaanderen gesegmenteerd [The fashion industry in Flanders, by segment]*. Study commissioned by Flanders Fashion Institute. University of Antwerp and the Antwerp Management School.

Schrauwen, J., Schramme, A. (2013b) *Annex: een gesegmenteerde bedrijfseconomische impactmeting [Annex: A segmented business management impact measurement]*. Unpublished study commissioned by Flanders Fashion Institute, University of Antwerp and the Antwerp Management School.

Schrauwen, J., Demol, M., Van Andel, W., Schramme, A. (2013c) *Creatieve Industrieën in Vlaanderen in 2010, Mapping en Bedrijfseconomische Analyse [Creative industries in Flanders in 2010: Mapping and business management analysis]*. Antwerp Management School/Flanders District of Creativity.

RECOMMENDED

Braaksma, R.M. (2009) *Kopstaartbedrijven. [Head-tail Companies]*. Zoetermeer: Panteia/EIM.

Corbellini, E., Saviolo, S. (2012) *Managing Fashion and Luxury companies*, Milano: Rizzoli Etas.

Derycke, L., Van De Veire, S. (ed.) (1999) *Belgian Fashion Design*, Gent: Ludion.

De Voldere, I., Maenhout, T., Debruyne, M. (2007) *Fashionate about Creativity*. Vlerick Management School/ Flanders District of Creativity.

Gimeno Martinez, J. (2008) Fashion, country and city: the fashion industry and the construction of collective identities (1981-2001). In: *Modus Operandi State of Affairs in current research on Belgian Fashion*. Momu – Fashion Museum Province of Antwerp, 51-67.

Greenwood, K.M., Murphy, M.F. (1978) *Fashion Innovation and marketing*. New York: Macmillan Publishing.

Guiette, A., Jacobs, S., Schramme, A., Vandenbempt, K. (2011a) *Creatieve industrieën in Vlaanderen: mapping en bedrijfseconomische analyse [Creative industries in Flanders: Mapping and businessmanagement analysis]*. Antwerp Management School/Flanders District of Creativity.

Guiette, A., Jacobs, S., Schramme, A., Vandenbempt, K. (2011b) *De creatieve industrieën in Vlaanderen en hun drivers en drempels [The creative industries in Flanders, and their drivers and barriers]*. Antwerp Management School/Flanders DC.

Hines, T. & Bruce M. (2007) *Fashion Marketing. Contemporary issues*. The Netherlands: Elsevier Ltd.

Hilger, J. (2008) The apparel industry in West Europe. In: *Creative encounters*, Working Papers n° 22. Online: www.cbs.dk/creativeencounters.

Jackson, T., Shaw, D. (2009) *Mastering Fashion Marketing*. Hampshire: Palgrave Macmillan.

Jacobs, S., Van Andel, W., Schramme, A., Huysentruyt, M. (2012) *Dominante logica in de Creatieve Industrie in Vlaanderen [Dominant logic in the creative industry in Flanders]*. Antwerp Management School/Flanders DC.

Karra, N. (2008) *The UK Designer Fashion Economy, Value relationships – identifying barriers and creating opportunities for business growth*. Centre for Fashion Enterprise. Report commissioned for NESTA.

Moons, A. (2008) To be (in) or not to be (in): the constituting processes and impact indicators of the Flemish designer fashion industry undressed. In: *Modus Operandi State of affairs in current research on Belgian Fashion*. MoMu – Fashion Museum Antwerp, 69-82.

Porter, M. (1985) *Competitive Advantage. Creating and Sustaining Superior Performance*. New York: Free Press.

Porter, M.(1980) *Competitive Strategy, Techniques for Analyzing Industries and Competitors*. New York: Free Press.

Pouillard, V. (2008) Before Antwerp? Re-producing fashions in interwar Belgium. In: *Modus Operandi State of affairs in current research on Belgian Fashion*. MoMu - Fashion Museum Antwerp, 1-15.

Sterlacci, F., Arbuckle, J. (2009) *The A to Z of the Fashion Industry*. Lanham: The Scarecrow Press.

Tungate, M. (2008) *Fashion Brands, Branding Style from Armani to Zara*. London & Philadelphia: 2nd edition, Kogan Page.

case # 1   Christian Wijnants

SS 14

"As a student, I never considered fashion to be art. Even back then, I wanted to make wearable collections"

Definitely a designer to watch... This became clear when Antwerp-based Christian Wijnants won the prestigious International Woolmark Prize in London in February 2013. Smart, talented and humble, Wijnants won his first accolade in 2000 (awarded by Belgian fashion stalwart Dries Van Noten) for his graduation collection at the Fashion Department of The Royal Academy of Fine Arts in Antwerp. He went on to win the Festival of Hyères and a number of other awards, including the Swiss Textile Award and Andam Awards. He set up his own label, Ben Nv, in 2003. In 2013, holding company CLdN Finance, owned by the Belgian shipping family Cigrang, acquired a 50 per cent share in Ben Nv.

Interview by
Trui Moerkerke

You are an alumnus of Antwerp's famous fashion school. How do you look back on your student years?
At the Antwerp Royal Academy you live on an island with so much creative freedom. The economic reality of a wearable collection is far away. This freedom is a unique opportunity to experiment and find your own voice. But every student has his or her own approach. As a student, I never considered fashion to be art. Even back then, I wanted to make wearable collections. In my student years I took a few freelance design jobs, but that was not really appreciated at the school. They wanted you to focus. The vision of the Fashion Department is clear: creativity and experimentation first, although they do invite guest speakers and organize visits to showrooms. And after all, it is a difficult gap to bridge: there are so many things in this business that school cannot teach you. Building up experience in one way or another is the magic trick.

"Awards give you huge visibility, which is important for attracting new clients"

You started your own label soon after graduating. How did you cope with the business side?

Initially, my own label wasn't my intention or ambition. But the year after I graduated, I won the Festival of Hyères. This got me a lot of press coverage and potential clients came to me asking for a collection. Great clients. People at Harvey Nichols, at Takashiyama... I wasn't ready and put the idea aside for a while, working instead as an assistant for Dries Van Noten. I learned a lot there' it was a fantastic "school".

But some clients continued to insist. I realized I couldn't wait too long. So I started in 2003, on my own. That was before the banking crisis and you could negotiate with banks to finance your production. They didn't want to invest in your collection or your fashion show or lookbooks, but if you could prove you had orders, they granted you a small, short-term loan to produce. I worked this way for years. Later, when we wanted to grow, we appealed to "Cultuur Invest", a Flemish investment fund for the creative industry.

On top of that I have always worked on different projects, since the beginning of my career. I did, and still do, a lot of consulting assignments. I have designed for Malo, for Natan and for the Hong Kong based company, G.R.I.. For years I was a lecturer at The Royal Academy. All these side jobs allowed me to finance collections or fashion shows.

In October 2013, it was announced that Christian Cigrang, heir of an Antwerp shipping family, became an investor in your company. How did this come about?

It happened very naturally. We met and we immediately connected. Cigrang believes in what we do and shares our vision of the company. The way I see it, he is an entrepreneur with respect for creative people, not only fashion people. If you ask me whether this structure will give me time to concentrate on all things creative, the answer is yes, to a certain degree. If the company grows, we can hire extra staff. But I will still have to be fashion designer and entrepreneur. That's my job.

You have won some prestigious awards. Can you elaborate on the financial impact of these prizes?

Although it's difficult to measure and prove the impact, the prizes really helped me. One of the rewards of the Woolmark Prize, for instance, was that five top retailers bought my collection. Awards also give you huge visibility, which is important for attracting new clients.

If you had to give just one piece of advice to a young fashion designer, what would you say?

Pursue your dreams, stay motivated even in difficult times and fight with passion.

"Pursue your dreams, stay motivated even in difficult times and fight with passion"

SS 14

case # 1   Christian Wijnants

Christian Wijnants
SS 14

THE EVOLVING NATURE OF SPECIALTY RETAIL FORMATS WITHIN THE FASHION SECTOR: FLAGSHIPS AND POP UPS

Karinna Nobbs

The fashion retail sector is one of the most dynamic and internationally competitive commercial industries (Moore and Docherty 2007, Tungate 2012). In order to maintain a point of differentiation, fashion brands increasingly have to seek new and innovative methods of capturing the hearts, minds and wallets of savvy consumers (Bhardwaj and Fairhurst 2010, Dillon 2012). This is particularly evident within retail, in which the growth of fashion e-commerce means that brands need to give consumers a reason to visit a brick-and-mortar store (Sorescu 2011, Nobbs et al 2012, Mintel 2013). This shift has forced change and innovation within the fashion retail sector.

The aim of this chapter is to outline this change with respect to the evolution of *specialty retail formats*. Specifically it will address two types of specialty retail format: firstly, the *flagship store* and secondly, the *pop up store*. The chapter begins by outlining and defining the retail format concept and explaining its wider purpose for a fashion brand. Then the history and characteristics of both the flagship and the pop up are discussed and interesting examples of each are presented.

Retailing occupies an important position in the economies of contemporary society. In terms of a definition of a retail format there is a lack of consensus however. Reynolds et al. (2008: 648) define it as "the physical embodiment of a retail business model: the framework that relates the firm's activities to its business context and strategy". This description is useful as it highlights the relationship between the corporate strategy to the tangible elements of the store design. The notion of *design* is therefore key to the concept of a retail format. Walters & White (1987) agree, underlining that the successful implementation of a positioning statement requires the appropriate use of retail design in order to translate the overall brand strategy.

According to Bruce et al. (2004) the main role of the retail format is to communicate a retailer's capability in respect to their marketing mix offer. It also serves as the unifying component of the competitive plan, i.e. bringing all parts of the business plan together (Goldman 2001). The retail format also has a positioning role, where we understand *retail positioning* to be "a co-ordinated statement to be made to the consumer through merchandise selection, trading format, customer services and customer communication" (Harris & Walters 1992:3). A trading format is also a strategy for growth, whereby as brands diversify their products and ranges they require differentiated store environments (Fernie and Sparks 2004). Furthermore, the retail format plays an operational role in determining both the purchasing requirements (i.e. stock) and the production management model (i.e. sourcing and replenishment) for a store (Guercini 2008).

The creation of a retail format strategy can be based on a number of internal and external environmental factors. From an internal perspective some successful formats can and do emerge from structured business models. However, often, winning formats can also materialise from an opportunistic and incremental process, based more on intuition than rational analysis. Guercini (2008) describes this approach as "organic". A brand such as *Comme Des Garçons* with their guerrilla, flagship and Dover Street Market store format can be described as such. From an external perspective Guercini (2008) argues that what ultimately drives change in retail formats are changes in consumer products and lifestyles. He specifically identifies that a fundamental polarisation in consumer behaviour has taken place whereby consumers today simultaneously have a preference for large-scale/convenience formats alongside a growing rise in specialty formats. This is evident in the retail format experiments of department stores like Selfridges in London, Lane

Crawford in Hong Kong and Barneys in New York. Walters & Hanrahan (2000) also look externally to state the importance of identifying the customer shopping mission (i.e. the decision making and behavioural process) as an initial step in deciding the format and trading environment strategy.

Retail formats have limited lives, thus supporting the need for a life cycle approach which is based on environmental analysis (Reynolds et al. 2008). Levy et al (2005) also previously identified the importance of self-monitoring a brands' stage of retail format "innovation" and "exit" within the market. A final challenge with respect to approaches to format innovation is the creative tension between market-led and finance-led motivations for change. For example, new geographic market opportunities, versus pressure from shareholders and investors to expand.

Reynolds et al. (2008) propose four features of contemporary format change in UK retailing. Generally these include: *a drive to scale, volatility in scale, a rise in specialty formats and a growth in "value"*, not discount retailing. They continue to identify three types of specialty retail format: *e-commerce, flagships* and *pop ups*. The last two will be discussed more in detail in this chapter, as e-commerce is addressed elsewhere in the book (see **CHAPTER THREE** Communicating fashion in the new era: understanding social media and corporate social responsibility).

E-COMMERCE

E-commerce has become one of the fastest growing retail formats globally, with the majority of fashion brands reporting year on year double-digit growth, while sector specialists like ASOS are about to hit their £1 billion sales target in 2013 (Reuters 2013). E-commerce is defined by Chaffey (2011:7) as "all types of electronic transactions between organisations and stakeholders whether they are financial transactions or exchanges of information or other services". The e-commerce retail format offers a lean profit margin and economies of scale and is both utilised as a *pure-play* (online only) or *omni-channel* ("bricks and clicks") model. If operating as a pure-play, a successful e-commerce model relies on an effective logistics and IT infrastructure combined with a strong public relations (PR) strategy. This is essential as the brand must have good exposure both online in search engine optimisation (SEO) and social media and offline in traditional media. If operating as an omni-channel, the same is true – however the physical presence in stores enhances brand exposure and therefore sales potential. Currently, mid-to-large fashion brands are investing in the integration of their back office systems in order to facilitate a true omni-channel experience for the customer (*The Guardian* 2013). For small fashion brands and emerging designers, the decision on whether to develop an e-commerce platform should be dependent on its business model and its position in the marketplace. E-commerce offers an increased degree of control in how the brand is presented and also allows the potential for a higher margin to be achieved due to the sales being direct.

FLAGSHIPS

A variety of definitions have been offered to describe a flagship store.

Kozinets et al. (2002:17)	"They carry a single brand, the brand manufacturer owns them, they are operated with the intention of building the brand rather than operating to sell product"
Mikunda (2004:228)	"The principal store of a retail chain"
Jackson (2004:177)	"Allows the brand to re-enforce its image communication through establishing a physical presence in a prestige shopping location and to influence the experience at the point-of-sale"
Diamond (2005:12)	"The most important in a chain"
Varley (2005:176)	"The pinnacle in retail chain, usually large and located in a high footfall prestigious location, with a full range of merchandise but an emphasis on the more expensive high quality and high fashion lines"
Mores (2006:25)	"A translation of the marketing strategy into a 360 degree experience of consumption, and is increasingly becoming the company's prime mass medium"
Fringis (2008:458)	"The largest and most representative store in a chain organisation"
Nobbs et al (2012:920)	"A larger than average specialty retail format in a prominent geographical location, offering the widest and deepest product range within the highest level of store environment and serving to showcase the brand's position, image and values"

Figure 1.
Definitions of a flagship store format.

The definitions offered by Mikunda, Diamond, Varley, Mores, Fringis and Nobbs et al are all deemed effective. The definition offered by Kozinets is less applicable and the reasons are threefold. Firstly, flagships can regularly carry more than one brand; for example the Armani and Sony store in Milan (Bingham 2005). Secondly, within luxury fashion, the brand manufacturer usually but does not always own the flagship. An example of this is Burberry in India who operates a joint venture with Genesis Luxury Group. Finally, Kozinets's assertion that the flagship's sole purpose is to build the brand is contradicted by emerging evidence that flagships may also increasingly be meeting a *commercial* purpose; i.e. generating revenue (Allegra Strategies 2005, Moore & Docherty 2007, Nobbs et al 2012).

HISTORY OF THE FLAGSHIP

Figure 2 illustrates the evolution of the flagship concept. This specialty format has developed out of two fashion strands: the private apartments of the couturier, and traditional small luxury shops. Paris has always been considered the true home of luxury and, historically, influential French fashion brands operated *maisons* which housed the atelier (workshops/studio), a showroom and a retail boutique. Often the creative director also lived there (Bingham 2005). According to Mores (2006), the next development appears to have been the opening of the Fiorucci store in Milan in 1967. This was seen as the designer's "personal inclusive vision of fashion" and it spawned the *concept store format*. Concept shops are clever stores which aspire to be striking but are on a smaller scale from flagship stores (Mikunda 2004).

The next step in the evolution of the flagship was the advent of the *lifestyle store* in the 1980s. Mikunda (2004) suggests that lifestyle stores have an under-rated cultural and social function to communicate style awareness and assurance. Ralph Lauren has been very successful at this, cultivating the aristocratic, classic lifestyle of the polo-playing/golfing classes by designing his stores as if they were inviting consumers into his home (Mikunda 2004, Diamond 2005). By the end of the eighties, in a counter reaction to the lifestyle store concept, directional luxury fashion stores became minimalist in design and stores resembled art galleries (Mores 2006). In the early nineties, fashion brands were increasingly diversifying their product range and they required large stores in which to display multiple product categories. In 1996, Nike opened Niketown first in New York and later in London and across the globe, effectively (it is suggested) inventing the concept of "flagships". At the time, many thought this just a marketing proposition; today, however, almost every fashion brand has a flagship in its store portfolio (Wgsn 2007). Mikunda (2004) notes that ubiquity of flagship store design has become a kind of avant-garde new popular culture. As a result, certain luxury fashion brands, most notably Prada and Louis Vuitton, realized that in order to maintain a point of differentiation they would have to enhance their flagship strategy. Prada created three "Epicentre" stores that set a new standard for flagships. The distinguishing feature of their flagship was not just the architecture per se but rather innovation and experimentation, in particular the fusing of commerce and culture. For example, in the New York store there is a flexible space where concerts and lectures can be held; to some degree the merchandise is secondary (Barreneche 2005). Due to the level of investment required, flagship stores tend to be utilised by more established brands or those using it as a market entry or growth strategy. For independent designers, the launch of a flagship store symbolizes a certain maturity in its stage of business as control over the store environment and marketing mix is taken back. This is also a high-risk strategy as inexperience can affect performance

Figure 2.
The evolution of the flagship retail format.

FASHION MANAGEMENT

and the longevity of the business. The most recent evolution of the flagship concept is driven by technology. *Digital flagships* have risen to prominence due to Gucci's high-profile (digital) launch in 2010. Since then, Zegna and Diesel have also rebranded their e-commerce offering as a "digital flagship". It will be interesting to see to what extent this strategy will be adopted by other fashion brands as if the difference between X and Y remains unclear.

FORM OF THE FLAGSHIP

Figure 3 illustrates the six main characteristics of the flagship store as synthesised from research by Kozinets et al. (2002), Mikunda (2004), Jackson (2004), Moore & Docherty (2007), Fringis (2008), Nobbs et al (2012).

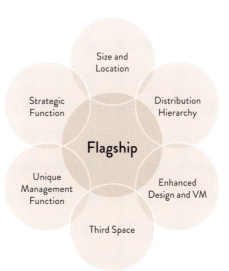

Figure 3.
The characteristics of a fashion flagship store.

Size and Location

Allegra Strategies (2005) agree that a prime location is a critical success factor and that flagships should be at prime sites in the most important shopping areas. Moore et al. (2000) identify that luxury fashion flagship stores are typically in capital cities on premium shopping streets (Bond Street, London; Fifth Avenue, New York and Avenue Montagine, Paris). Moore and Docherty (2007) support this, adding that flagships tend to be concentrated on specific streets accessible to HNWI (High Net Worth Individuals), fashion innovators and tourists. Walters & White (1987) postulate that the success of a retail formula rests on the appropriateness of its location. For example, some brands may choose the most prestigious streets while others enjoy an "attention grabbing alternative" in fringe areas that add *"frisson"* (Bingham 2005). The location serves to make sure the right customer profile is being reached and the "right" statement is being made about the brand (Allegra Strategies 2005).

Distribution Hierarchy

A flagship store tends to offer the full range of products, both in terms of breadth and depth within a range and across categories (men's, women's, accessories, home and childrenswear) (Moore & Docherty 2007, Varley 2005, Fernie et al. 1998). A flagship store should also hold the potential for exclusive ranges, as in the case of brands like Tiffany & Co, Marc Jacobs and Comme des Garçons (Verdict 2007). Allegra Strategies (2005) found that a critical success factor of a flagship store is sufficient space to offer the full product range and possibly additional products and services not offered in other stores. Store size and distribution dimensions are therefore linked.

Enhanced Design and Visual Merchandising (VM)

Architecture and design play a significant role in reflecting and helping build the identity of a brand (Barreneche 2005). Interestingly, as the boundaries between retail, art and architecture have blurred, architects and artists have increasingly wanted to work with fashion brands (Bingham 2005). Of course, fashion designers have been turning to architects to magnify the image of their labels since the seventies (Mores 2006). However, it was the collaboration between John Pawson and Calvin Klein in 1996 that gave momentum to this collaboration (Barreneche 2005). Visual stimulus within a flagship induces customers into a silent dialogue with the fashion designer's broader vision (Bingham 2005). Future Systems (2008) said of their design of the Marni flagship that the clothes become part of an overall composition; i.e. not separated from the design, but part of it. Allegra Strategies (2005) found that flagships are used as a role model within the chain to trial new visual merchandising concepts and ideas. Furthermore, due to the importance of the flagship within the distribution hierarchy, it must have the highest standards and the most impressive and emotive window and interior displays.

Third Space

Over the past five years the notion of "third space" or "place" has emerged within the retail context. Third space is defined by Mikunda (2004: 11) as "somewhere which is not work or home but a comfortable space to browse, relax and meet people, even enjoy a meal". There is a public garden at Prada in Tokyo, you can get a massage in Kenzo's Paris flagship, and at Dolce & Gabbana in Milan you can get a shave and then have a cocktail at the Martini and Rossi Bar. Allegra Strategies (2005) suggest third space is a critical success factor for a flagship store and may involve events and/or entertainment elements. Experiences form an integral part of third place as they activate psychological experience mechanisms (Mikunda 2004). Nobbs and Manlow (2013) identify a taxonomy of third space within flagship stores which evolves in terms of *complexity*, *risk* and *cost*. Rest/lounge areas are the simplest, followed by space for art/culture, then food and drink and, finally,

FASHION   MANAGEMENT

the specialist space, which is diverse (and additional to the core fashion business) and may include, for example, health and beauty or technology. The Armani Centre in Milan has all of these aspects of third space within its 129,000 sq ft, offering all its clothing lines, as well as a home furnishing section, flower shop, confectionary counter, bookstore, restaurant, bar and Sony electronics gallery. This "total Armani lifestyle experience" was enhanced by the addition of an Armani hotel in 2011. Third space is a blend of retail and leisure, where there is an emphasis on socialization and which ultimately functions to enhance dwell time in store.

Unique Management Structure

As a result of their unique status within a firm and the increased pressure on standards and performance, many flagship stores operate a differentiated management structure in terms of operations, sales and VM. For example, within luxury fashion flagship retail, sales advisors sell in a specific product category so that they can provide depth of knowledge. With respect to VM, most fashion flagship stores will have a dedicated full-time team within the branch due to the need for the store to always look its best. Flagship stores tend also to have an extended management team, with multiple assistant managers who focus on a specific business function like stock, human resources or administration.

Strategic Function

The significant financial investments into flagship stores by fashion brands are indicative of their strategic purpose (Moore & Docherty 2007). There is no clear consensus as to what the ultimate objective of a flagship store should be, however they do play an important role in retailer's strategies to represent the brand's identity, values and philosophy internally and externally (Allegra Strategies 2005). Similarly Riewold (2002) argues that the primary objective is not to sell the product but to generate a fascination with the brand, creating a deep-set emotional anchor. Varley (2005) too suggests that the role of the flagship store is essentially about retail brand building and reinforcement rather than profitability. However Allegra Strategies (2005) and Nobbs and Manlow (2013) have discovered that, whereas many flagship store formats were formerly covered by the marketing budget, flagship stores are expected increasingly to not only represent the brand but also to generate profit, which in turn makes them a potentially effective and cost-efficient marketing tool.

POP UPS

The pop up format is a relatively new retail concept and this is reflected in the nature of the academic coverage of the subject. The majority of definitions of the concept are found in recent journal articles and in textbooks on retail and marketing communication, however these are scarce (Spena et al. 2012). Pop up stores can also be referred to as "temporary", "guerilla", "flash retail" or "nomad" stores (Surchi 2011), although, as we will discuss later, each has unique format connotations.

Neihm et al (2007:1)	"A new experiential marketing format intended to engage consumers. It is a short term promotional/retail setting designed to offer an exclusive and highly experiential interaction for the consumer"
Kim et al (2010:134)	"A marketing environment which is highly experiential, focused on promoting a brand or product line, available for a short time period, and generally in smaller venues that foster more face-to-face dialogue with brand representatives"
Surchi (2011:257)	"The establishment and operation by established manufacturers of short-term retail premises"
Norsig (2011:11)	"A short term retail location"
Posner (2011:219)	"A temporary store set up for a limited time frame...often including some kind of event to create buzz"
Lea-Greenwood (2012: 28)	"A short term lease in a location that the retailer might not normally consider"
Spena et al (2012:21)	"Short-lasting brand stores located in highly representative locations that aim to develop brand awareness and strengthen brand loyalty and value through a recreational happening"

The most common feature evident within each of the definitions, and the pop up store's definitive facet, is the non-permanent (temporary) or short-term nature of the store. The next most important aspect is that of its experiential function. Neihm (2007), Kim et al (2010) and Posner (2011) all note that the atmosphere and environment of the store should generate engagement and excitement with the consumer. Finally, location is key. Kim et al (2010) and Lea-Greenwood both highlight that "un-typical to the brand" size or geographic location strategies are characteristic of pop up stores. The most comprehensive definition of the pop up is proposed by Neihm et al (2007) as it includes each of these three aspects and also mentions the dual marketing/retail role of a pop up. Therefore this definition will be used within the context of this chapter.

Figure 4.
Definition of pop up stores.

HISTORY OF THE POP UP

The first brand credited with starting the pop up phenomenon is an LA-based company called Vacant who, in 1999, after observing consumers queuing in Japan for limited edition products, were inspired to buy and curate exclusive products in small quantities and sell them in a unique location in London for a month, closing the store after the goods had sold out (Boxhall 2012). Neihm et al (2007) and Hopkins (2012) highlight Target as an early pioneer and leader of pop up retail, their first experiment being on a barge on the Hudson River in 2002. They have since experimented with a variety of different product lines and locations. Vacant opened their second pop up store in New York in 2003 with the tag line "is it a store? or is it a gallery?" thus exposing the dual-functional nature of the store (Tzortiz 2004). In 2004 Commes Des Garçons (CDG) created a series of "anti-concept" concept stores (which they called "guerrilla stores"), so called because they were open for a year, had an artistic store interior and were located in raw urban yet-to-be gentrified areas (Neihm et al 2007). What is interesting about this unconventional retail model was the stock: CDG chose out of season (or old) stock, effectively using the store as a means of reducing inventory (Horn 2004). Adopting this approach increased the value of the stock and changed its meaning from old to exclusive. Also in 2004, trend agency Trendwatching.com tracked the "pop up retail" trend, highlighting it as a global movement seen at all levels of the market (Trendwatching.com 2013).

After 2005 the trend tricked across to other industries, like leisure (food and beverage brands) and automotive (Zmunda 2009). In 2007 Japanese fast fashion retailer Uniqlo operated travelling pop up stores in New York to promote the launch of its new flagship store. Using shipping containers, Uniqlo dropped these unique pop up stores during the night and then moved them to another location the next night, thereby creating buzz and hype about the previously unknown brand (Gogoi 2007). Since then, due to their low cost and flexibility of the store interior, brands from Hermes, All Saints and Puma have also used shipping containers. Taking this to the next level is Boxpark, the world's first pop up mall, which opened in East London in 2011. Created by Rodger Wade, the founder of fashion brand Boxfresh, he created it to be the antithesis of homogenized high streets and out-of-town shopping malls (Boxpark 2011). The mall is populated by a curated mix of 60 lifestyle, niche and emerging brands and has become a destination location within the already hip East London retail scene.

The pop up concept has since been criticized for being ubiquitous. However, in a difficult economic environment, pop ups can be a way to regenerate falling high street occupancy levels (Zmunda 2009, Cochrane 2010). Thompson (2012) and Spena et al. (2012) note that in developed retail locations the number of pop up stores have significantly increased. The benefits to a landlord of having a property occupied are that it is less likely to attract antisocial behaviour, and that it contributes to the overall health of the location it sits on. Furthermore if the pop up is successful it may be made permanent, which ultimately benefits all stakeholders (Zmunda 2009).

The most recent incarnation of the pop up store has been online: digital pop up stores have been trialled (with mixed success) by Rachael Roy, Bvulgari and H&M (Mashable.com 2012). There are a variety of platforms to choose from, with a flurry of Facebook pop ups occurring in 2011. The most commercially successful of these was Rachel Roy, who used the concept to promote a new product collaboration. She offered both exclusive product and editorial content thereby giving consumers a reason to visit the online pop up. The product sold out within hours and the publicity generated on social media was invaluable. H&M have created a pop up e-commerce microsite for each designer collaboration. These sites have been praised for their visually appeal, but criticized for their poor logistical support, as the sites tend to crash due to underestimations of traffic (Fashionista.com 2011).

It is clear that the pop up is used by fashion brands at all levels of the market place – from luxury to mass market – and that its strength lies in its versatility as a marketing and retail tool. Furthermore, pop up stores are an especially useful strategic option for small or emerging fashion brands (or independent designers) who don't have the budget to open a permanent store and who are still testing the market for demand. In the past two years we have seen the emergence of pop up co-operative stores in Europe and Northern America. These are often supported by government or trade bodies and function as a cumulative showcase of talent while also providing a vehicle for brand awareness for the designers.

FORM OF THE POP UP

A review of the literature highlights *six main characteristics* (and *four main types*) of pop up format (see Figure 5).

Figure 5.
Characteristics and formats
of pop up stores.

Time

This refers to the length of time the store is open. Limited life spans and pre-determined timeframes are key (Surchi 2011). The shortest timeframe for a pop up is a few hours. An example of this are the stores created for Vogue's fashion night out in September, undertaken by brands like ASOS and Net-a-Porter. The longest type of pop up sign leases for a year, on average they tend to be open for 1-3 months, enough time to be discovered, shopped in and written about before the demand wanes. Their temporary nature is their most definitive feature and the one which generates the greatest call to action from consumers i.e. visiting the store.

Size

The academic literature and industry press indicate that pop ups tend to be smaller in size than normal format stores (Neihm et al 2007). It is suggested that this is because it adds to the sense of exclusivity and buzz. Because there is not a full product range expected, brands are also able to keep costs lower.

Location

Surchi (2011:27) highlights the importance of location: "[it] is part of the packaging and the store itself becomes the product". Thus location contributes to the overall identity and experience of the brand. Traditionally, pop ups tend to be located in high-traffic city centre locations in order to maximise sales and consumer exposure (Kim et al 2010). The counter strategy to this is exemplified by Vacant and CDG, who choose offbeat underground locations to act as destination store and add to the allure of the brand. Both options suggest the importance of choosing a location based on a combination of market positioning, target market and the objectives of the pop up. Furthermore the format of the pop up will influence the location choice.

Design

Ryan (2010) suggests it is important to use brand colours to convey the brand personality and values. Ryan (2010) also states that the design and visual merchandising do not require as much "polish" and can have a temporary feel. This is evident in Prada's pop up store in 2010 in which cardboard, basic wood and *trompe l'oeil* were used to maximum effect.

Experience and Interactivity

Another important feature of the design and layout is that it should provide opportunity for interactivity (Neihm et al 2007). Having some aspect of "third space" is also evident within pop up stores (this is discussed in more detail below). The notion of experience and interactivity is suggested to be essential within pop ups as they operate not just to retail products but also to market the brand. In contemporary society the roles of consumer and producer intermingle and this is demonstrated in the trends of co-creation, customization and experiential retailing (Solomon and Rabolt 2003). Most commercially sucessful pop up stores appear to have two, if not all, of these aspects. Kim et al's (2010) study of pop up store consumers found that they valued novelty and hedonic features, and based future store patronage on these. Furthermore Spena et al (2012) noted that pop up stores are an ideal vehicle for the co-creation of value through the experience of the consumer's level of interaction within the store.

Viral Promotion

Due to their "guerilla" nature it is logical for pop ups to adopt a similar approach to their communication mix. A fundamental tool of their unconventional marketing communication is the generation and exploitation of word-of-mouth promotion, both online and offline (Posner 2011). Indeed there is generally little to no above the line promotion and social media in particular which adds a "cool factor" and contributes to the novelty and discovery values that a pop up hopes to promote (Surchi 2011).

FORMAT OF POP UP STORES

Based on Surchi's (2011) classifications, there are *four main typologies* of pop up stores. The first is the *traditional* pop up, which describes a store which has all six of the above-mentioned characteristics and uses an existing store or conventional space which can be converted. This is a low-risk option followed by the majority of pop ups, especially those targeting the mass market. Examples of the traditional pop up include Liberty's 2012 Olympic pop up in a shopping centre close to the games; United Colours of Benetton's Art of the Knit pop up in a disused garage in Soho NYC; and Phillip Lim's 3.1 four-stage technologically enhanced pop up in Hong Kong. Another version of the traditional pop up is the *shop-in-shop concept*, whereby a supermarket, department or multi-brand store will allow space for a pop up. An example of this is the Missoni for Target pop up in New York in 2010 which has been heralded as one of the most successful pop ups in fashion retail (*Wall Street Journal* 2011).

The second type of pop up is the *nomad* and its key differential is that the store is outside and mobile i.e. there is always flexibility of location (Surchi 2011). This is one of the most dynamic types of pop up in a variety of forms that have been designed and adapted into retail stores. As mentioned earlier, shipping containers have been a popular choice, as have forms of transport, including boats, buses, vans, cars, trains and even aeroplanes. Temporary structures like tents, pavilions and marquees have also been utilised. Shanghai Tang's 2011 Mongolian Yurt in Hong Kong, which was operated whilst their flagship store was being refurbished, is a good example of the Nomad pop up. Another celebrated example is by Uniqlo (masters of the pop up concept), who created LED ice cube pop up stores that travelled around New York in 2011 to promote their heat-tech range of products.

The third type is the *mono-event* pop up store. Similar to the *Nomad*, it is outside, though its definitive feature is that it happens only once and usually operates as part of an event or festival. Therefore this format of pop up store has the shortest life span. As with the other types of pop up, location remains a key characteristic as it has a direct relationship with the consumer's experience and associations while in the pop up (Kim et al 2011). Sponsorships and celebrity endorsements are particularly effective in this context as a brand will want to gain mutual benefit by choosing to retail a pop up at an event or festival which is complementary to the brand. For example, in 2012 Puma converted a food van into a mobile lounge at SXSW (music and digital festival in Texas) where consumers could customise t-shirts, play games and get refreshments. The SXSW festival brand is innovative and youthful and by operating here those values can be transferred to the Puma brand. Another example is Oxfam's pop up in a tent at Glastonbury in 2011, where they offered DIY fashion workshops and fair-trade refreshments.

The final type of pop up is *digital*. As mentioned previously, these stores can be hosted on a variety of platforms, from Facebook and Second-life to conventional extensions of e-commerce sites. Even though these pop ups are in a radically different format to offline pop ups, they nonetheless share the six main characteristics. Digital pop ups are time-bound and range from a few hours to a maximum of three months. They are smaller in terms of content and product range than traditional e-retail stores, tending to focus on a specific product range. The location refers to which technology platform is used, the choice of which depends on the function of the pop up store. The design of a digital pop up offers more freedom than the other typologies (anything can be created), but it is suggested that, for consistency, brand colours and logos should be utilised. An exception is if the pop up aims to take the brand in a new direction or has a niche focus. Space for interactivity is also essential in a digital pop up and this is normally facilitated through links to social networks and the inclusion of a facility for comments and discussion. Finally, digital pop ups of course lend themselves to viral promotion and electronic word of mouth (eWOM). An example is Nicola Formichetti's 2011 NicoPanda e-pop up, which was open for three months and sold a curated mix of his brand and other brands (like Versace and Mugler) that he works with. This concept was a follow on from two commercially successful traditional pop up stores (in New York and Hong Kong) and demonstrates a way to increase the longevity of the pop up.

FASHION MANAGEMENT

SUMMARY

This chapter has served to illustrate two types of specialty retail format which have come to be adopted by fashion brands at all levels of the market, from mass market or independent designers to luxury market. A retail format essentially functions as a representation of the brand's business model and communicates its core values and personality. This can be done tangibly in the form of a brick-and-mortar store or intangibly from an e-commerce platform. As a result of intense competition between brands and increased choice for consumers, fashion brands have developed a variety of retail formats. The majority have experimented with the flagship and the pop up concept, in particular. The flagship format was described as evolving from the luxury *maisons* of Paris and the lifestyle stores of the 1980s. It was suggested that, to be classed as a true flagship, a store needs to have a combination of six features, with the notion of third space being an emergent aspect. The pop up store, on the other hand, is a more recent phenomenon that has gone from trend to accepted marketing/retail tool. Six key features of a pop up were described in this chapter, with length of time it is open for being its definitive one. Additionally, four types of pop up were classified: traditional, nomad, mono-event and digital. Each of these specialty retail formats can play distinct and strategic roles for fashion brands and, provided they are not exhausted or abused, they will continue to be in existence. Finally, for both the flagship and pop up, their potential lies in the complex convergence of the digital and material worlds.

REFERENCES

Allegra Strategies (2005) *Project Flagship: Flagship Stores in the UK*. London: Allegra Strategies Limited.

Barreneche, R, A. (2008) *New Retail*. London: Phaidon Press.

Bingham, N. (2005), *The New Boutique*. London: Merrell.

Bhardwaj, V. and Fairhurst, A. (2010) Fast fashion: response to changes in the fashion industry. In: *The International Review of Retail, Distribution and Consumer Research*, 20(1), 165-173.

Boxpark (2011) *The worlds first pop up mall*. Press Release 02/08/11. Accessed at http://www.worldretailcongress.com/press-releases/2012/BOXPARK-release Sept.pdf Accesssed on 04/01/13.

Boxhall, N. (2012) Are pop up stores the answer to empty high streets? In: *The Guardian*, Accessed at http://www.theguardian.com/ money/2012/jul/20/pop-up-shops empty-high-street Accessed on 02/02/13.

Bruce, M. Moore, C and Birtwistle, G. (2004) *International Retail Marketing: A Case Study Approach*. London: Butterworth Heinemann.

Chaffey, D. (2011) *E-Business and E-Commerce Management*. London: Financial Times/Prentice Hall.

Cochrane, K. (2010) Why pop ups Pop up everywhere. In: *The Guardian*, Tuesday October 10th, accessed at http://www.guardian.co.uk/lifeandstyle/2010/oct/12/popup-temporary-shops-restaurants. Accessed on 31/01/13.

Diamond, E. (2005) *Fashion Retailing: A Multi-Channel Approach*. New Jersey: Prentice Hall.

Dillon, S. (2012) *The Fundamentals of Fashion Management*. London: AVA Publishing.

Fashionista.com (2011) *Versace for H&M crashes retailers e-commerce site in the UK*. Accessed at http://fashionista.com/2011/11/versace-for-h-us-site-to-launch-in-fall-2012/ Accessed on 04/01/13.

Fernie, J., Moore, C.M. and Lawrie, A. (1998) A tale of two cities: an examination of fashion designer retailing within London and New York. In: *Journal of Product & Brand Management*, Vol. 7 No. 5, 366-78.

Fernie, J. and Sparks, L. (2004) *Logistics and Retail Management*. London: 2nd edition, Kogan Page.

Frings, G, S. (2008) Fashion: *From Concept to Consumer*. New Jersey: Prentice Hall.

Future Systems (2008) *Architecture-Marni*. Accessed on 08/02/08. Accessed at <http://www.future-systems.com/architecture/architecture_13.html>

Gogoi, P. (2007) *Pop up Stores – All the Rage*, Business Week, February 9th, Accessed at http://www.businessweek.com/stories/2007-02-09/pop-up-stores-all-the-ragebusinessweek-business-news-stock-market-and-financial-advice accessed at 04/01/13.

Goldman, A. (2001) The Transfer of Retail Formats into Developing Economies: the example of China. In: *Journal of Retailing*, 77, 221-241.

Guercini, S. (2008) Matching format strategy and sourcing strategy in clothing retail: a conceptual representation. In: *International Journal Process Management and Benchmarking*, Vol. 2, No. 3, 185-196.

Harris, D. and Walters, D.W. (1992) *Retail Operations Management*. London: Prentice Hall.

Horn, C. (2004) A store made for right now: you shop till its dropped. In: The New York Times, February 17th. Accessed at http://www.nytimes.com/2004/02/17/nyregion/a-storemade-for-right-now-you-shop-until-it-s-dropped.html?pagewanted=all&src=pm accessed on 3/01/13.

Hopkins, H, D. (2012) Living in a Pop up World. In: *Huffington Post*. Accessed at http://www.huffingtonpost.com/matthewdavid-hopkins/pop-up-shops_b_2082841.html accessed on 2/01/13.

Jackson, T. (2004) A contemporary analysis of global luxury brands. In: Bruce, M., Moore, C. and Birtwistle, G. (Eds), *International Retail Marketing: A Case Study Approach*. Oxford: Elsevier Butterworth Heinemann.

Kozinets, R.V., Sherry, J., DeBerry Spence, F., Duhachek, A., Nuttavuthisit, K., Storm, D. (2002) Themed flagship brand stores in the new millenium. In: *Journal of Retailing*, Vol. 78., 17-29.

Kim, H., Fiore, A.M., Neihm, L. and Jeong, M. (2010) Psychographic characteristics affecting behavioral intentions towards pop-up retail. In: *International Journal of Retail & Distribution Management*, Vol. 38 Iss: 2, 133-154.

Levy, M., Grewal, D., Kopalle, Praveen K., & Hess, James D. (2004) Emerging trends in retail pricing practice: Implications for research. In: *Journal of Retailing*, 80(3), xiii-xxi.

Lea-Greenwood, G. (2012) *Fashion Marketing Communication*. London: John Wiley & Sons.

Mashable (2011) *Five ways retailers are winning big with Facebook commerce*. Accessed at http://mashable.com/2011/03/22/facebook-commerce-retailers/ accessed on 3/01/13.

Mintel (2013) *Clothing Report*. London: Mintel Retail Intelligence.

Mikunda, C. (2004) *Brand Lands, Hot Spots & Cool Spaces*. London: Kogan Page.

Moore, C., M. Fernie, J., Burt, S. (2000) Brands without Boundaries: The Internationalisation of the designer retailer's brand. In: *European Journal of Marketing*, Vol. 34, No. 8, 919-937.

Moore, C, M. and Doherty, A. M. (2007) The International Flagship Stores of Luxury Fashion Retailers. In: Hines, T. and Bruce, M. *Fashion Marketing: Contemporary Issues*. 2nd Edition. Oxford: Butterworth-Heinemann.

Mores, C, M. (2006) From Fiorucci to the Guerrilla Stores: Shop Displays. In: *Architecture, Marketing and Communications*. Oxford: Winsor Books.

Niehm, L., Kim, H., Fiore, A., M,. and Jeong, M. (2007) Pop-up retail acceptability as an innovative business strategy and enhancer of the consumer shopping experience. In: *Journal of Shopping Center Research*, Vol.13 No.2, 1-30.

Nobbs, K., Moore, C., and Sheridan, M. (2012) Luxury Fashion Brand Strategy: The Role of the Flagship Store. In: *International Review of Retail and Distribution Management*, Vol. 40 Iss: 12, 920-934.

Manlow, V. and Nobbs, K. (2013) Form and function of luxury flagships: An international exploratory study of the meaning of the flagship store for managers and customers. In: *Journal of Fashion Marketing and Management*, Vol. 17 Iss: 1, 49-64.

Norsig, C. (2012) *Pop up Retail: mastering the global phenomenon*. New York: Bauhaus Press.

Posner, H. (2011) *Marketing Fashion*. London: Lawrence King.

Reuters (2013) ASOS *Full year profit jumps by 23 per cent*. Accessed at http://uk.reuters.com/article/2013/10/23/uk-asosresults idUKBRE99M04S20131023 Accessed on 23/10/13.

Riewolt, O. (2002) Brandscaping: *Worlds of Experience in Retail Design*. Switserland: Birkhauser Verlag AG.

Reynolds, J. Howard, E, Cuthbertson, C. Hristov, L (2007) Perspectives on retail format innovation: relating theory and practice. In: *International Journal of Retail & Distribution Management*; Volume: 35 Issue: 8, 647-660.

Sorescu, A. et al. (2011) *Innovation in Retail Business Models*. In: Journal of Retailing, Vol 1., 3-16.

Spena,T. R, Carida, A. Colurcio, M. and Melia, M. (2012) Store experience and co-creation: the case of temporary shop. In: *International Journal of Retail & Distribution Management*, Vol. 40 Iss: 1, 21-40.

Surchi, M. (2011) The temporary store: a new marketing tool for fashion brands. In: *Journal of Fashion Marketing and Management*, Vol. 15 Iss: 2, 257-270.

The Guardian (2013) *Omni channel retail – joining up the customer experience*. Accessed at http://www.theguardian.com/media-network/media-network blog/2013/jul/22/omni-channel-retail consumer-experience Accessed on 01/10/13.

Thompson, J. (2012) Pop up shops are licking the high street blues. In: *The Independent*, Monday December 6th, accessed at http://www.independent.co.uk/news/business/news/popup-shop-sare-licking-the-high-street-blues-8420078.html accessed on 31/01/13.

Trendwatching.com (2013) Pop up Retail. Accessed at http:// trendwatching.com/trends/popup_retail.htm accessed on 01/01/13.

Tungate, M. (2012) Fashion Brands: *Branding Style from Armani to Zara*. London: Kogan Page.

Tzortis, A, (2004) Pop up stores, here today and gone tomorrow. In: *The New York Times*, Monday October 25th accessed at http://www.nytimes.com/2004/10/24/business/worldbusiness/24ihtpopups25.html?pagewanted=all&_r=0 Accessed on 5/01/13.

Varley, R. (2005) *Retail Product Management*. London: Routledge.

Verdict (2007) *Global Luxury Retailing. Datamonitor*, October.

Wall Street Journal (2011) *Madhouse for Missoni*, September 9th. Accessed at http://online.wsj.com/article/SB10001424053111903285704576558850941728260.html. Accessed on 4/01/13.

Walters, D. & Hanrahan, J. (2000) *Retail Strategy: Planning & Control*, London: Macmillian.

Walters, D. & White, D. (1987) *Retail Marketing Management*. London: Palgrave MacMillan.

Wgsn (2007) Nike. Accessed at: http://www.wgsn-edu.com/members/retail-talk/features/rt2007sep03_081658?from=search Accessed on 05/01/13.

Zmunda, N. (2009) Pop up Stores pop as an inexpensive way to build buzz. In: *Ad Age*, August 31st, Accessed at http://adage.com/ article/news/marketing-pop-stores-brands-build-buzz/138704 Accessed on 5/01/13.

case # 2   Edouard Vermeulen

"Abroad, I am called the European Oscar de la Renta, or Carolina Herrera. Nobody will ever refer to me as the Prada of the North. That's perfectly fine by me"

In 2013, Belgian fashion house Natan celebrated its 30th anniversary. Edouard Vermeulen is the founder, designer and owner of Natan. The company is run independently, but Vermeulen is open to collaboration. "If Natan wants to become an international player, I can't do this on my own," he says.

Interview by
Trui Moerkerke

Natan has both a couture line and a ready-to-wear collection. Vermeulen is the favourite designer of the Belgian and Dutch royal families. But a lot of Belgian women are fans too: Natan has eight stores, sells in 120 multi-brand stores and has a team of 60 employees, 10 of which work in Natan's Brussels atelier. Natan is known for its contemporary classics.

You have been in this business for 30 years, as a fashion designer and entrepreneur. Would you say the fashion landscape has changed radically?

Totally. In the past five years, the business has completely changed. Thinking about two seasons a year? Think again. Now you need to adjust everything at least four times a year: not only your collection, but also your store presentations and your budgets.

Apart from that, your customers have changed and their consumer behaviour is different. High-street chains advertise rock-bottom prices. This affects the perception of prices. A pair of trousers for 250 euro now seems expensive, even if it is well made in fine materials. In our collection we constantly have to look for a balance between what we offer and our prices.

But I love the dynamics of our times. You can't sit back anymore and decide to do more of the same if a piece has sold well. Today, it doesn't work that way.

"I love the dynamics of our times"

Natan Couture FW 13-14

FASHION MANAGEMENT

"You need to know that a fashion designer does more than just sketching and styling. That's only a small part of the job"

When Natan turned 30 you announced that you wanted to expand the company and look for an international market. What are your plans?

I do not have specific plans yet, but I am considering some possibilities. This year, I want to take a decision. I will be 56 and I have to decide how I want to work in the next 10 years. I want it to be 10 happy years. You know, life whizzes by.

Continuing to focus on the Belgian market remains an option. Why not? The company is doing fine. But if I do decide to sell internationally, I will not do it alone. I've already been contacted by investment companies; that's their job. But if I decide to go that way, I want a clear project. One of the options is to hire an independent manager for half a year and let him or her prepare a plan: where are we going and how will we do that. With such a report, I can get the necessary funding.

In the coming months, I will also have meetings with some top executives in the luxury business. They surely will have interesting opinions and advice.

Do you want Natan to go on when you retire?

I don't think that's the most important question. Why should that have to happen? I have a family member who could take over. But this isn't easy. The heart and soul of a fashion house is often associated with its designer.

If you had to give advice to young fashion designers, what would it be?

Be passionate about what you do and be patient. You also have to realise that no one is waiting for you to arrive. You also need to know that a fashion designer does more than just sketching and styling. That's only a small part of the job. The collaboration between Yves Saint Laurent and his business partner Pierre Bergé is considered the textbook example of success. But times have changed. And besides, how many fashion designers do you know that have worked in the same way and succeeded?

Looking back at your career from a business perspective, do you have any regrets?

No. I am really proud that I was able to maintain the DNA of our label with success. I think that's quite an achievement. The best decision was to start the company with my own resources. My grandfather always said: "better to be a small boss than a major servant." I took that to heart. You could argue that I could have achieved more by now, but in that case I probably would have had to take big risks. The 30th anniversary of Natan is a great motivation to look forward. It's like making resolutions on New Year's Eve. You make plans, you look at the future with confidence. For Natan, 2014 will be an exciting year.

COMMUNICATING FASHION IN THE NEW ERA: UNDERSTANDING SOCIAL MEDIA AND CORPORATE SOCIAL RESPONSIBILITY

Francesca Romana Rinaldi

In this chapter the two main challenges that nowadays fashion brands have to face in communicating their identities will be addressed presenting the ground theory, some best practices and relevant questions about social media communication, corporate responsibility programmes, commitment to environmental and social sustainability.

THE SOCIAL MEDIA CHALLENGE IN FASHION

In the past decade fashion companies have been experiencing a dramatic transition in their relationship with consumers. The new consumers – it would be better to say "consum-actors" or "consum-authors" – increasingly trust online recommendations and feel comfortable sharing their choices and ideas. They want to be more informed about the origin of the product, manufacturing process and the labour used. The new consumer is willing to participate more and more in direct communication and dialogue with the company. Social media galvanised this revolution.

Communicating fashion in this new era requires that companies develop new competences, exhibit greater transparency of their supply chain and increasingly invest in the online channel.

Fashion and luxury companies allow people to dream and satisfy their certain needs of identification and association. Traditionally, the world of luxury brands denied access to a large portion of admirers. Social media however provides a sneak peek into the fashion system and society, thereby satisfying curiosity and interest. For this reason most fashion companies will have to face the complexities and challenges of communicating online.

COMMUNICATION IN FASHION

Communicating in fashion differs from communicating in other consumer goods industries in that it relies on a highly visual kind of communication. Preferred tools of communication include photographs, shows, showrooms, models, displays, videos and sample collections. According to Saviolo & Testa (2002) communication tools can be classified as follows:

- *seasonal* communication tools (for example: fashion shows, media, catalogues and fairs), which mainly communicate the *product*;

- *institutional* communication tools (for example: the brand, its headquarters, shops, sponsorship and business magazines), which mainly communicate the *brand*;

- *relational* communication tools (for example: social media, website, direct marketing, relational marketing, mailing, events), which communicate both *the product and the brand*.

- A further distinction is applied by Saviolo & Testa (2002) between "hot" and "cold" media: social media is an example of *hot media* (users are active and able to engage directly); television is perhaps the best example of *cold media* (users are passive and unable to engage directly).

A final distinction is made among product, brand and corporate communication. *Product communication* has the objective of increasing the *sell in* (wholesale) or *sell out* (retail) and its main tools include advertising, editorials, fashion shows and events, videos, catalogues, materials available in the stores, website. *Brand communication* has the objective of working on the *brand identity* and its main tools include: logo, heritage, designer/entrepreneur, spokesperson, celebrity marketing, flagship, website, viral marketing. *Corporate communication* has the objective of increasing the *reputation* of the company and its main tools include: internal communication, investor relations, foundations and sponsorships, charity, exhibitions, website.

SOCIAL MEDIA LANDSCAPE

THE WORLD WIDE VARIETY OF SOCIAL MEDIA

The social media space is highly fluid: it is represented by a variety of platforms from social networks such as *Facebook* to blogs such as *Tumblr* and micro-blogs such as *Twitter* to video-sharing platforms such as *YouTube* (see Figure 1).

The variety of social media is even higher if we consider country-by-country differences. In China, for example, the social media landscape is dominated by local social networks (see Figure 2). *Facebook* is not available and is substituted by *renren*; *Youku* is used instead of YouTube.

Social media has achieved universal penetration for the population with access to internet: its usage is relatively high worldwide, with the majority of online users (90% or more) accessing social sites.

Figure 1.
The Conversation Prism
(Source: Brian Solis
& JESS3, 2012
www.theconversationprism.com).

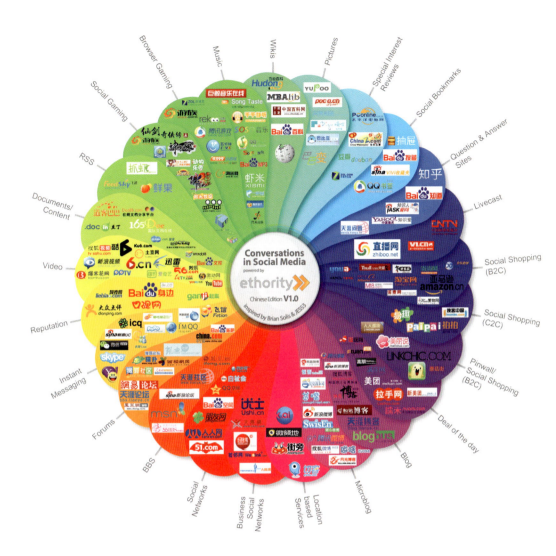

Figure 2.
Chinese Social Media Prism
(Source: www.ethority.net/blog/
social-media-prism

Companies – fashion companies among them – are paying careful attention to (online) traffic patterns as these reveal unexploited integration opportunities. Indeed social media is largely more important than the sites themselves for generating the traffic going to and coming from the fashion brand sites. Furthermore there is a strong relationship between the amount of traffic that brands generate from and to social media and their online performance in terms of traffic. For now, mobile applications and m-websites (websites specifically created for the mobile access) opportunities are exploited only by a minority of fashion brands.

HOW TO BE INNOVATIVE IN SOCIAL MEDIA

The level of *social media progress* of a fashion company can be determined by several *key social indicators* (see Table 1):

··· presence of social media platforms
··· type of language used
··· diversity of content among social platforms
··· level of interaction among social platforms
··· level of interaction with the fans

Key social indicators	Items	Evaluation
Presence of social media platforms	• number of social platforms that a brand has	Fashion companies should manage Facebook, YouTube and Twitter at least. Instagram and Pinterest are the next step.
Type of language used	• use of web-oriented language	Online language should be smart, synthetic and with a frequent use of questions to involve the fan.
Diversity of content among social platforms	• number of differentiated posts among platforms	The diversity of the contents among social platforms should be high.
Level of interaction among social platforms	• number of contents with sharing option among platforms	The level of interaction among social platforms should be high thanks to sharing tools.
Level of interaction with the fans	• number of likes • number of comments • number of comments that receive immediate reply	The level of interaction with the fans should be high: this is related to the "quality" and "shareability" of the contents.

Figure 3. | Key social indicators for the social media progress of a fashion company (Source: Francesca R. Rinaldi, Social Media Fashion Monitor, SDA Bocconi 2011).

The success of a social media communication is based on the coherence of its contents (what kind of projects/events do we select for the communication? Which products do we want to communicate?) and tone of voice (ironic? fairytale?) with the *brand identity*.

THE PARADOX OF SOCIAL MEDIA COMMUNICATION IN A LUXURY BUSINESS

The greatest challenge for luxury companies willing to invest in online communication is communicating to an elite group of people (the "creation of the dream") while simultaneously being open and transparent to a multitude of fans (potential customers) on social networks. This is a complex dilemma that high-end companies are obliged to solve. There is for example a high-end jewelry brand that on a first step decided not to open an account on Facebook: an e-tailer decided to open an independent account in the brand's name managing the conversation and especially the traffic generated thanks to the high brand awareness of this player. This is a very simple reason why managing the online conversation is fundamental for luxury brands as well.

How does one best use new media, and social networking's characteristic one-to-one communication, to resolve the trade-off between elitism and democracy? Some brands answered this question by making the brand "cool" in the digital world and finding ways to recreate elitism *online*, for example, by giving fans the opportunity to attend a live fashion show or talking directly with the creative director on social media platforms.

In its "Gucci E-Connect" campaign in 2010, the company invited fans to sign up for a unique virtual fashion show via Facebook. Facebook fans increased by 500,000 in just one week. In the same year, Louis Vuitton gave "behind the scenes" access in its Women's Live Fashion Show and a video narrated by Marc Jacobs (creative director at the time). The virtual experiences were arguably even better than the real ones.

In 2011, Burberry posted a video on Facebook showing their head designer Christopher Bailey who asked fans to post questions. He answered questions five days later in another video. Almost 3,000 people reacted to the two posts by commenting, asking questions and "liking" the post.

Of course the path is not always easy or smooth. High-end companies also need to find ways to reduce the risks of talking to a multitude of consumers, which means receiving positive or negative comments visible to all, actual clients and other potential clients. Managing the online conversation involves a lot of effort and time dedicated to planning and monitoring. The key rule is that content must be perfectly coherent with the brand identity and relevant to the community.

TIPS FOR EFFECTIVE SOCIAL MEDIA COMMUNICATION IN FASHION

Social media has huge potential to make communication between brand and consumer in a *two-way conversation*. The consumer/user of social media has the power to choose which messages to receive. By stimulating fan involvement, companies can establish a connection with fans, keep communication ongoing, and obtain a feedback directly from them.

Best practice for brands is to use a *web-oriented language* when communicating through posts or tweets. Brands should use an engaging, fairly informal language that is not purely commercial. Taglines, which are short slogans to define the contents posted online, must also be explicative; they must, in a simple and interesting way, give a description of the post and a preview of what the fan is going to read. Meaningless taglines and excessive formality may decrease the effectiveness of the content and reduce the level of interest of the fans thus generating lower traffic.

The company should publish content that explicitly invites the fan to participate (e.g. competitions or quizzes). To catch the fan's attention it is also useful to post topics on everyday life, as well as comments or questions on current affairs. Posts that advertise the brand's products are insufficient: content should stimulate fans and be in line with the brand's *lifestyle*.

It is interesting to notice that both mass and high-end brands can use a web-oriented language i.e. both can employ the informal means of expression typical of the web. Due to their target client, mass brands may also use slang to communicate.

An example of effective fan involvement is to set up (online) events connected to real-life events. A brand may advertise an event or invite fans through social networks or online communities.

Finally, the brand should always answer fan posts or comments, even if by simply "liking" a comment. A negative comment left unanswered may bring a multitude of negative comments from the online community. It is advisable, however, to have a strategy for responding to negative comments, rather than to reply impulsively. Italian premium brand Patrizia Pepe learned this lesson in 2011: accused on Facebook of using anorexic models, the brand immediately replied that their models were not anorexic but simply very skinny and that this was consistent with the brand's target market (below size 42). This generated a slew of negative reactions and publicity (mostly by bloggers,

FASHION MANAGEMENT

who are very active online). A few days later, the company acknowledged in its official blog that it should have taken the time to listen first and that it learned a lot from the experience (http://inside.patriziapepe.com/it/2011/patrizia-pepe-impara-dai-social-media/). Since then the company has put in place a social media strategy and is also active in the innovation of the customer's in-store shopping experience, thanks to the use of technological tools such as the "smart assistant", a multimedia totem with RFID (radio-frequency identification) technology installed in the stores to create a better interaction with the products in the physical space which can be recognized by this digital device which provides additional information and suggestions of looks to the final clients. The advantages for the company are the following: cross-selling, possibility to use all the communication material on the product, giving a useful tool to the sales assistant to engage the final clients. The advantages for the final clients are the following: a direct interaction with the product, WOW-effect and "retailtainment" (entertainment in the retail space) and the opportunity to have visibility on the complete collection. In the future these digital tools used in the retail spaces will always be more connected with social media influencing the shopping experience and making it always more interactive and interconnected.

CONCLUSION: TOWARDS EMOTIONAL TRANSMEDIA STORYTELLING

In communicating online, fashion companies have to face an additional challenge of keeping a strong coordination with the other communication channels and media. As a result, fashion companies today tend towards "transmedia storytelling": telling their stories across multiple platforms and formats using digital technologies. The most successful brands will be those able to take advantage of opportunities arising from the dialogue of both online and offline channels.

Given the difficulties of being remembered in a wider and more complex media environment, coherence of the brand identity and the creation of an *emotional relationship*, building "intimacy" with the consumers, is fundamental.

Kevin Roberts, worldwide CEO of Saatchi & Saatchi, writes about the creation of "sisomo" (sight, sound, motion): seamless communication involving sight, sound and motion with an international programming for television, internet and mobile devices to create a powerful intimacy (Roberts, 2005). Strong brands are those able to develop *emotional communication*.

Some may decide to take the direction of the emotional values working on the so-called *responsible communication*: the following section will present the logics around the opportunities of managing and communicating sustainability in fashion.

MANAGING AND COMMUNICATING SUSTAINABILITY IN FASHION: THE MULTI-STAKEHOLDER APPROACH

A company that operates in the fashion industry should be prepared to answer a series of questions. How does it reduce environmental impact? How does it contribute to the economic development of the area (district, region, country) in which it operates? How should it interact with stakeholders through new media? What can be given back to the territory of origin, local art and culture as sources of inspiration for the stylistic identity of the brand? Given the current process of globalization and outsourcing, how does the company ensure that the rights of workers in all countries in which it operates (produces) are respected and that their skills are developed? Does it respect consumers?

A *responsible fashion company* (Rinaldi & Testa 2013) is continuously interacting with many contexts and stakeholders to achieve a systemic balance: environment, society, art, culture and territory. This can be done, for example, through programmes to reduce environmental impact of its activities; promotion of the territories in which it operates; healthy and challenging work environments; the quality of the products guaranteed to consumers; promotion of culture through philanthropic actions, artistic collaborations, funding and donations, and company museums.

The communication of sustainability (which means the long-term balance with all the stakeholders) can only start from a responsible vision on the society. Those who interact with the brand want to be treated like people and not consumers or customers. This means that companies must learn to engage, inspire and motivate towards responsible behaviour. An increasing number of consumers is using smartphones and tablets that gives them the power to declare the death of a product in just a few minutes. The challenge for companies is to create real benefits and values in line with the new desires and new priorities around sustainability. *The real opportunity lies in giving people the power to feel part of a community.*

As we saw earlier, thanks (especially) to social media, brands can ensure a high level of transparency and interaction with consumers, laying foundations for a genuine relationship. In particular, a big advantage of the social media is that they allow the consumers access to a wealth of information about products and brands, as well as data related to the supply chain.

COMMUNICATING SUSTAINABILITY IN FASHION

Communication is a key aspect of corporate responsibility for at least two reasons:

- ··· It enhances the behaviour and maximizes the benefits from the adoption of socially responsible strategies and actions to establish lasting relationships with the relevant stakeholders.

- ··· It creates/builds reputation.

Communicating the company's approach to sustainability is important because, with the support of all stakeholders, it helps to define the identity of the company.

Depending on the key stakeholders one can speak of *external communication* (with consumers, local communities and government agencies) to promote, inform and advertise or *internal communication* (to employees/workers, shareholders/investors, suppliers) to train and inform (see Table 2). Depending on the stakeholder, each company prepares a range of different communication tools, activates discrete channels, and uses different languages.

Stakeholder	Main communication tools	Purpose of the communication
Purpose of the communication	• Website, magazines, brochures, events and social networks	• Promote, inform and advertise
Investors	• Website, reports, direct mail	• Inform
Employees	• Intranet, training courses, manuals and guidelines, business magazine, social networks	• Develop and inform
Supplier	• Codes of conduct, guidelines, training sessions, questionnaires	• Develop, monitor and inform
Local community	• Big events, donations, social networks	• Promote, inform and advertise
Public administration	• Reporting	• Inform

Figure 4. | Stakeholders of responsible communication (Source: Rinaldi & Testa 2013).

Social networks are an especially valuable tool when directed to the community of consumers and employees. The best practices in social media communication are moving from the concept of "target" to that of "stakeholder": a communication that can be defined as socially responsible need not consider his recipients as a "target" but as "actors".

Yet companies in the fashion industry, if they started working on sustainability practices, still do not communicate their responsible behaviour. This is probably because the responsibility is a notion of fear: fear of pollution, consumption, increasing or highlighting social differences. Unfortunately fear threatens to overshadow an opportunity to assume a crucial role that today drives change. The opportunity exists for the company to establish and maintain a new and more authentic relationship with its customers and general public opinion – and social media is the perfect tool with which to achieve this goal.

To cultivate and nurture a brand is an ongoing process that requires attention. Companies – at least the most innovative ones – are becoming aware that responsibility is a new and different way of doing business to continue to thrive over time. Communicating the sustainability is an opportunity to realign the reference values with their stakeholders. Porter and Kramer in their article "Creating Shared Value" published on Harvard Business Review in 2011 confirm that "The solution lies in the principle of shared value, which involves value for society by addressing its needs and challenges. Businesses must reconnect company success with social progress. Shared value is a new way to achieve economic success".

The communication of responsible behavior creates value for the company by generating demand, reducing its environmental or social risks and contributing to reputation. A program of responsibility that is consistent with the positioning of a brand creates potential value for the company and the brand itself. The more a company is able to offer and enhance the attention of financial markets and of all stakeholders' paths of responsibility, the lower the risk associated and the better its reputation. To behave responsibly today is to become a spokesperson for new values and lifestyles placed at the center of the brand identity: this can provide a platform on which emotion can renew the promise and the relationship of trust with its customers and all stakeholders.

The fashion brands are key players in media attention: they can recognize the important role of new and important influences in society. Creating products and services relevant to the new consumer, helping them to live more responsibly, means accepting a social sense, which offers a positive influence and at the same time increases the demand for the brand, creating value for the company (Rinaldi & Testa 2013).

RESPONSIBLE COMMUNICATION IN FASHION: GOOD PRACTICES

Brands like Levi's (Water<Less™ Jeans) and Patagonia (Common Threads Initiative) can be considered as good practices in fashion thanks to their responsible communication (see the case studies below).

Good practices in responsible communication: case study 1

Levi's Water<Less™ Jeans

Water<Less™ Jeans created by Levi's are using a lower amount of water in the finishing process. The company decided to launch a behavioural campaign directed at consumers in order to create awareness of water usage issues and drive more responsible behaviour in product care.

The Waterless campaign aims to change the attitude and behaviour of the consumer. The company has decided to use video and point-of-sale materials that are effective and emotionally engaging.

http://store.levi.com/waterless/

Good practices in responsible communication: case study 2

Patagonia Common Threads Initiative

The Common Threads Initiative is an integral project that influences the consumers towards the following behaviours:

Reduce: using tools such as Patagonia Care Guide, the company provides all the advice needed to treat the product after purchase and prolong its life;

Repair: although the quality is high, the product may sometimes require repairs, even after washing it. The repair service is guaranteed by Patagonia both in case of manufacturing defects and in case of problems arising during the use.

Reuse: Patagonia is committed to donating unsold products to charity. One of the implementation of this commitment is Patagonia's partnership with eBay for reselling used clothes.

Recycle: Patagonia provides an in-store service of items that have reached the end of their life cycle, in order to recycle the fabric.

Re-imagine: thinking with the consumer the way in which we consume and produce to protect the land and the water that we love is the last effort of the Common Threads Initiative.

http://www.patagonia.com

FASHION MANAGEMENT

Communicating the messages of responsibility with the techniques of traditional media is probably not effective: if a consumer has limited time, she/he can manage less information. Appropriate communication can improve purchasing decisions within minutes. Communication needs to inform and excite, educate and innovate through images and words. Companies need to develop the ability to tell stories that are compelling.

THE DECALOGUE

In *The Responsible Fashion Company* (Rinaldi & Testa 2013) the main principles of effectively communicating a brand's environmental and social responsibility are presented. Both mass market and luxury brands, small and big companies, can follow these guidelines in order to communicate in a responsible manner:

Positive messages
Only positive messages enable change. The new story should be attractive, exciting and, above all, credible. It should not repeat clichés.

Walking the talk
"Do as you say" should guide the communication, not vice versa.

Transparency
For a brand, credibility is equivalent to transparency. Transparency means having a vision with commitments, setting goals and sharing not only the positive results but also the failures. Companies should not be shy: if the company is transparent people are willing to give their trust.

Accessible, concise and interactive information
Transparency also involves the need to provide extensive and complete information. People want to know what's behind a brand, a product, a company, and what the implications are in their lives. For this reason they must be able to access information when and how they want. The network and various devices (mobile, tablet) allow a free consultation: the content should be designed to be enjoyed to the fullest, and to be synthetic and interactive.

Credibility
The information must be visual, tangible and guaranteed by a credible third party, such as an NGO or a certification authority (N.B. there are more than 800 certifications in the world). A company should not fall prey to

self-certification and/or "green washing". Certification or no certification, the information must have a solid foundation and evidence of what has been done.

Relevance

Companies need to know the recipients of the message and become relevant to them. Who is this for? Who am I? Are they a niche or large segment? But above all, what moves them? Being "green" in itself is not enough. Consumers will continue to choose a product or service firstly for its performance, its price over quality ratio. The value of responsibility, which should be integrated into the DNA of a brand, is a great accelerator, however, and remains a key reason for the choice. Communication must be able to decline the value of the responsibility in the benefit for the consumer. If I buy a chocolate I do so because it's good. If it is hyper-sustainable but the taste is not good then I leave it on the shelf. The fact that a product is sustainable should instead be the foundation for its excellent quality.

Narrative

The most innovative brands are already driving an approach from the "what" to the "how" and it's based on shared values and on the relationship: choosing the path of responsibility demonstrates their competitive advantage by telling how products are made, as they come on the market, how they build relationships, what responsibility means in their industry of reference and what impact they have on society. Think of a bottle of wine that narrates its origin: from the grapes obtained during cultivation, to the production process and taste. Information should not only allow us to choose or buy with awareness, but also enable the buyer to continue the story with the consumer until the end (if the wine is purchased by a restaurant) or with some friends (if purchased by the consumer).

Courage and innovation

To communicate the responsibility, courage and innovation are necessary. Courage can mean declining trivial paradigms or facing a crisis with great irony, or speaking openly about the failures. And finally, using the first person plural rather than singular: not "I do" but rather "together we can do."

Simplicity. Simplify, simplify, simplify

If we talk about issues perhaps people don't know the difference between grams and tons of carbon dioxide, but everyone knows what it is like to travel in an airplane, to do the laundry in a washing machine, or to make coffee. We must then translate numbers and complex concepts in easy examples so everyone understands.

FASHION MANAGEMENT

Emotion

Communication will never be effective unless it's emotional, if it does not create a mindful and emotional connection with the listener or viewer. The video is the most effective way to tell a concise, simple, direct and engaging story. Emotion is the basic ingredient of responsible communication.

RESPONSIBLE COMMUNICATION IN LUXURY

As seen previously, luxury companies are trying to solve the dilemma of communicating to an elite group of people the "creation of the dream" and going towards a more direct and "transparent communication" with a multitude of fans (potential customers). A similar paradox can be found in communicating responsibility.

Kering holding (since 2012, formerly PPR) instigated a rebranding that grappled with this challenge. This corporate rebranding was not only necessary (PPR refers to Pinault-Printemps-Redoute and the latter are no longer owned by the group), but also symbolic: the group wishes to communicate a certain type of image. Indeed, Kering is pronounced "caring" and "Ker" in Breton, the home region of CEO François-Henri Pinault, means "home". "It is my conviction that sustainable business is smart business. It gives us an opportunity to create value while helping to make a better world," François-Henri Pinault said (mission statement published on the sustainability section of the Kering website http://www.kering.com/en/sustainability).

Among all the brands of Kering, Gucci represents a good practice in managing responsibility towards the stakeholders.

Gucci and the stakeholders

Gucci was among the first luxury brands that decided to invest in sustainability. In 2004 it created its Corporate Social Responsibility (CSR) department, which was in charge of numerous sustainability projects involving various stakeholders: environment, supply chain, society and territory, culture and cinema.

The culture of high craftsmanship and the quality of Gucci products are increasingly combined with economic, social and environmental principles.

In 2004, Gucci distinguished itself as one of the first companies in its sector to start a voluntary certification process of Corporate Social Responsibility (SA8000) along the entire pipeline. The brand has always placed a responsible attitude towards the people, the landscape, the environment and the community, with particular attention to the value of sustainability.

Quality craftsmanship, always a key element of the Gucci brand, is being combined with socially and environmentally responsible practices.

As a matter of fact Gucci started numerous projects concerning environmental sustainability such as the use of more eco-friendly packaging, incentives to the use of electric vehicles among the employees and for the delivery of the goods, to reduce the consumption of paper and plastic and compensation of emissions of CO_2. Those related to the commitment to the traceability of the entire supply chain and at the same time the attention that the brand dedicates to the territory to small and medium-sized enterprises and have been working with them for years.

In 2012, Gucci signed a voluntary agreement with the Italian Ministry of the Environment and Protection of Land and Sea to evaluate the environmental impact and calculate what are known as "eco-costs" of some of Gucci's signature products in order to implement processes and products that are certified under the law and international standards. Gucci – the first company in the luxury goods business to sign this type of agreement – is therefore pledging to measure CO_2 emissions produced by its manufacturing supply chain with an eye to reducing them.

In 2013, the brand launched the Green Carpet Challenge (GCC) collection with the establishment of new certification standards in the field traceability and eco-sustainability. The GCC Gucci is in fact the first line of bags to be made with leather coming from the Brazilian Amazon forest avoiding deforestation of the natural environment. Each bag of the new line is accompanied by a passport, which traces the history from the birth of the animal to the beautiful finished product. The bags are made with leather from farms certified by the Rainforest Alliance, which establishes compliance with environmental criteria of social justice and ethical breeding of livestock.

In 2013, Gucci also founded Chime for Change, a new campaign to raise funds and awareness for girls' and women's empowerment, aiming to convene, unite and strengthen the voices speaking out for girls and women around the world. THE SOUND OF CHANGE LIVE concert event, held on June 1st in London, has helped raise funds to support 210 projects for girls and women across the globe. After VAT, the concert raised $3.9M USD to support projects in the three key focus areas of the Chime for Change campaign: Education, Health and Justice. Donations were allocated to 84 different non-profit partners, across 81 countries.

FASHION MANAGEMENT

Some independent designers are also fighting for a "business of truth": a more responsible supply chain and more transparent communication to consumers. Being an independent designer usually gives more freedom and more space to personify the brand, with the designer as spokesperson. This makes it easier to inspire and motivate the consumer, who can listen to and read the words of the designer. Among the independent designers going in this direction is Belgian Bruno Pieters, CEO of Honest by.

Bruno Pieters TED 2013 speech, "The business of truth"

My purpose in life is to be human and how do I fulfill that purpose? By being human in my relationships, in my diet in my consumption, and in my work… In my work, I think that is where I have made the biggest change: Honest by. I launched Honest by last year in January. Honest by is the first 100% transparent company in the world. We offer our customer sustainable fashion made in Europe. We share all the information about a product with our customer. From the origin of the raw material to the entire price calculation including the mark up that we take a product. The reason why I created Honest by is because this is something that I wanted as a consumer. Because I believe one needs that level of transparency to be able to make the right choices and consume more humanely. At the moment we are the only brand offering 100% transparency to the public. Which makes me very happy as a CEO, but as a consumer it doesn't. So what I try to do in my personal life is help other companies to become more sustainable and transparent by only buying products from brands that are in sync with my values and by using my voice. When I'm in a store I always ask the people who work there the same questions: who made it, where it was made and how it was made. Because I need to know what I'm paying for and who I'm financially supporting through my purchase. Another thing I've learned is that all that matters today besides love, is money. And that doesn't need to be a sad thing. Money has become a universal language that is understandable to all. And If we learn to speak money well, it can become a very powerful and positive tool for change. Now there are moments when I do doubt if my shopping really makes a difference. But then I try to remember all the crazy things we do for money. We abuse our children, we abuse our animals, our environment sometimes just to get a dollar, or a euro for someone. That is how important every purchase is. That is how important everyone is.

Everyone matters.

I would like to finish with a quote from Gandhi: "Be the change you want to see in the world".

Source: Transcript available at | http://www.honestby.com/en/news/150/ted-speech-full-transcript.html (Bruno Pieters 2013)

CONCLUSION: TOWARDS A MULTI-STAKEHOLDER APPROACH

It is fundamental to underline that communicating responsibility should be the last step of a set of *coherent actions towards the different stakeholders in the fashion industry*. To be credible, a brand must back up all forms of promotion with concrete behaviour in line with that promotion. A responsible brand is willing to create a balance with a multitude of stakeholders: the environment, society, art, culture and territory and through the media with consumers.

In order to see concrete results it is necessary for the companies to go from a few random launches of individual products and surprising advertising campaigns to ongoing and coherent actions that take into account all stakeholders, integrating ethics and aesthetics along the entire value chain. The only way forward is to be part of the solution instead of being part of the problem.

REFERENCES

Bendell, J., Kleanthous, A. (2007) *Deeper Luxury Report*, http://www.wwf.org.uk/deeperluxury/_downloads/ DeeperluxuryReport.pdf

Berry, Christopher J. (1994) *The Idea of Luxury: A Conceptual and Historical Investigation*. New York: Cambridge University Press.

Carroll, Archie B. (1991) The Pyramid of Corporate Social Responsibility: Toward the Moral Management of Organization Stakeholders. In: *Business Horizons*, 34(4), 39-48.

Cerana, N. (edited by) (2004) *Comunicare la responsabilità sociale. Teorie, modelli, strumenti e casi d'eccellenza [Communicating social responsibility. Theories, models, tools and best practices]*. Milano: Franco Angeli.

Chadha R. and Husband P. (2006) *The Cult of the Luxury Brand: Inside Asia's Love Affair with Luxury*. London, UK: Nicholas Brealey International.

Chevalier, M., & Mazzalovo, G. (2008) *Luxury brand management: A world of privilege*. Singapore: Wiley.

Corbellini, E., Saviolo, S. (2009) *Managing Fashion and Luxury Companies*. Milano: Etas.

Garzoni, M. and Donà, R. (2008) *Moda & tecnologia [Fashion & Technology]*. Milano: Egea.

Kapferer, N., Bastien, V. (2009) *The Luxury Strategy: Break the Rules of Marketing to Build Luxury Brands*. London: Kogan Page.

Okonkwo, U. (2007) *Luxury fashion branding: trends, tactics, techniques*. New York: Palgrave Macmillan.

Ornati M. (edited by) (2011) *Oltre il CRM [Beyond the CRM]*. Franco Angeli.

Pickton, D. & Broderick, A. (2005) *Integrated marketing communications* (2nd ed.). Essex: Pearson Education Limited.

Porter, M. E. and Kramer, M. R. (2011) Creating Shared Value. In: *Harvard Business Review*, 89 (1-2).

Pomering, A. and Dolincar, S. (2009) Assessing the Prerequisite of Successful CSR Implementation: Are Consumers Aware of CSR Initiatives? In: *Journal of Business Ethics*, 85, 285-301.

Qualman, E. (2009) *Socialnomics: how social media transforms the way we live and do business*. John Wiley & Sons.

Reina, D., Vianello, S. (2011) *GreenWebEconomics. La nuova frontiera [GreenWebEconomics. The new frontier]*. Milano: Egea.

Rinaldi, F.R. (2012) Getting the E-Shopping experience right: Tips and Traps in multi-channel distribution. In: *Detail on Retail*.

Rinaldi, F.R., Hutter (2010) *Social Media Fashion Monitor*, http://www.lescahiersfm.com/en/artices/99-social-media-fash-ion-monitor2010-.html

Rinaldi, F.R., Testa, S. (2013) *L'impresa moda responsabile [The responsible fashion company]*. Milano: Egea.

Roberts, K. (2005) *Lovemarks, The future beyond brands*. powerHouse Books.

Sacerdote, E. (2007) *La strategia retail nella moda e nel lusso [The retail strategy in fashion and luxury]*. Franco Angeli.

Saviolo, S., Testa, S. (2002) *Strategic Management in the Fashion Companies*. ETAS.

Saviolo, S., Marazza, A. (2013) *Lifestyle Brands: A Guide to Aspirational Marketing*. Palgrave Macmillan.

Thomas, D. (2007) *Deluxe: How Luxury Lost its Luster*. New York: Penguin Group USA.

Online resources

Young Digitals, Digital in the Round (blog & interviews): http://www.digitalintheround.com/

case # 3   Veronique Branquinho

FW 13-14

"I wanted to do it on my own terms"

Veronique Branquinho worked as an independent fashion designer for more than 10 years. Based in Antwerp, she was an established name on the Paris ready-to-wear schedule (with both womenswear and menswear). She also designed collections for the Italian leather company Ruffo Research, as well as for 3 Suisses and for lingerie brand Marie-Jo, and worked as a creative director for Delvaux. But in 2009 she had to shut down her company, due to financial problems.

Then, in 2012, she made a fashion comeback in Paris, welcomed by fans and critics alike. The Italian clothing manufacturer Gibo (now part of The Onward Luxury Group) soon invested in her brand. After seeing the SS14 collection in Paris, *New York Times* critic Cathy Horyn wrote that "Ms Branquinho has not lost her mysterious ability to get under the skin."

Interview by
Trui Moerkerke

You started your own label soon after graduating from the Fashion Department of the Royal Academy of Fine Arts in Antwerp. Were you prepared for the business side of fashion?

Of course I wasn't prepared. I think there is only one way to learn and that is by creating a fashion collection. Regardless, it is difficult. I started with a business associate, so I wasn't on my own, but having my artistic freedom was one of the conditions. And sometimes it is important not to agree to all the proposals of your business partner. Some discussions I remember vividly: do we go to a fair with tons of brands or do we show the collection individually? I was inspired by the previous generation of Belgian fashion designers (like Dries Van Noten and Ann Demeulemeester) who did it on their own terms.

case # 3   Veronique Branquinho

Should fashion schools include business in their curriculum?

I am not sure. You need talent to create a collection, but the business side requires talent as well. Because few people can combine those qualities, it is perhaps far more important to be surrounded by the right people, or to have a solid network in the fashion world... much better than believing you can do it on your own. Besides, you don't have the time to do everything.

From early on in your career, you took on design assignments for brands like Ruffo Research, and later 3 Suisses, Marie-Jo... Can you elaborate on those collaborations?

Such collaborations are a typical win-win situation. As an independent designer, you get the chance to show your work and gain brand awareness. For 3 Suisses, for example, you can reach other markets. As a result many people get to know your name. The financial aspect is just as important. You need that money to run your business. In all the collaborations I did, I appreciated being part of a well-oiled machine. I only had to focus on the creative part. And I learned a lot. Working with leather at Ruffo Research, working in a strict price frame at 3 Suisses...

In 2009, after a good 10 years in business, you shut down your company. How tough was that decision?

It was incredibly hard. I started a fashion label from scratch, worked like a dog and felt responsible for the whole team. But I had no choice. The worldwide economic crisis set in motion a vicious circle: you have a collection produced but your client files for bankruptcy or doesn't pay. At the same time you have to invest in your next collection. But as you sell less, your collection becomes more expensive, because of the shrinking volume. You have to let go some of your team; you cannot pay them anymore...

One tends to forget that even a smaller collection requires the same amount of work. So the workload became really unbearable, both for me and my team. I had four collections a year, a complete shoe line, all the projects and collaborations I did for the sake of brand awareness. Nice and interesting projects, but a lot of work. And to make ends meet, I took a teaching job too [at the fashion department of the University of Applied Arts in Vienna].

Eventually I tried to bring a manager into the company, but it didn't work out. I couldn't handle it anymore. I was far too exhausted and lost my drive.

In 2012 you made a highly publicized and well-received comeback. Were you surprised?

In 2009 I couldn't imagine that I would start again, ever. The previous years had left me with a hangover. After two years though, I was happy to discover something was missing in my life. I am a fashion designer and I wanted to make collections. But I, in no way, wanted to start on my own; I had been there.

I started considering options. My connections with the company Iris (which has been producing my shoe collections for 15 years) brought me to Gibo. Now both companies are part of the Onward Luxury Group. It wasn't an easy step. I was used to working very independently; now I have to compromise. But the return is worth it. I have incredible creative freedom, but I don't have to think about production, human resources, sales, distribution... I can focus. Of course you have the responsibility not to work only with the finest and most expensive fabrics, but that's the logic of a collection – I worked like this before.

The only disadvantage, in my view, is the fact that you have to design pre-collections (cruise collections). That makes four collection deadlines a year, instead of two. Of course, I understand: Onward has a big production capacity and clients want to receive the clothes earlier, but it isn't easy to juggle the different deadlines.

If you had to select one piece of advice for aspiring designers, what would it be?

Pursue your dreams. Some years ago, I would have answered: follow your dreams and don't compromise. In these difficult times, I would advise trying to find a balance between your artistic integrity and choices that make your work possible.

"Try to find a balance between your artistic integrity and choices that make your work possible"

FW 13-14

SS 14

FW 13-14

case # 3   Veronique Branquinho

Veronique Branquinho
SS 14

INTERNA-TIONALIZATION STRATEGIES OF THE FASHION INDUSTRY

Walter van Andel

Marlies Demol

Annick Schramme

As a result of globalization, the field of international trade has become increasingly accessible over the years. Due to exponential advancement in technology and digital media, companies from all over the world can communicate, collaborate and compete. The (Flemish) fashion industry includes many small and medium-sized enterprises (SMEs) with limited resources in terms of capital, management and time, yet they succeed in internationalizing their activities. The internationalization of fashion brands is apparent on multiple levels, *foreign market expansion* being one aspect and the *internationalization of the value chain* – from creation to sourcing and manufacturing to distribution and marketing – a second and more fundamental evolution. During the past two decades, the international expansion of fashion brands has been unprecedented, facilitated by several factors and driven by push and pull factors.

The first and most prevalent dimension of internationalization in the fashion industry is the sourcing of raw materials and finished or semi-finished items from abroad. International (out)sourcing and manufacturing is a long-established activity in the fashion industry and is mainly prompted by economics, as fashion brands attempt to take advantage of low labour costs in less developed countries. The second and most obvious aspect of fashion internationalization is the expansion of sales in foreign markets through direct exports, cooperation with local partners abroad or even the operation of retail shops within foreign markets.

This chapter describes the current state of globalization in the independent and high-end fashion industry and includes an overview of the key locations for both international production and sales. Furthermore, this chapter provides insight into the process of internationalization, as well as its drivers and barriers. Finally, the operational management of internationalization is discussed by zooming in on business models and the effect internationalization has on them.

World trade in textiles and clothing is on the increase. According to the World Trade Organization, the total value of world exports of textiles and clothing in 2011 amounted to US$ 706 billion, a 17 percent increase compared to the year before indicating a vastly grown international trade and production. The top 10 exporters (countries) each registered 13 percent growth or more, with Bangladesh recording the highest increase (27 percent). China is the leading exporter of textiles and clothing in 2011 with a 32 percent share in world exports of textiles and 37 percent in clothing.

In terms of sales, a different picture emerges. The European Union and the United States are the major markets for clothing, accounting for 45 percent and 21 percent respectively of world imports. However, the sale of high-end fashion seems to revolve around certain so-called "fashion capitals". A fashion capital is a city which has a major influence on international fashion trends and is a key centre for the fashion industry, in which activities including the design, production and retailing of fashion products, fashion events (such as fashion weeks and awards), and fashion-related trade fairs generate significant economic output. Fashion capitals usually have a broad mix of business, financial, entertainment, cultural and leisure activities and are internationally recognized for having a unique and strong identity (Gemperli 2010).

The Global Language Monitor (GLM), a US-based media analytics company, releases an annual ranking of the top fashion capitals of the world. GLM's Narrative Tracking technology analyses the Internet, blogosphere, top 250,000 print and electronic news media, as well as social media sources (such as Twitter) as they emerge. The technology tracks fashion-related words, phrases and concepts in relation to their frequency, contextual usage and appearance in global media outlets, which leads to a ranking of importance. Table 2 shows the top 15 fashion capitals in 2012.

It's interesting to note the continued dominance of London and New York at the top ranks of fashion in recent years, beating out established centres of fashion and fashion design, Paris and Milan. This seems to reflect a shift in fashion away from historical centres of cutting-edge design to the world's leading financial centres.

Country	Textiles*	Clothing*
China	94.4	153.8
EU27	76.6	116.4
India	15.0	14.4
Turkey	10.8	13.9
Bangladesh	1.6	19.9
United States	13.8	5.2
Vietnam	3.8	13.2
Republic of Korea	12.4	1.8
Pakistan	9.1	4.6
Indonesia	4.8	8.0

Figure 1.
Major exporters of textiles & clothing, 2011 (World Trade Organization 2012)./ *US $ billion.

INTERNATIONALIZATION STRATEGIES

There are different manners in which fashion companies execute their international expansion strategy. Internationalization theories try to explain why companies decide to operate sales strategies outside of their home market and describe the approaches and structures they develop to do so. The first scientific publications on international business stem from the 1950s and 1960s, when American companies were expanding their activities to countries in Europe and Asia in particular. Since then, spurred by rapid developments in the opportunities and possibilities of international entrepreneurship, many new insights have arisen. In the case of the fashion industry, recent emphasis lies on the so-called "Born Globals": companies who develop direct and extensive export into several markets right from their start-up phase (Rasmussen & Madsen 2002).

A study of Flemish fashion brands shows the importance of both the segment and the life stage of the brand in its approach to internationalizing distribution and sales (Demol, Schramme & Van Andel 2013). Concerning segmentation, important differences are found between independent designers on one hand and middle segment and high-street labels on the other hand in terms of their internationalization strategy.

Furthermore, the way companies deal with internationalization is to a high degree linked to their stage in the life cycle. On the basis of Hagoort's (2007) insights on life cycles in creative and cultural organizations, the researchers distinguish four phases. The first one is the *idea phase*, in which the organization is centered on artistic leadership and ideas. In this stage, that can last up to 5 years, the internationalization process is an experiment and organizations learn by trial and error. International fashion weeks and fairs are expensive and young designers often lack the know-how to successfully bring their brand to a new market. This first phase is followed by the *structure phase*, in which a division will be made between artistic and strategic activities. In this second phase the organization develops a strategic vision concerning its internationalization, regarding both production and distribution. Finally, when the organization has established itself in its industry, it has reached the *strategy phase* with artistically inspired new future-focused initiatives, for example several international target markets or collaborations with foreign partners. The last phase according to Hagoort is the *festival phase*, this phase evolves around teamwork and innovative projects. When an organization does not naturally evolve to the next phase, a crisis occurs. Hagoort's insights are similar to Greiner's (1998) life cycle model that can be described as a sequence of crises. As, according to Greiner, every phase in the life of an

Rank	City (*)
1	London (1)
2	New York (2)
3	Barcelona (7)
4	Paris (3)
5	Madrid (12)
6	Rome (13)
7	Sao Paulo (25)
8	Milan (4)
9	Los Angeles (5)
10	Berlin (10)
11	Antwerp (44)
12	Hong Kong (6)
13	Buenos Aires (20)
14	Bali (21)
15	Sydney (11)

Figure 2.
Top 15 fashion capitals in 2012. *
Previous year's rank.

organization ends with a typical crisis before evolving into the next phase. Over the years, several theories have been developed to explain how fashion companies internationalize their operations and sales. However, former research has almost exclusively been focused on large multinational organizations – mainly clothing chains and luxury companies – and their international strategies. Yet most independent designers have a less extensive organizational structure and a smaller market and are therefore subject to different factors from their multinational counterparts. Fortunately, in past decades some interesting models and theories have been formulated to better understand and describe the process of international sales in small and medium fashion companies. This section will discuss the *Uppsala model*, first posed by Johansson and Vahlne in 1977 and later revised by them to ensure its currency; the *Born Global Theory* as introduced by Rasmusen and Madsen in 2002; and drivers and barriers within the process of internationalizing sales.

THE UPPSALA MODEL

Swedish scholars Jan Johansson and Jan-Erik Vahlne found that the internationalization process in both large and small businesses is often an incremental process that follows different stages. Their "Uppsala model" (named after the researchers' university) suggests that companies increase their commitment to new markets the more knowledge they gain of those markets – the latter occurring primarily through experience.

According to this model, companies follow a certain process when internationalizing their sales activities. After a period of having operated in the domestic market only, they tend to start their international activities with *direct export*. As exports increase through middlemen (for example, agents or distributors), their market knowledge increases, as does their commitment. This leads the company to take on further commitments by setting up own sale subsidiaries in those markets. This way, the outcome of one cycle of events provides the input for the following cycle. In general the Uppsala model shows that increased commitment to a certain market leads to new knowledge of the market, which leads to more commitment, etc...

An important concept in this model is "psychic distance" or the perceived distance between a foreign market and a company. This psychic distance, which is different from geographical distance, is determined by language differences, differences in cultural norms and values, political systems, level of education and the level of industrial/economic development. Johansson and Vahlne conclude that enterprises primarily focus on countries whose culture is similar to that of their home country for their internationalization attempts, opting for small psychic distances. The incremental or gradual nature of the internationalization process can then be explained by the fact that a company intensifies its commitment to a foreign market as the psychic distance is increasingly reduced by accumulated knowledge of this market. For example, many designers first work with a sales agent or a distributor for their international sales and only sell their products in multi-brand stores. Once they get to know the market – the customers and competitors – the next step is often to hire exclusive sales employees for certain markets or areas. In recent revisions of the model, Johansson and Vahlne have argued that "outsidership" in relation to relevant networks also adds to uncertainty of expanding into a foreign market. As the current business environments can be viewed as a web of relationships – a network – rather than as a neoclassical market with many independent suppliers and customers, belonging to the right networks is essential to a company's ability to successfully expand in unknown territories. Trust building within these networks, as well as knowledge creation developed through external relationships, are therefore additional change mechanisms crucial for gaining ground in foreign territories.

Knowledge deficiency is considered to be the main inhibiting factor in this internationalization process. Three types of knowledge can be distinguished: business knowledge, institutional knowledge and internationalization knowledge. *Business knowledge* refers to knowledge about competitors and customers in foreign markets. *Institutional knowledge* includes information on laws, language, norms and standards in those markets. *Internationalization knowledge* refers to the knowledge the organization has gained from previous experiences with internationalization. Insufficient knowledge in (one of) these areas will result in a flawed internationalization process (Eriksson, Johanson, Majkgard & Sharma 1997).

Research shows that the internationalization process of many high-street brands and middle segment labels continues to follow the Uppsala route – even though the original model is over three decades old and despite the fact that the strategic decision-making of internationalization processes has changed as market changes, internet and globalization have forced companies to operate differently and in a fast-paced environment (Demol, Schramme & Van Andel 2013).

THE BORN GLOBAL MODEL

A second, more recent theory that explains the internationalization process, and one that arguably relates more to high-end independent designers, is the concept of "Born Globals". As stated previously, in today's fast-paced competitive environment, fashion companies operate in different contexts than designers of the past few decades and often must find quick ways of internationalizing. Networking and relationship building the key to achieving this, according to the Born Global theory. Born Global companies typically see the entire world as a possible market and, rather than following a gradual internationalization process, show a strong international commitment in the early stages of their business. Thus they often focus on distant markets or several countries at a time. Usually Born Globals consider the domestic market only as a support for their international activities.

In this case, strong personal networks in foreign markets and previous experience are important drivers of an internationally oriented start-up. The secret to the success of these companies is the uniqueness of their network. Born Globals are involved in different professional relationships at the same time, with a large number of weak ties.[3] These weak ties are the key to their success. Born Global firms are also open to change and continuously adapt their internationalization process based on the conditions they face in each new market. They are keen to improvise and see the expansion process as an experiment as they learn through trial and error. Finally, Born Globals tend to enter the markets that have connections to their network, not necessarily targeting the largest and most profitable markets first.

ENTRY MODES

When expanding into new markets, fashion companies have the choice of several distinct entry modes. These modes can be placed upon a continuum from low to high commitment.

Low commitment →	Medium commitment →	High commitment
Distributor	Acquisitions/mergers	Fully owned subsidiaries
Agent	Joint Venture	—
Direct export	Franchising	—

Figure 3. | Entry mode options.

Low-commitment entry modes are wholesale agreements with a middleman (distributor or agent) or without one (direct export). These entry modes are mainly chosen in circumstances of high uncertainty when companies attempt to keep the risks as low as possible. Agents and distributors for example ensure that companies can perform their business activities in different markets, without having to integrate their business entirely into those markets. Effectively this prevents companies from risking too much of their business. Most high-end designers and middle-market brands that enter a new market use (one or more of) these strategies. The young Belgian designer Kim Stumpf for example works with an international sales agent because she neither has the knowledge of the distant markets and possible client network, nor does she has time or money to travel all over the world to visit and follow-up (possible) clients and interesting contacts.

Medium-commitment entry modes mostly involve a local partner and are generally used when entering a rather difficult and/or culturally distant market. In the case of a strategic acquisition, a company takes over a fully operating company that has full knowledge of the intended market. In a joint venture, a firm co-operates with one or more local companies for its sales activities. In this way, they can exchange know-how and expertise of foreign operations, share risks and costs, but still retain adequate control. A final common medium-commitment option is a franchise agreement: the concept of a store or label (the franchisor) moves abroad and is performed by a local operator (the franchisee) in exchange for a fee or other financial arrangement. Most independent designers are very fond of their identity and image, and therefore prone less to mergers or joint ventures and although franchises are common in the international fashion world, Belgian brands rarely have franchised stores abroad.

When companies engage in the *highest levels of commitment*, cost and control, they open their own foreign subsidiaries. This can range from a wholly owned subsidiary to less expensive and high-risk alternatives such as a store-in-store in a department store. In the latter case, the labels take full responsibility for the results, but don't have the need to invest in expensive retail space. Belgian designers with flagship stores abroad are scarce. Only the biggest Flemish names, such as Ann Demeulemeester or Dries Van Noten, have their own (flagship) stores in foreign cities. It's important to point out that firms can adopt different sets of market entries on different markets. In that way, companies can diversify their activities and spread risk. Moreover, they utilize the optimal market entry mode and international strategy for each market. A second important observation is that many fashion companies expand their sales activities in different stages: first through various business-to-business agreements such as direct export and/or through an agent or distributor, later through more committed entries like mergers or even wholly or partly owned subsidiaries. Wholesaling gives the companies the chance to enter new markets without major investments. Furthermore, it allows firms to take their time to test the market, build their brand image and establish a relationship with customers. When the company feels it has enough knowledge of, and coverage in the market, it could then move forward with increasing its commitment.

DRIVERS AND BARRIERS IN INTERNATIONALIZING DISTRIBUTION AND SALES

For many fashion designers, the focus is not limited to the local (domestic) market for product sales. As the local market for designer fashion is often small and highly competitive, an urgency to seek international sales can be prevalent even in the early stages of entrepreneurial development. Many of these designers are therefore Born Globals who not only feel the necessity to go international, but also often feel the desire to succeed in important fashion hotspots such as Paris, Milan, London and New York. Other drivers for pursuing international sales are interest from foreign markets/distributors (for instance, based on fashion shows), and an instinctive match between certain international markets and the designer's brand characteristics. Finally, large growth markets such as the BRICS countries (Brazil, Russia, India, China and South Africa) can have an important pull-effect towards international sales for fashion designers due to these countries' increasing purchasing power and their interest in Western luxury products.

Studies (Moore 1997) on the internationalization of French fashion retailers (among others) suggest that the motivation for internationalization depends on the age of a company and the foreign market it wants to enter. Young retailers tend to be more proactive in their internationalization process. They are driven by business opportunities in other countries, unlike the incumbent firms, who seek foreign market expansion in response to limitations of the domestic market. Proactive firms also appear generally to use more aggressive strategies to penetrate a new market.

If we apply these insights to the internationalization theories described earlier, we could say that Born Global firms often apply a proactive strategy, while home-based businesses, which are more cautious and internationalize incrementally, have a more reactive approach. This distinction between a proactive and reactive approach is related to the push-pull dichotomy. High competition and a small market are often cited as *push factors* for fashion companies to internationalize. Examples of *pull factors* are large or niche markets abroad and favourable economic conditions in foreign markets. These push and pull factors operate simultaneously: the factors "pushing" companies to move abroad wouldn't be sufficient ground for international expansion unless foreign opportunities didn't "pull" these companies to those international markets.

An important barrier to internationalization of sales are its *high costs*, especially for young designers. Numerous investments in time and resources are required to expose products to the international market. For instance, prices for fashion shows and showrooms during international fashion weeks are substantial, making entry more difficult for novice designers without large financial reserves and for whom the return on investment is uncertain.

A second barrier to international sales and distribution is a *lack of knowledge* on fundamental issues such as foreign markets (both business and contextual knowledge) and executing international business in general. Discovering and penetrating new markets is often accompanied by great uncertainty. The internationalization theories previously discussed highlight knowledge deficiency as a major barrier to the internationalization of sales activities. This can be partly mitigated by employing an agent with contextual knowledge. However, this requires investing time and money into searching for a correct agent, training the agent in understanding the essential details and values of the designer, and monitoring the agent (as he or she is an official representative of the company).

Finally, pursuing international sales can lead to a *loss of control* on certain levels. As international markets are more difficult to closely monitor, important values regarding the brand image can be interpreted differently abroad. Control over intellectual property also weakens, placing the company at risk of piracy of designs and brand values (see **CHAPTER FIVE**).

Drivers	Barriers
• Small home market (and limited possibilities for expansion)	• High costs
• Attraction of major fashion cities	• Lack of business, internationalization, and contextual knowledge
• Interest from foreign markets	• Control over brand image and intellectual property
• Match between foreign market and brand identity	
• Growth markets/countries with high purchasing power	

Figure 4. | Drivers and barriers in internationalizing sales.

INTERNATIONALIZING PRODUCTION

Due to the high labour costs in most of the Western world, combined with a shortage of technically trained staff, most labels outsource their manufacturing operations to a number of supplying contractors in Asia, South and Eastern Europe and North Africa. The decision-making process regarding these outsourcing activities mainly focuses on optimizing the combination of *product attributes*, *speed to market* and *production cost*.

The coordination of an international supply chain can be challenging and requires solid relationships between organizations as they facilitate communication within an industry operating on a global level. Although companies can obtain significant benefits from a global supply network, there are several thresholds to overcome before these benefits can prevail. Some key challenges are:

- identifying suitable foreign partners
- monitoring and evaluating manufacturers abroad
- cooperating and negotiating with foreign partners
- training foreign suppliers
- cultural differences and language
- lost sales caused by late delivery of merchandise

It should be noted that some of the cited risks are inherent to the process of outsourcing, regardless of the location. Nonetheless distance can make it more difficult to identify and solve problems concerning those risks in the early stages. The aforementioned challenges can be more generally described within three main groups:

Logistic support
International production involves longer distances, which creates longer delivery times. Longer lead times require more resources and increase the opportunities for problems. Delays in delivery, for example, can be disastrous for a flexible inventory. Fast fashion company Zara chose to locate a big part of its production nearby to counter these logistic issues and to be able to react as fast as possible on new trends and sales statistics.

Cultural differences
Differences in values, language, religion, attitudes and habits can cause communication problems and potentially complicate the evaluation of the products, the conclusion of contracts and the maintenance of international relations.

Regulation
Government regulations may affect international production both directly and indirectly – the most direct effect being tariffs and quotas, while a complex administration (for example) could be an indirect threshold to internationalization.

DRIVERS AND BARRIERS IN INTERNATIONALIZING PRODUCTION

Many independent fashion designers are organized such that creation, distribution and communication are kept in-house, while production is mainly outsourced. Until a few decades ago, production could usually be outsourced locally, or rather, regionally. However, many Western countries have seen a trend towards a reduction of trade capacity in various fields, including fashion. It is becoming increasingly difficult to find high-quality fashion production regionally as skills such as stitching, pattern drafting, and embroidering become increasingly rare and quality of such production progressively inconsistent. Moreover, costs of regional production in Western countries have risen due to developments in wages. In comparison to developing nations, wages in Western countries are high (especially in disciplines in which certain skills are becoming increasingly rare), leading to a large disparity in production costs.

However, there are also several barriers to fashion companies outsourcing production internationally. As we saw earlier, these barriers are mainly associated with logistic difficulties and cultural differences, as well as some context-specific regulatory dissimilarities. The barriers to internationalization of production for independent designers apply to companies at each stage of the company's life cycle. However, more mature companies may have the organizational structure and resources to more easily deal with these challenges. For more established companies, the risks and barriers often do not outweigh the benefits, while the opposite is true for novice entrepreneurs. High minimum order sizes and the need for detailed planning and preparation of the design process can be extra hurdles for the latter in particular. Even though most young designers first gain experience in larger, established fashion houses, they nonetheless often lack the business knowledge needed to successfully undertake outsourcing plans. Moreover, they have neither the capital nor the staff to regularly check on the spot, making production more difficult to control, which adds an extra element of uncertainty.

Thresholds that confront both novice and experienced designers include manufacturer's neglecting to adhere to delivery times and investment of time and resources to identify and train new manufacturers. Another influencing factor is the production country's reputation among wholesale customers. A negative reputation may arise as a result of unethical working conditions, perceptions about (lack of) quality and/or political tensions between certain countries. Anne Chapelle, CEO of BVBA 32 (see also case #8), the company behind Belgian designer Ann Demeulemeester until 2013 and still of Haider Ackerman, mentions her wholesale clients won't buy anything that is labeled "made in China" or even "made in Turkey". But reputation isn't an issue reserved for high-end designers. Disasters such as the collapse of several production units in Bangladesh in 2013 for example, show all labels that produce their clothing in low-wage countries in a bad light.

Drivers	Barriers
• Quality of production at home country cannot be guaranteed • Insufficient production capacity locally • High costs of production at home	• Difficult quality control • Negative reputation • Difficult communication • Longer delivery time • Less flexibility • Complex (tax) regulations • Large minimum order size (especially for starting independent designers)

Figure 5. | Drivers and barriers in internationalizing production.

INTERNATIONAL BUSINESS MODELS

Over the past few years, the term "business model" has become prevalent in management vocabulary. Indeed, it is more widely used and researched nowadays than almost any other concept related to strategy, and for good reason: a good business model is essential to a successful organization, whether a new venture or an established player. Indeed, some suggest that the same idea or technology taken to market through two different business models will yield two different economic outcomes.

But what does this term mean exactly? Its meaning is regularly assumed to be implicit and thus seldom defined explicitly. There are many different thoughts on the matter, but most often the concept refers to a loose conception of how a company does business and generates revenue. On a basic or practical level, there is general agreement that a business model is simply a *description of how a firm does business*. The notion therefore refers to an operational model (with a focus on practices), rather than a financial model.

For our purposes, we will assume the following approach to business models: *a business model is a logical story explaining who your customers are, what they value, and how you will make economic returns in providing them that value* (see also Osterwälder & Pigneur 2013). This definition highlights some of the fundamental issues that underlie a business: how it identifies, creates and captures value for customers. Focusing on these elements, it becomes clear that a business model can be seen as the operationalization (application) of a company's strategy. It also defines how a company can execute its strategy on a daily basis. The business model is as such a bundle of specific activities that are conducted to satisfy the perceived needs of the market, including the specification of the parties that conduct these activities, and how these activities are linked to each other.

Noted business model researchers Ramon Casadesus-Masanell and Joan Ricart (2011) depict business models – on a more abstract level – as a bundle of choices a company makes about how they (should) operate, and its corresponding consequences. Companies can make choices on three levels: on a (organization-wide) *policy level*, on an *asset allocation level*, and on the *level of governance of the company*. Consequences can be either flexible (easy to change by making other choices) or *rigid* (not easy to change).

Let's say a high-end fashion designer operates under the strategy of differentiating itself from competitors by being the most luxurious in the market. The operationalization of this strategy would dictate that the company makes well-defined choices in its suppliers (high-end fabrics and high-quality production), outlets (high-end stores), marketing, etc. All these choices would have clear consequences (high price, limited outlet options, certain brand image, etc.) that, combined, would form the (operational) business model of the company.

As we have seen in this chapter, there are two main ways in which a fashion company can increase its internationalization. On the one hand it can internationalize its production, on the other hand its sales. Either way, the decision to further internationalize a fashion company has large-scale effects on all elements of the organization, including its business model.

IMPACT OF INTERNATIONALIZING PRODUCTION ON THE BUSINESS MODEL

An increasing number of fashion companies chooses to internationalize part or all of their production (motivated by pull or push factors or a combination of both). This entails a series of choices (and corresponding) consequences. These choices are specific to each organization. Most importantly, these choices are determined by essential characteristics of the partner (such as speed and quality of production, reliability, location, ability to monitor development and price).

As every choice has its consequences, choosing specific internationalization options can have a significant impact on the business model of the organization. Casadesus-Masanell and Ricart distinguish three key considerations to ensure that the correct choices have been made:

- **… are the choices and consequences aligned with company goals and values?** The choices made while designing a business model should deliver consequences that enable an organization to achieve its goals.

- **… are the choices and consequences self-reinforcing?** The choices that organizations make while creating a business model should complement one another. There must be internal consistency.

- **… are the choices and consequences robust?** The choices made should help improve the competitiveness of the company and should help over time in fending off competitive threats.

IMPACT OF INTERNATIONALIZING SALES ON THE BUSINESS MODEL

The second way a fashion company can increase its internationalization is through seeking international sales. This is a step that many independent fashion designers are forced to undertake due to the often small size of, and limited possibilities for expansion in the local market. From a business model point of view, the fashion company can decide between two global directions. It can choose to 1) replicate its current sales strategy in the new international markets, or it can 2) reposition its strategy. Each choice has different implications on the company's business model.

Replicating the business model strategy

Many organizations will opt for replicating their current (domestic) sales strategy in their international endeavours. For example, a company that currently sells its designs mainly via department stores can choose to replicate this strategy and find department stores abroad to use as its sales channel. This approach has several advantages; for example, the fashion designer is used to the processes that are involved in such channels. However, it is important to note that pure replication is almost never possible. Each market has its intricate workings and requires a (to some degree) specialized approach. Dunford, Palmer and Benveniste (2010) have developed a model consisting of four stages that help organizations in successfully replicating a business model in a new setting. The four processes are *clarification*, *localization*, *experimentation* and *co-option*. By applying the four stages, organizations can replicate their business model while making the necessary localized adjustments.

Clarification: establishing the core business model elements

Early business model clarification is key to understanding what exactly the company wants to replicate. What are the core values that underlie the business and its business model? What specific choices have been made in the day-to-day operationalization of the company's strategy, and why? What processes are essential for defining and clarifying what the organization stands for? Insights into these fundamental questions – and therefore the core elements of a business model – are essential before being able to replicate a strategy internationally.

Localization: responding to contextual conditions

Localization refers to those changes that are required if the demands of specific local conditions are to be met. Local regulations, for example, may require a business to change certain approaches. Changes may also be required in the more operational aspects of your business model. For instance, a fashion brand that is unknown in the new market will require a different marketing approach. Responding to local contextual differences is critical to being able to operationalize a business model on a country-by-country basis.

Experimentation: trying something new

The experimentation phase involves being innovative and trying out new processes or products not previously part of the business model operationalization. Business models do not emerge "fully formed" – rather they continue to evolve from their initial conception and throughout their repeated application. Therefore, continued experimentation, which in this case refers to innovations that can broadly be characterized as "optional" in comparison to the required adjustments in the previous phase, is important. This phase is usually a continuous process in which the company tries to find, through continuous trial-and-error and fine-tuning, an optimal business model configuration for each context.

Co-option: taking advantage of others' experience

The final phase in a successful replication strategy, co-option refers to the process whereby organizational practices and ideas originating in one country through localization or experimentation are applied in operations in the home country or in other locations. This is the learning and application phase in which a continuous and thorough evaluation of successful practices can help fine-tune the overall operation and business model of the organization. This is a vital process for companies that are considering further expansion in different markets as it helps refine and clarify the fundamental business model elements of the company.

Repositioning the business model strategy

Trying to operate more than one business model at a time is difficult – and frequently cited as a leading cause of entrepreneurial failure. However, there are many situations in which a company may wish (or need) to address several customer segments, using a particular business model for each. A fashion designer who sells his products through one or more privately owned stores in his home country is able to create an atmosphere that is in line with the company's core values, thereby adding an extra dimension to the product-sales experience. It is unlikely, however, that the company will be able to recreate this in foreign markets, as it can prove to be difficult to open a store abroad and to translate a local experience to a foreign culture. The company will therefore be forced to use a different channel and method of distribution.

Or let's say a designer positions himself and his products in his home market as a medium-priced, mid-segment brand, but, relying on "foreign mystique", as a luxury, high-end brand in markets elsewhere. The Belgian label Essentiel is a good example of this mixed strategy. In most markets, the brand can be labeled as middle segment, in Italy however, its sales agent placed Essentiel (see also case #6) successfully in a more high fashion segment. In this case, using a different business model for the different markets will be useful, even necessary.

A combination of distinct strategies and business models can, however, be difficult to manage, as it adds additional complexity to the organization; requires broader organizational skills, for instance in sales and marketing; and requires additional investments. Research by Casadesus-Masanell and Tarziján in 2012 indicates that to determine whether two business models are complements or substitutes, executives should consider two questions:

··· To what extent do the business models share major physical assets?

··· And to what extent are the resources and capabilities that result from operating each business model compatible?

Successfully managing complex portfolios of business models can be difficult, as it is more common for two business models not to have critical assets, capabilities, and resources in common. Successfully applying different business models relies on a leadership that can make dynamic decisions, build commitment to both overarching visions and agenda-specific goals, learn actively at multiple levels, and engage with conflict.

SUMMARY

Within the past two decades, globalization has become inherent to much of the fashion industry. Independent and high-end fashion companies have taken note of the consumption patterns of global consumers, and have expanded their businesses in areas where consumer spending on fashion is high often revolving around the world's leading financial centres. Furthermore production activities are increasingly being outsourced to low-cost areas, such as China, India, Turkey and Bangladesh.

Over the years, several theories have been developed to explain the manner in which fashion companies internationalize their operations and sales. The Uppsala model suggests that companies, after a period of operating in the domestic market only, increase their commitment to new, relatively similar, markets, the more knowledge they gain of that market through experience. The more recent Born Global model states that firms operate in a different context and in a fast-paced competitive environment and must therefore find quick ways of internationalizing. The latter theory arguably relates more to high-end independent designers, who tend to quickly face limitations in their domestic market and perceive value in fast expansion abroad, both in terms of production and sales.

A decision to expand operations or sales abroad has significant consequences for a fashion company's business model. In internationalizing sales, an organization has the option to either replicate its current sales strategy in its international endeavours, or to completely reposition its strategy.

The globalization of the fashion industry has had an enormous impact on fashion organizations and the manner of operating and expanding. Insights into the process of internationalization, its drivers and barriers, and its strategic consequences can help fashion companies to understand the industry and better deal with the complexities of operating in a globalizing context.

REFERENCES

Casadesus-Masanell, R., & Ricart, J. E. (2011) How to Design A Winning Business Model. In: *Harvard Business Review, 89* (1/2), 100-107.

Casadesus-Masanell, R., & Tarziján, J. (2012) When One Business Model Isn't Enough, in: *Harvard Business Review, 90* (1/2), 132-137.

Demol, M., Schramme, A., & Van Andel, W. (2013) *Internationalisering van de Creatieve Industrieën in Vlaanderen. Case: De Vlaamse Mode-industrie [Internationalizing the Creative Industries in Flanders. Case: The Flemish Fashion Industry]*. Leuven: Flanders DC – Antwerp Management School kenniscentrum.

Dunford, R., Palmer, I., & Benveniste, J. (2010) Business Model Replication for Early and Rapid Internationalisation: The ING Direct Experience. *Long Range Planning, 43* (5-6), 655-674. doi:10.1016/j.lrp.2010.06.004.

Gemperli, N. (2010) *Fashion World Mapper: Your City on the Trend Radar.* Master Thesis, University of the Arts Zurich, Zurich.

Greiner, L. E. (1998) Evolution and revolution as organizations grow. In: *Harvard Business Review, 76* (3), 55-68.

Hagoort, G., Thomassen, A., Kooyman, R. (2007) *Pioneering minds worldwide. On the entrepreneurial principles of the cultural and creative industries.* Utrecht: Eburon.

Johanson, J., & Vahlne, J.-E. (1977) The Internationalization Process of the Firm-A Model of Knowledge Development and Increasing Foreign Market Commitments. In: *Journal of International Business Studies, 8* (1), 23-32. doi:10.2307/254397.

Johanson, J., & Vahlne, J.-E. (2009) The Uppsala internationalization process model revisited: From liability of foreignness to liability of outsidership, in: *Journal of International Business Studies, 40* (9), 1411-1431. doi:10.1057/jibs.2009.24

Moore, C.M. (1997) La mode sans frontières? The internationalisation of fashion retailing. In: *Journal of Fashion Marketing and Management, 1* (4), 345-356.

Osterwalder, A. & Pigneur, Y. (2013) *Business Model Generation.* Hoboken: John Wiley & Sons.

Rasmusen, E. S., & Madsen, T. K. (2002) The Born Global concept. In: *SME internationalization and born globals – different European views and evidence.* Presented at the 28th EIBA Conference 2002, Athens.

Teece, D. J. (2010) Business models, business strategy and innovation. In: *Long Range Planning, 43* (2-3), 172-194. doi:10.1016/j.lrp.2009.07.003.

The Global Language Monitor (2013, September 6) London Edges New York for Top 2012 Global Fashion Capital. *The Global Language Monitor.* World Trade Organization. (2012). *International Trade Statistics.* Geneva: WTO.

RECOMMENDED

Books

Prahalad, C. K., & Krishnan, M. S. (2008) *The new age of innovation: Driving cocreated value through global networks* (1st ed.). New York: McGraw-Hill.

Priestley, D. (2013) *Entrepreneur revolution: how to develop your entrepreneurial mindset and start a business that works.* Oxford: John Wiley and Sons Ltd.

Articles

Casadesus-Masanell, R., & Ricart, J. E. (2011) How to Design A Winning Business Model, In: *Harvard Business Review, 89* (1/2), 100-107.

Johnson, M. W., Christensen, C. M., & Kagermann, H. (2008) Reinventing your business model. In: *Harvard Business Review, 86* (12), 50-59.

Ofek, E., & Wathieu, L. (2010) Are you ignoring trends that could shake up your business? In: *Harvard Business Review, 88* (July-August), 124-132.

case # 4   Tim Van Steenbergen

FW 13-14

"I work away from the spotlight"

Investor Bart Van den Eynde

Antwerp-based Tim Van Steenbergen graduated from the city's fashion department of the Royal Academy for Fine Arts. He launched his first fashion collection in Paris in 2001. He worked as the first assistant to Olivier Theyskens for a few seasons before launching his own label, Tim Van Steenbergen. In 2003, he started to cooperate with investor Bart Van den Eynde. The brand is a "creative lab": Van Steenbergen doesn't limit himself to his fashion collections – he has also designed shoes for Ambiorix, glasses for Theo, lamps for Delta Light and the costumes for numerous plays. For three years, he created costumes for the world famous opera house La Scala in Milan. Here, Bart Van den Eynde chats about the pair's collaboration.

Interview by Trui Moerkerke

You and Tim Van Steenbergen have a special collaboration. Can you describe your role?

I'm not a traditional investor, the kind you are likely to find in large fashion groups, the ones I call "label fashion". These groups are not different from any other businesses: they focus on strategies to make money. I want to play a different role. I work away from the spotlight. You know, sometimes I compare creative people to cluster bombs: their ideas and initiatives go in all directions. This can be a good thing, but it does complicate running a business. What I try to do is to limit the endless possibilities they see, from 360 degrees to, let's say, 180 degrees, still a wide range in which to work. You need some focus to realize a fashion business. I think I can help there.

"Define how and in which structure you want to work"

Investor Bart Van den Eynde

How does this work on a day-to-day basis?

I stick to the rule that I never ever interfere with the creative part. But I try to show Tim the business opportunities. It's a jungle out there and I see myself as the driver of a bulldozer, preparing the road in the jungle. I go in front and hope that Tim wants to follow and does not veer into the bushes or in the direction of a dangerous cliff. Of course, creative people can discover exciting things off-road. But if I see any danger, my role is to advise him not to go there.

Tim Van Steenbergen works as a creative lab. If there is a request for a collaboration, he considers whether or not he wants to do it. If he thinks it is an interesting project, then I come in and deal with the contracts. Tim is an intelligent man, which makes my job easier. He knows how he should expand his own collection in terms of numbers and pricing. Of course we talk a lot. The collaboration was uncharted territory for both of us; we learned by doing.

What do you find most difficult about working in the creative industry?

You should be able to convince creative people that they live in the world and not only in their own world. Creatives have to dream, but they need to wake up too. All that shines is *not* gold. One sees financial tragedies often in the creative industry. It's heartbreaking that some creatives build up so many debts and when things go wrong, they are just left on their own.

The economic environment is tough, times are uncertain. It's difficult to plan ahead. Moreover, there is no precise recipe for success. There are a few things you really shouldn't do, but apart from that, there is no such thing as a magic formula. It's easy to comment on the winner of the Tour de France at the arrival. But at the start of the Tour, nobody knows for sure who will make it. In fashion, there are very few people who succeed.

If you had to give advice to investors or fashion designers, what would that be?

For investors: don't use money you can't afford to lose. For designers: define how and in which structure you want to work. It's an option to go for the management style of "label fashion". In that case, you have to know that you give up at least part of your independence in exchange for money, a network and customers. That's the way it works. If you'd like to approach an investor as an independent designer, then you should have what I call a track record. By that I mean that you have to be experienced and must have had a business for some years. An investor wants to avoid risks and sees dangers everywhere. That's somehow deadly for the creativity and identity of a fashion designer who is starting up his own collection. But if you already have a track record, you can approach an investor. Last but not least: go your own way and decide whether you really want to be someone who is there to stay. And who wants to work hard all the time. There is no other way to do this job.

Blood and Roses

Macbeth

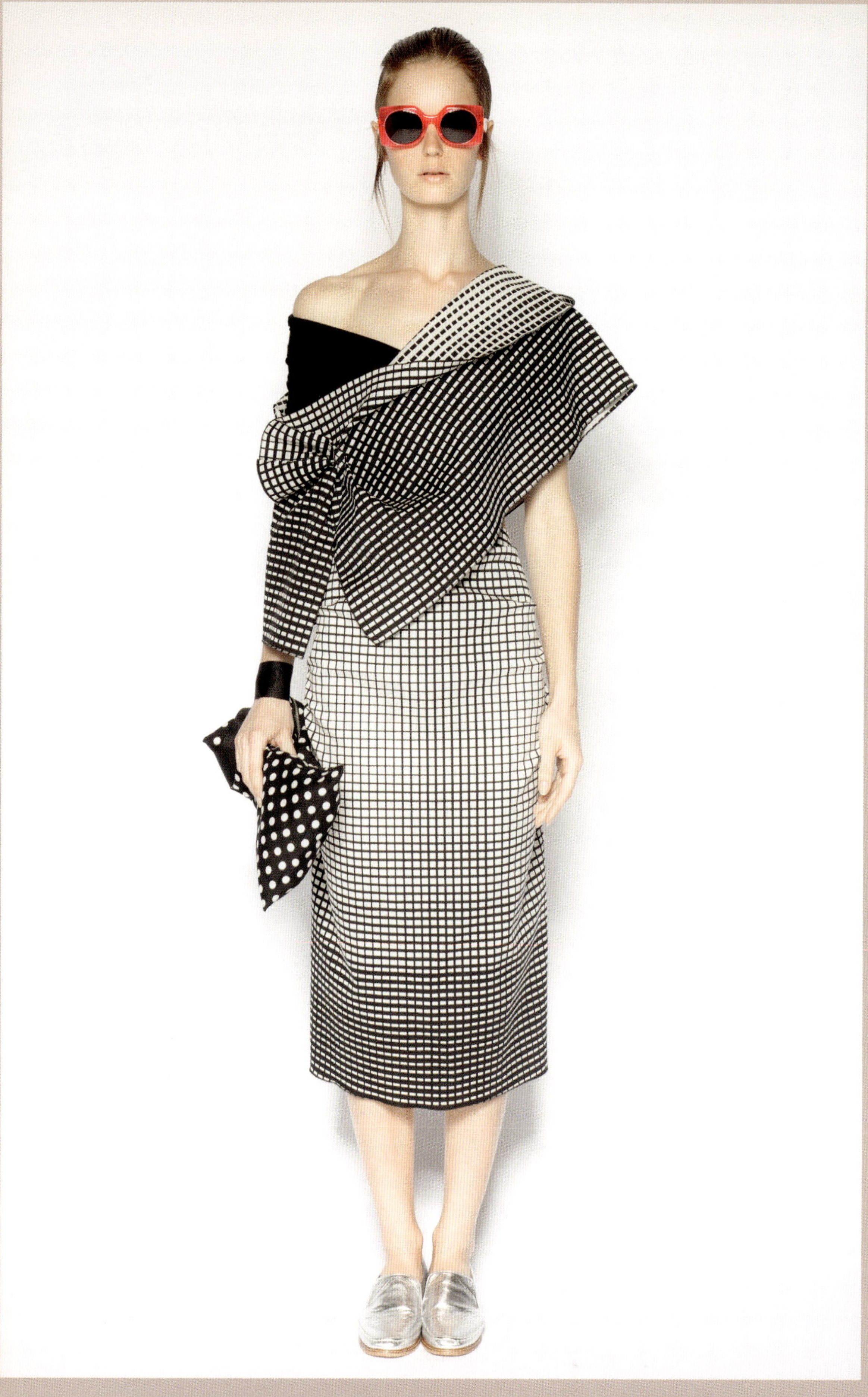

Tim Van Steenbergen
SS 14

FASHION LAW

Dieter Geernaert

In this chapter, we will explore a number of legal issues that a fashion designer or a fashion business (the brand) may have to deal with at some point in the course of business: be it at the very beginning, after the business has expanded or when the business is being sold or closed.

Although legal matters may be the last thing on a designer's mind, each designer should reflect on how his *intellectual property*, i.e. the manifestation of creative efforts (a name, an image, a design...), can be protected optimally. Intellectual property is a legal concept and refers to the laws and regulations that give exclusive rights to owners of *trade marks, domain names, copyrights, industrial design rights and patents*. In section 2 we will briefly explain these five categories. Intellectual property includes many other rights (e.g. database rights and plant breeders' rights), but these are less relevant for the fashion industry and will therefore not be treated here.

The next step is to exploit your intellectual property, by entering into agreements with third parties who are given the right to use it, preferably in return for a financial consideration. This will be dealt with in section 2. Several agreements – such as *license agreements, manufacturing agreements* and *commercial agency agreements* – will be briefly discussed and key provisions will be highlighted.

In section 3 we will conclude with some practical tips and tricks for aspiring fashion designers. As intellectual property is a complex legal matter, the rights differ from country to country and each business requires tailor-made advice, we recommend taking expert legal advice. The tips and tricks in this section are meant as points of interest that you could keep in mind when seeking such advice.

PROTECTING YOUR INTELLECTUAL PROPERTY

Would Gucci still be successful today if it had not registered Guccio Gucci's surname as a *trade mark*? Who would have heard of Diane von Fürstenberg if she had not created (and documented the designing of) the original work of art that is the iconic wrap dress? Would YKK ever have been incorporated if the inventor of the zipper had not bothered applying for patent protection of his *invention*?

These are just a few examples of how the legal concept of intellectual property interacts with commercial business. All successful fashion stories start with protecting your intellectual property. No matter how creative a designer, if he does not provide for any legal protection for his original creation, name, logo or invention, the story will come to an abrupt end sooner rather than later:

- ... Third parties will try to benefit from these creative efforts without making any investment themselves and may cause serious damage to the brand image if the market is inundated with cheap copies of your product.

- ... Investors may be put off from investing in your business if your intellectual property is not protected. Investors will look for designers with strong intellectual property rights. You will have to demonstrate that you took the necessary steps – which can be tricky because of the intangible nature of intellectual property.

Each designer (or brand) must determine which intellectual property right(s) will best suit his (or its) business needs. Having a distinctive *trade mark* is relevant to every type of fashion business so we will elaborate on this shortly. If you intend to design and market an iconic bag that will be sold over more than one season (the new Birkin bag?), you may want to consider an *industrial design registration*. Otherwise you can rely on *copyright*. For those creative people who invent a new high performance sports shoe, patent protection could be useful.

TRADEMARKS

What? A trade mark is a distinctive sign that is capable of distinguishing the goods or services of one undertaking from those of other undertakings.

Conditions? When deciding which sign to use as a trade mark, a designer or brand will look for a strong trade mark that will help create the brand identity, distinguish it from competitors and guarantee quality. One should not forget to take into account the legal requirements in order to avoid a refusal of the trade mark application. Even if the trade mark does get registered, lack of distinctiveness could be a reason for its cancellation.

Generally, a trade mark must (i) be capable of being represented graphically and (ii) have a distinctive character. Signs that are capable of being represented graphically are, for example, words (including personal names), designs, letters, numerals and the shape of goods or of their packaging. Because of this requirement, it remains under discussion whether a specific scent (of a perfume) can be registered as a trade mark.

The *distinctive character* of the sign in question will also have to be assessed. Distinctiveness is not only a business requirement but also an important legal requirement. The assessment is done in relation to the goods or services for which the sign will be used. For example, the word "Aqua" will probably not be a valid trade mark for water because it is descriptive. However, the word "Aqua" is perfectly capable of distinguishing jeans of one undertaking from those of other undertakings. It would therefore make a valid trade mark for clothing.

Below a trade mark registered for fashion goods:

Word (here in a specific font)

PRADA

Figure 1. | Community trade mark n° 011918331 owned by Prada S.A.[4]

It is common practice in the fashion sector to use and register *a person's name* as a trade mark (Dior, Saint Laurent and Chanel, to name but a few). Some names may initially not be the strongest trade marks, particularly if the name is common. They are, however, capable of distinguishing clothing or shoes from one company from those of a competitor, as opposed to a descriptive sign such as "shoeshoe" for shoes.

This principle was confirmed by the European Court of Justice, which is the highest judicial body to rule on the validity and interpretation of the laws of the European Union, in a judgement of 30 September 2004 about the trade mark (and surname) "Nichols" for food products:

In the same way as a term used in everyday language, a common surname may serve the trade mark function of indicating origin and therefore distinguish the products or services concerned.

(...) the assessment of the existence of the distinctive character of a trade mark constituted by a surname, even a common one, must be carried out specifically in relation, first, to the products or services in respect of which registration is applied for and, second, to the perception of the relevant consumers.[5]

If a designer registers his (sur)name as a trade mark, under certain circumstances he could subsequently lose the right to continue to use it as a trade mark.

This could occur when the designer has become a brand. Most often the trade mark registration will be held by a company set up by the designer. If the business is sold or the designer is no longer a majority shareholder, he could lose control over his personal name. This was the case for a Ms Elizabeth Emanuel, a designer of bridal gowns. She transferred her trade mark application for "Elizabeth Emanuel", which she had filed for clothing, to the company she set up. That company subsequently transferred the trade mark, including the goodwill attached to it, to another company. As a consequence of subsequent assignments, the trade mark registration ended up at an owner with whom Ms Emanuel had no dealings.

When this latest owner applied for a new trade mark registration ("ELIZABETH EMANUEL" in upper case), Ms Emanuel tried to oppose that application. She argued that consumers would be deceived and led to believe that she was involved in the new owner's clothing business.

University of South Wales
Prifysgol De Cymru

Library Services
FASHION LAW

The European Court of Justice pointed out in its judgement of 30 March 2006 that:

> A trade mark corresponding to the name of the designer and first manufacturer of the goods bearing that mark may not, by reason of that particular feature alone, be refused registration or be liable to revocation on the ground that it would deceive or mislead the public, in particular where the goodwill associated with that trade mark, previously registered in a different graphic form, has been assigned together with the business making the goods to which the mark relates.[6]

The new owner was therefore, in principle, allowed to keep the trade mark, unless (or until) it could be proven that he was misleading consumers.

This does not necessarily mean that every designer who transfers his trade mark would lose the right to use his name for business purposes. In the absence of contractual arrangements, generally trade mark laws expressly allow a person to keep using his conflicting name in circumstances such as those set out above, provided that person does not use the name *as a trade mark*. This means that, for example, the designer could use *"X designed by Elizabeth Emanuel"* as the words "designed by Elizabeth Emanuel" are descriptive and refer to the name of Ms Emanuel. The words are therefore not considered part of the trade mark as such. However, the word combination *"X by Elizabeth Emanuel"* (without the word *"designed"*) would not be acceptable if the public's perception is that these four words constitute a trade mark.

Image (with or without words)

Figure 2. | International trade mark n° 767729 owned by Levitas S.p.A.[7] owned by Levitas S.p.A.[8].

Figure 3. | Community trade mark n° 005509823.

Shape / colour

Figure 4. | U.S. trade mark n° 85700861 owned by Christian Louboutin[9].

FASHION MANAGEMENT

Readers may recognize this red shape as the distinctive feature of a Louboutin shoe, known for its red sole. In litigation before the United States Court of Appeals, Christian Louboutin relied on a similar red trade mark to oppose the marketing by Yves Saint Laurent of a "monochrome" shoe. The Yves Saint Laurent shoe in the monochrome style featured the same colour on the entire shoe: the red version was all red, including a red insole, heel, upper, and outsole.

The United States Court of Appeals decided in September 2012 that Louboutin's trade mark was a valid trade mark for shoes[10]. However, the court pointed out that it is the contrast between the sole and the upper that causes the sole to stand out, and to distinguish its creator. The court therefore limited the red sole trade mark to a red lacquered outsole that contrasts with the colour of the adjoining upper. Accordingly, it declined to prohibit Yves Saint Laurent from using a red lacquered outsole as applied to a monochrome red shoe.

Registration? Rights to trade marks are obtained through registration in a national or regional register, for which you pay a registration fee.

The Office for the Harmonisation of the Internal Market is a regional office that is based in Alicante, Spain and takes care of the *Community Trademark* registration[11]. This trade mark is valid in the European Union as a whole. The basic fee for a Community Trademark is between EUR 900 and EUR 1,050[12]. If you use the services of a trade mark attorney to take care of the registration for you, you will have to add his fees. If you have a large portfolio of trade marks to manage worldwide, it may be a safer option to outsource this to a trade mark attorney, who has the necessary systems in place to keep an eye on all the different renewal deadlines, payment terms, etc.

When applying for trade mark registration, the applicant must indicate for which products or services the trade mark will be registered. Most countries use the "International Classification of Goods and Services for the Purposes of the Registration of Marks" (the "Nice Classification")[13]. The 2013 edition consists of 34 classes of products (class 1 to class 34) and 11 classes of services (class 35 to class 45).

For the fashion business, relevant product class headings of the Nice Classification are:

- class 3: soaps, perfumery, cosmetics;
- class 9: eyewear;
- class 14: jewellery and watches;
- class 18: leather goods, trunks and travelling bags;
- class 22: bags; and
- class 25: clothing, shoes and headgear.

These class headings describe in broad terms the nature of their products. Each class has a sub-level that contains detailed alphabetical lists of products that are included in that specific class (for example, in class 25, clothing: aprons, ascots, babies' pants, bandanas, etc.). One can choose from about 10,000 indications of products. Internet search engines are available to assist with selecting the right class heading or sub type.

The more class numbers a trade mark owner designates, the higher the registration and renewal fees. Typically, one to three class numbers will be included in the basic fee. Additional fees will be due for each class number added.

Where? It is recommended to register your trade mark in all countries and regions where you are doing business or may do business in the future. Even though you may not expect to be doing business in countries like China, South Korea or India in the near future, they are major markets where all well-known fashion brands are present. Typically, in those countries so-called "trade mark squatters" will be on the look-out for European brands. When you become successful in Europe, they will register your trade mark in their country and they will try to sell this trade mark registration to you for excessive amounts of money as soon as you decide to explore those markets too. To avoid this, it is better to proactively register your trade mark in those territories from the start.

To avoid having to register with each national office of each country in which you intend to use your trade mark, the World Intellectual Property Organisation (WIPO) administers a system of international registration of marks. WIPO is a United Nations agency that is dedicated to the use of intellectual property[14]. This system, known as the "Madrid System for the International Registration of Marks", will allow a person who has a trade mark registration or application with the trade mark office of a member state, to obtain an international registration having effect in some or all of the other member states[15]. This is done through a single procedure with his national trade mark office. This way you can avoid having to contact all the other offices separately and it will substantially reduce registration costs. Not all countries are members though. For example, only a few Asian and Latin American countries are members of the Madrid Union.

Who? The trade mark application can be in the name of a physical person or of a company. However, because of a legal obligation to put a trade mark to *genuine use*, it may be better to let the trade mark be registered in the name of a company. Generally, within a period of time following registration (for example, 5 years in the E.U.[16]), if the registered owner has not put the trade mark to genuine use in connection with the goods or services in respect of which it is registered, a third party may request that the rights of the trade mark owner be revoked. If the trade mark is registered by an individual, it may be difficult to prove that he made genuine use of it in the course of trade. If the trade mark is not registered in the name of a company, the individual should at least grant licences to one or more companies to use his trade mark *in the course of trade* and register these with the trade mark office.

Term? A trade mark registration is generally valid for 10 years but is renewable indefinitely, provided the owner pays the renewal fees in time each subsequent period (usually also of 10 years). This is where trade mark rights differ from copyright, rights to industrial designs and patents, which are *limited in time*.

Infringement? A trade mark confers on the owner the exclusive right to prevent others from using *a sign which is identical or similar* to the trade mark, *in relation to goods or services which are identical or similar* to those for which it is registered.

Additional conditions may apply, such as the requirement that the infringing sign is used in the course of trade, as opposed to a non-commercial use. Often it will be required too that there is a likelihood of confusion on the part of the public or that the use of the infringing sign takes unfair advantage or is detrimental to the distinctive character or the repute of the trade mark, especially if the younger sign is being used for products that are not similar. For example, a trade mark "DRIES VAN NOTEN" that is used for beverages (i.e. for products that are not identical or not similar to clothing) may take unfair advantage of the Belgian designer's original trade mark for clothing.

Before applying for the registration of a trade mark, the applicant should verify whether he will not be infringing the older trade mark rights of a third party. Some trade mark offices will perform *ex officio* searches for identical or similar registrations. If the trade mark office does not perform such a search, it is advisable to let a trade mark attorney do this for you. This way you can anticipate possible problems and avoid nasty surprises after having developed a brand identity based on your (possibly invalid) trade mark.

A fairly affordable tool to monitor infringing trade mark applications is to ask a trade mark attorney to look out for similar words or logos that third parties try to register in the registers of countries that you designate. *This surveillance* is done by means of a computer program that will warn you about possible infringing applications, which you can oppose in administrative procedure before the national or regional office.

DOMAIN NAMES

What? A domain name is a name that will lead you to a specific website. It maps to a unique Internet Protocol address (IP address) of a server or computer. The domain name gives every Internet server an easy-to-remember and easy-to-spell address, instead of the underlying IP address, which consists of a number (for example, 123.456.789.0) and which is harder to remember.

Conditions? Unlike a trade mark, a domain name generally does not need to be distinctive. One can register the domain name "fashion.com" to sell clothing on a website, whereas it will not be possible to register the word "fashion" as a trade mark for clothing.

Registration? Registration of a domain name is only done through official intermediaries, which are named *registrars*. They are commercial undertakings that are accredited by the Internet Corporation for Assigned Names and Numbers (ICANN)[17]. ICANN is responsible for managing and coordinating the domain name system by overseeing the distribution of unique IP addresses and domain names. Unlike the other intellectual property registers set out in this chapter (trade mark register, patent register, and so on), which are managed by government authorities, the registers in which the domain names are kept are managed by private not-for-profit organisations.

Who? In principle, anyone with a legitimate interest in a name has the right to register it as a domain name. In some countries you must own a trade mark that is identical or similar to the domain name that you want to register.

Where? The best known domains are generic top-level domains (gTLDs), such as .com, .info, .net and .org. Recently, new gTLDs rules came into force, and as a result it is now also possible to register your trade mark as a domain (for example, .balmain) – though this will cost more than EUR 100,000. Country code top-level domains (ccTLDs) are, for example, .uk, .jp and .br and refer to a specific country. For some ccLTDs, it may be required to have an address in the relevant country.

We recommend registering your domain name with as many gTLDs as possible (that is, the classic gTLDs such as .com and .net) and with all ccTLDs of all countries where you are doing business or may expect to do business in the future. Registering too many names will be more cost efficient than having to litigate to get your name back from a so-called "cyber squatter" who has no legitimate interest in the name, but whose only purpose is to sell it to you or to take unfair advantage of your business by luring consumers to his website.

Term? Generally, a domain name registration is valid for one year and it is renewable each year against payment of a renewal fee.

Infringement? Domain name disputes are usually dealt with in arbitration proceedings, to which a domain name applicant must agree when applying for a domain name. These procedures, which are conducted 100% electronically, allow the dispute to be resolved without the cost and delays often encountered in court litigation[18]. The deadline for exchanging written briefs is short (a couple of weeks), you do not need to be represented by a lawyer and you will not have to travel to court or spend additional time pleading the matter.

If the rightful owner of the domain name files a complaint under the applicable arbitration rules, that owner can request that the domain name be transferred to him or that the registration be cancelled, if he proves that the name is registered and/or used in bad faith. It is recommended to request a transfer to avoid a third party registering the disputed domain name again after it is cancelled.

In the vast majority of cases, the complaint is accepted. Examples of domain names that were the subject matter of arbitration proceedings are[19]:

··· transfer: christiandior.net, dolcegabbana.com, salvatoreferragamo.org
··· cancellation: chez-agnes-b.info, oakleyspree.com;
··· request denied: aberzombie.com, armaniexchange.net, azzaro.com.

COPYRIGHT

What? Authors, artists and other creators of *literary and artistic creations* are granted copyrights to their works. Although from this definition it may appear that this only applies to novels, plays, films, painting, sculptures or photographs, copyright protection extends to all sorts of expressions of the mind, which can include clothing designs. Ideas, trends or styles are not protected because they are not a *concrete expression*.

Copyright confers economic and moral rights on the author of the work. The *economic right* implies the exclusive right to reproduce or adapt the work (or authorise others to do so) in any manner or form (for example, to make a picture of a bag or sell reproductions of a dress). Each author (physical person) also has a *moral right* to his work. This includes the right to (i) claim authorship of the work (i.e. to have his name mentioned on it) and (ii) object to any changes to the work that would harm the creator's reputation.

Conditions? Copyright generally applies only in relation to a work that is *original* in the sense that it is the author's own intellectual creation. In the E.U., this protection is given a fairly broad interpretation and copyright protection may be easily granted.

Originality of a work is often proven by means of a comparison with other works, from which it should sufficiently differ. It is important to document the entire creative process (from first design to final product) and to date all documents, in order to prove how and when the original work was created.

Registration? Under the Berne Convention[20], copyright protection is *obtained automatically* without the need for registration or other formalities. Copyright exists from the moment the work is created – hence the need to keep proof of the date of creation.

In some countries, like the USA, you will have to register the work before you can bring a lawsuit for infringement of the work.

Who? The creator of the work will be the initial owner of the economic and moral rights. The economic rights can be transferred to another person or a company; the moral rights always remain with the initial creator.

The author or right holder of a literary or artistic work will be deemed to be the copyright owner vis-à-vis a third party if his name appears on the work in a manner that is customary for the product in question. Therefore, it is recommended to use a copyright notice © with your name/trade mark on labels, lookbooks, pictures and all other protectable items. This not only makes it easier to prove that you are the copyright owner, third parties will also be warned that you deem your products to be original works that are protected by copyright and that cannot be reproduced without your consent. The third party may provide proof that somebody else is the actual owner of the rights, in which case the legal presumption will no longer apply.

Always verify the chain of rights when using a work that is protected by copyright. Many different people and companies may have been involved in the creation of a work. For example, the designer who creates a piece of clothing, the photographer who shoots that item for an advertising campaign and the website designer who incorporates the pictures of the clothing in the brand's website. Ideally, the brand makes sure that all relevant rights are transferred to it. It should have standard clauses for the transfer of rights in labour contracts of employees and in service agreements with, for example, photographers and website designers, who usually reserve these rights in their general terms and conditions.

If a transfer of copyrights is not possible, the brand must at least obtain the right to use the work in all formats and for all purposes that it wants to use it for (for example, the use of a picture online and/or in advertisements in print magazines, in one country or worldwide).

Term? The term of copyright protection is generally limited from the creation of the work until 50[21] to 70 years after the death of the creator. However, national laws may establish longer terms of protection.

This term should enable creators and businesses to benefit financially from their creations for a sufficiently long period. Given the fact that clothing collections change at least twice a year, and even though certain trends may reappear every couple of years, it is rather unlikely that a designer or brand would need such long-term protection, except for the occasional timeless piece.

Infringement? Copyright protects the original work from being reproduced, distributed or adapted without the right owner's consent. This does not mean that it is permitted to market reproductions that differ slightly or that, for example, have seven differences or more (a common misconception). If the original features of the older work are found in the younger work, there will be copyright infringement, even if there are many differences between the two products.

Copyright infringements are dealt with by the national courts. The copyright owner will have to litigate in each country where he deems that his rights are being infringed, in accordance with the copyright laws of that jurisdiction. The infringing party is not always some dodgy manufacturer but might as well be a popular clothing chain or other luxury brand. An example of the latter is found in a ruling of the court of The Hague (The Netherlands) of 19 April 2011 in a dispute between the Dutch brand owner G-Star and the Swedish clothing chain H&M[22]. The court found that G-Star could rely on its copyrights to the design of its pair of trousers named "Elwood" to prevent H&M from selling jeans that were considered a reproduction of G-Star's "Elwood" jeans below: :

Figure 5. | Benelux trade mark n° 0624.182 owned by G-Star Raw C.V.[23] Benelux trade mark n° 0662.447 owned by G-Star Raw C.V.[24] Design rights.

Figure 6.
Community design
n° 000084223-0001[25].

INDUSTRIAL DESIGN RIGHTS

What? An industrial design is the *appearance* of (the whole or a part of) a product that results from the features of, in particular, the lines, contours, colours, shape, texture and/or materials of the product itself and/or its ornamentation.

A *product* can be any industrial or handicraft item, including textile designs, clothing, bags, or shoes. Alongside are examples of a textile pattern and a bag that Louis Vuitton Malletier S.A. registered as an industrial design.

Figure 7.
Community design
n° 000084223-0003[26].

FASHION MANAGEMENT

Conditions? To be protected, under most national or regional laws an industrial design must (i) be new and (ii) have individual character

A design shall be considered to be new if no identical design has been made available to the public. Designs are deemed to be *identical* if their features differ only in immaterial details. A design will be considered to have *individual character* if the overall impression it produces on the informed user differs from the overall impression produced on such a user by any design that has been made available to the public.

If the features of the product's appearance are dictated solely by its *technical function*, it will be excluded from protection. This is similar under copyright law. It is unlikely that, for example, a shoe's appearance will be *solely* dictated by technical requirements. Each shoe must have a sole, an upper and a heel, yet despite these requirements, most shoes' appearances will differ and therefore most shoes will qualify for protection (provided they are new and have individual character).

Registration? Generally, an industrial design must be registered in a national or regional register in order to be protected under industrial design law. In the E.U. a single application for a design costs EUR 350[27].

The design registration uses a classification system that is somewhat similar to the Nice Classification. When registering a design, for example, in the E.U., the applicant must designate the relevant product class in accordance with the *Locarno classification*[28]. Articles of clothing are part of class 2 of this classification.

Registration is not always required. For example, in addition to the registered E.U. Community Design, the E.U. grants design protection to unregistered Community Designs, provided they are new and have individual character[29]. These conditions are the same as for registered designs, but the duration of the protection is *limited to three years* from the date on which the design was first made available to the public within the Community.

Such unregistered design can be of interest to fashion brands, whose products have a short market life given the seasonal character of collections, and who do not wish to spend their resources, or do not have resources to spend, on registering all designs they create.

Who? Generally, the rights to a design will initially be vested in the designer. National laws may provide that the rights to a design that is developed by an employee in the execution of his duties shall immediately vest in the employer. In each event, the brand should stipulate that each third party (in-house design team or external designers) expressly transfer to the brand all rights to the designs that these parties develop for the brand.

Furthermore, the brand should make sure that the design application is filed in its name. This way the brand will be deemed the owner of the design rights. Under certain laws, the brand may also be deemed the owner of the copyrights to that design if the design is registered in its name. An industrial design may be protected concurrently under design law and copyright law. Where possible, the owner should rely on both copyright and design law in infringement procedures, in case the claim based on either copyright or design law fails (for example, because the owner forgot to renew the design registration in time). In countries where these are mutually exclusive, the owner must choose which kind of protection he will rely on.

Term? The initial term of protection is generally 5 years from the application, but this term is renewable from up to 15 to 25 years.

It is important to apply for design registration before showing the design to the general public. If a design has been publicly displayed before the application was filed, for example at a fashion show of which pictures and images are distributed to the public, it may no longer be considered to fulfil the requirement of *novelty*. Consequently, it will not be possible to obtain a valid registration.

Infringement? A registered design confers on its holder the exclusive right to use it and to prevent any third party not having the owner's consent from using it. This includes any design that does not produce a different overall impression on the informed user.

Such use includes making, putting on the market, importing, exporting or using a product in which the design is incorporated or to which it is applied. This right is limited to the country or region where the design is registered. We recommend performing a search of the registered design databases where you intend to file a design application, before filing it. This will give you some idea as to whether your design may infringe on older design rights.

PATENTS

What? A patent is an exclusive right granted for an *invention*, i.e. a product or a process that offers a new technical solution to a problem or that provides a new way of doing something.

Conditions? A patent shall, in general, be granted to an invention that (i) is new, (ii) involves an inventive step and (iii) is susceptible of industrial application:

··· *Novelty* means that it must have some new characteristic which does not form part of prior art. Prior art is all information that has already been made available to the public before the patent application was filed.

··· *Inventiveness* means that the result could not be deduced by a person skilled in the technical field concerned, based on the available prior art.

··· An invention shall be considered as *susceptible of industrial application* if it can be made or used in any kind of industry, hence including the clothing industry. However, some results are expressly excluded from patent protection, such as aesthetic creations because they will not fulfil the two previous criteria.

Registration? A patent must be registered with a national or regional office in order to be granted protection.

The patent application will have to contain a description of the invention, with sufficient detail to allow an individual with an average understanding of the technical field concerned to use or reproduce the invention. Often drawings are included to help explain the invention. The drafting of the patent information and claims requires the expertise of a specialist patent attorney and can therefore be quite costly.

In addition, the registration fees can be high, depending on the territory. According to the European Commission, to protect an invention throughout the E.U., a company could pay up to EUR 32,000, mostly because of translation costs and other formalities with different national registers. Under a new unified system that will be implemented in 2014 in 25 of the E.U. member states[30], the Commission hopes to reduce the filing cost to EUR 680.

Where? In general, the patent applies and can be enforced only in the country or countries where the application was filed and granted. This means that the application must be filed in each country where the applicant intends to use the invention.

Member states to the *European Patent Treaty* have agreed on a simplified procedure whereby the European Patent Office grants patents that have the same effect as if the patents were applied for and granted in each of the member states[31]. A somehow similar system under the *Patent Cooperation Treaty* simplifies the filing of an international patent application in designated countries worldwide[32].

Who? The inventor will be the owner of the rights to the invention but these rights can be transferred to another person or company.

Some legislation provides that these rights are transferred automatically to the employer if the employee invented the invention under an employment agreement. As with other intellectual property, we recommend providing a transfer of patent rights in employment and service agreements.

In some countries (for example, the USA), the patent application must be filed in the name of the inventor. In other countries, the inventor keeps the right to be mentioned in the patent application, even if his rights were transferred to another party that files the application in its own name.

Term? Patent protection is granted for a limited period only, generally 20 years from the filing date.

As with industrial designs, it is important to file a patent application before publicly disclosing the details of the invention. In general, if an invention is made public before an application is filed, it will be considered prior art. Consequently, the patent would no longer meet the novelty criterion and the applicant's own disclosure of the invention will prevent him from obtaining a valid patent.

Infringement? Patent protection means that a third party may not commercially make, use, distribute or sell the invention without the patent owner's permission. In case of infringement, the patent owner will have to initiate (costly) litigation in each country where the patent is being infringed.

EXPLOITING YOUR INTELLECTUAL PROPERTY

Intellectual property is not an end in itself. It should be used and its value should be maximised by means of commercial agreements. In addition to the (negative) protection against infringements set out above, brands can make (positive) usage of their intellectual property in agreements with third parties.

In this section we discuss the main agreements that a brand may conclude from the manufacturing of the product until its online sale to a consumer. We will focus, on the one hand, on the licensing of intellectual property in each agreement and, on the other hand, on a number of other provisions that are relevant per type of agreement.

MANUFACTURING AGREEMENT

Typically a brand will conclude manufacturing or production agreements with manufacturers to have its products manufactured.

This implies the right for the manufacturer to use the brand's intellectual property *for the purpose of manufacturing* the products. When a manufacturer produces a skirt in line with the brand's designs and instruction or puts the brand's trade mark on a piece of clothing, the manufacturer is using the brand's intellectual property with the consent of the brand. It should be provided in the agreement that the manufacturer is not allowed to use the brand's intellectual property for any other purpose. This is to avoid a situation in which the manufacturer produces, for his own account, excess products under your trade mark or markets your designs under another trade mark.

In addition to the license arrangements, the brand should also provide that:

••• The manufacturer transfers to the brand all intellectual property rights to the designs that he develops.

In the production process the manufacturer may co-design (elements of) the products and, consequently, could be considered to be co-author or co-designer. This is a situation that you want to avoid as a brand. Therefore, it should be expressly provided that all intellectual property rights are vested in the brand, in order to have complete freedom to market these products without any restrictions.

··· The manufacturer must comply with minimum rules about labour conditions and product safety.

Even though a start-up will not have the resources to verify compliance, it is essential to at least put such provisions in the agreement. As a brand with no knowledge of applicable laws in the country of production, you can refer to the rules and standards set by the International Labour Organisation, which is an agency of the United Nations[33]. It has created minimum international labour standards in respect of (among other things) child labour, working conditions and safety at work.

In addition, the agreement should contain clauses that prohibit the use of harmful or toxic products and that oblige the manufacturer to comply with product safety of the laws of both the country of production and of the countries where the goods will eventually be sold to consumers.

To ensure compliance, you must provide that the brand will have the right to immediately terminate the agreement if the manufacturer breaches these provisions and that the manufacturer shall indemnify the brand against all damage that it may suffer as a consequence of the manufacturer's breach. This may (at least partly) remedy the substantial damage that is done to the brand in such an event. If workers were to die in a Bengali factory fire, besides the regrettable loss of life, the brand image of the companies whose clothing was being manufactured in that factory, will no doubt be adversely affected too.

Other relevant provisions are:

··· The obligation on the manufacturer to deliver on time, especially with respect to the samples for the fashion show and order taking. Consider providing penalties in case the manufacturer does not comply.

··· The right to audit the manufacturer's books or the right to visit the plant, in order to verify the manufacturer's compliance with the agreement.

FASHION MANAGEMENT

- Restrictions on the manufacturer's right to use subcontractors. Even if the manufacturer is allowed to use subcontractors, he should remain responsible for their actions vis-à-vis the brand.

- Information about the composition of each product that the manufacturer must provide and that is used to make the care label.

AGENCY AND DISTRIBUTION

A brand can opt to sell its manufactured products directly to retailers or to a local distributor or to use the services of a local commercial agent. That choice will be mainly business driven. In this section we will briefly discuss some legal aspects that should be taken into account.

Sale/purchase – Direct sales are generally done in respect of the (more expensive) first lines, for which buyers will travel to the brand's offices in Milan, Paris, London or New York during the fashion weeks.

The agreement concluded between the brand and the retailer is a fairly straightforward sale/purchase agreement. To this end, the majority of brands use their general terms and conditions of sale, which the buyer must accept and sign when placing an order. These general terms should be carefully drafted, preferably with the help of a legal expert. It will be the main contractual document between the parties to which will be referred in case of a dispute. It should cover all possible issues (right to cancel orders, use of the brand's intellectual property in the retailer's shop, and so on).

Distribution agreement – If the brand chooses to work with a distributor, the brand enters into a sale/purchase agreement with the distributor, who in turn will enter into sale/purchase agreements with retailers. The agreement between the brand and the distributor is usually a distribution agreement, which will contain provisions about the sale and distribution and provisions about intellectual property. The distributor usually applies his general terms and conditions of sale in his relationship with the retailers.

The distributor is given a license by the brand to sell certain products in a specific territory. The brand should provide examples of any other use the distributor is allowed to make of the brand's intellectual property. For example, may the distributor register the brand's name as a trade mark or domain name? Is he allowed to register the license that the brand has given him? Ideally, all intellectual property registrations are done in the name of the brand. However, if the distributor registers certain intellectual property in his own name, the parties should agree in advance that all registrations are transferred automatically to the brand if the agreement ends and the distributor is unwilling to collaborate to transfer these registrations.

In the distribution agreement, the brand:

··· Should reserve the right to cancel orders, for example if the numbers ordered by all customers is too low to manufacture the product;

··· Could provide for a minimum purchase obligation by the distributor;

··· Should make sure that it keeps control of approval of retailers to whom the distributor may sell, to maintain the right brand image;

··· Should clearly define the extent of the exclusivity, if any: Will the distributor be the only distributor of the brand in the territory? Will the brand still be allowed to sell directly to retailers (multi brands or mono brands) in the territory? What about online sales by the brand to end-consumers? And vice versa: Will the brand be the only supplier of the distributor or will he be allowed to sell products of competing brands?

··· Should set out who is responsible for the delivery, from where to where. Most businesses use *Incoterms*, which are standard trade terms set by the International Chamber of Commerce and commonly used in international contracts for the sale of goods[34]. They define the respective obligations, costs and risks for the delivery of goods.

··· Should make sure that it does not impose any obligations that can be considered anti-competitive. Generally, competition laws do not permit imposing minimum retail prices on the distributor. The brand can only *recommend* retail prices. Equally, restricting or prohibiting Internet sales by authorised retailers with a brick-and-mortar shop may not be acceptable.

FASHION MANAGEMENT

Commercial agency agreement – A commercial agent is a self-employed intermediary who is given the right by the brand to negotiate the sale of the brand's products, on the brand's behalf, in a specific territory. In this relationship, the contract party of the agent (i.e. the brand) is called the "principal".

The relationship between the brand and the retailer is a sale/purchase agreement, to which the brand's general sales conditions are applied (as set out above). The agent has the duty to make the retailer accept and sign the brand's conditions. There will not be a direct agreement between the agent and the retailer.

Because of the agent's limited role and the fact that he will not have to store, deliver and sell products, his right to use the brand's intellectual property is more limited than the distributor's right. Other than that, his situation is similar to the distributor's with respect to licensing intellectual property and the same recommendations apply.

Other issues to be taken into account when concluding an agency agreement:

- A clear definition of the products. If a line is added (second line, men, kids...), will the agent automatically have the right to negotiate these sales too? What if a product range is reduced?

- A clear definition of the territory: Define the countries by name instead of referring to "E.U." or "the Middle East" to avoid ambiguity. Also, the brand must provide whether it has the right to sell directly to all or certain customers (for example, mono brands only) without using the services of the agent (and consequently, without having to pay him in respect of these sales).

- Sample collections: Sample collections are expensive to manufacture so the brand should provide whether the agent has to purchase them (at full or reduced price) or return them after order taking.

- The remuneration of the agent: The commercial agent will be entitled to receive remuneration for his services. This remuneration can be a fixed fee or a commission on the transaction that the agent successfully negotiates.

Provide clearly when the commission is due (usually if and when the retailer has irrevocably paid the goods) and if any amounts are to be deducted from the commission base (discounts to the retailer, transport charges, taxes, credit notes...). The principal will have to supply the commercial agent regularly with a detailed commission statement, which the agent must be able to verify.

The brand must be aware that, generally, the agent will be entitled to receive remuneration for some time after the agreement has ended. Given the fact that orders and deliveries do not occur in the same season, commercial agent A may have been replaced by commercial agent B when the retailer receives and pays the goods that agent A negotiated the sale of. In that event the principal will owe a remuneration to agent A, and possibly also to agent B. To avoid paying twice, the agreement must clearly agree on which tasks the old and the new agent must perform in case of a transition.

··· Indemnities or compensation for the agent. Terminating the agency agreement may be expensive for the brand, especially if the agent has been a long-standing partner who has generated a lot of business.

Generally, the commercial agent is entitled to an *indemnity* if (i) he has significantly increased the volume of business and (ii) the principal continues to derive substantial benefits from that business after the termination of the agency agreement. In the E.U., the amount of the indemnity is capped at a figure equivalent to an indemnity for one year calculated from the commercial agent's average annual remuneration over the preceding five years[35]. If the commercial agency contract goes back less than five years, the indemnity must be calculated on the average for the period in question.

If the commercial agent proves that he suffered damage as a result of the termination of his relations with the principal (for example, because he had to pay severance fees to employees whom he had to fire), he may be entitled to additional *compensation*.

LICENSING

A license agreement is an agreement whereby a party (the "licensor", generally the brand) gives the other party (the "licensee") a temporary right to use the former's intellectual property, for a specific purpose, in a specific territory. For example, a European fashion brand whose core business is apparel, can grant a specialist third party the right to manufacture and distribute leather shoes in Asia.

The licensee is required to pay a royalty to the licensor based on the licensee's sales and the licensor must provide the right to audit the licensee's books to verify whether the numbers given by the licensee are correct. The licensee may also be asked to invest an agreed amount in marketing.

Basically, the licensee is given the right to manufacture, distribute and sell the licensed products. Consequently, all points of attention set out above will have to be included in the license agreement (respect of the brand's designs, quality of production, safety and timely delivery of the products, exclusivity of the distribution, transfer of intellectual property rights, termination...). The licensor will impose upon the licensee the obligation to cause his contract parties (his manufacturers, agents, distributors and retailers) to comply with these obligations and restrictions. Subsequently, the licensee will have to make sure that these obligations and restrictions are imposed on his contract party in each manufacturing, agency, distribution or sales agreement that the licensee enters into.

FRANCHISE

Many aspiring fashion designers dream of opening a mono brand store. Often this will be a franchised operation instead of a company-run operation, given the resources opening a shop requires.

Under a franchise agreement, in addition to licensing the intellectual property, the brand licenses its retail know-how to a partner, to enable that partner to successfully exploit the brand's intellectual property.

The agreement will contain extensive provisions about the use of the intellectual property in and on the shop interior and exterior, packaging and displays. This will mainly concern the use of the trade mark but also the copyrights to the store design or to furniture, pictures and images used in the store. The retail partner will be required to regularly update this (for example, refurbish the store or adopt the brand's new look and feel).

Other relevant provisions will deal with:

- Territory: Is the retail partner given the exclusive right to operate a store in a specific city or country? Does that mean that the brand may no longer supply multi-brand stores within a certain radius of the mono brand store?

- Know-how: This should be set out in detail in a manual that the retail partner must comply with (interior, how to run the shop, how to present products, staff training...). For brands with limited experience with respect to retail, this may initially prove to be an obstacle.

- Sourcing: Where will the retail partner have to source the products if the brand has licensees who manufacture and distribute certain lines or if the brand and its licensee use agents or distributors?

- Business plan: The retail partner may be required to present a business plan that the brand will accept, with or without modification. The plan will include information on (amongst other things) advertising and launch events. It is important that the brand does not provide any representations or warranties (and declines all responsibility) in respect of the commercial feasibility of the project.

- Termination: When the agreement ends, the brand may want to continue operating the store from the same location. To this end, the brand should obtain a right of priority in the franchise agreement to take over the lease of the rented space, provided the owner of the space permits this. If the retail partner wants to continue operating a different store from the retail space, it should be provided in the agreement that he must substantially alter the store's interior and exterior, to avoid all references to the brand's store.

E-COMMERCE

Brands wanting to sell online can opt to outsource this activity to a specialist third party or to operate the web shop directly.

The brand can sell its products to a third party, who in turn sells them online to the consumer in its own name and for its own account. For example, the Italian Yoox Group operates the web stores of Giorgio Armani, Dolce & Gabbana, Dsquared and other high-end fashion brands. Generally, in that case the web shop is a distributor of the brand and the rules set out above with respect to distribution agreements will apply. In addition, consumer protection laws that apply to *distance selling* will have to be taken into account. It is advisable to expressly provide in the agreement that it is the responsibility of the distributor/third party – and not that of the brand – to comply with those laws.

If the online sale is concluded directly between the brand and the consumer (possibly with the assistance of a third party who operates the website but acts as a commercial agent or service provider), it will be up to the brand as seller to comply with these applicable consumer laws in its general terms and conditions of online sale.

Such consumer protection laws[36], as well as privacy laws, may:

⋯ Impose obligations with respect to the information that must be given online (for example, the seller's name, address and contact details) or the documentation that must be provided in a durable format (sales terms and order information);

⋯ Give the consumer the right to return goods free of charge within a certain period (usually 15 or 30 days from delivery) without having to give a reason;

⋯ Prohibit charging the consumer for returning products or for the use of other services (customer service);

⋯ Restrict the use of the consumer's personal data for purposes other than processing the customer's order;

⋯ Prohibit the sending of unsolicited marketing messages to the consumer who did not opt in to receive such messages;

⋯ Give jurisdiction to the courts of the consumer's country, even if the general sales conditions provide that only the courts of the seller's country have jurisdiction.

In principle, legal advice should be sought in each country where consumers can access the online store, in order to verify compliance of the website's terms and conditions with local laws. This is why a brand may decide not to sell in a given country or why it may apply different terms and conditions depending on the consumer's location.

Before operating a web shop, the website must be developed. If a third party creates the website design (and possibly also the software), we reiterate that the brand must make sure to have any intellectual property rights created by the web designer assigned back to the brand. If not, the brand may end up having to pay again when it wants to make changes to the website or when it wants to use another developer. Generally, website developers will reserve those rights in their general terms and conditions of service. Therefore, the brand should reject those terms and insist on entering into a specific development agreement in which the intellectual property rights are transferred from the third party to the brand.

TIPS & TRICKS

- ⋯ Choose a distinctive trade mark and check if no one else has already registered a similar name or logo.
- ⋯ Document and date all steps in the design process, from the first sketch until the production of the finished product.
- ⋯ Register key designs, but do so before showing them to the public.
- ⋯ Make sure that third parties (employees, suppliers and service providers) transfer the intellectual property rights to you.
- ⋯ Where possible, rely on copyright, industrial design and trade mark protection concurrently.
- ⋯ Clearly define the rights that you license to a third party (product, territory, duration, exclusivity...) and the consideration that is owed by or to you.
- ⋯ Be aware that even after termination of an agreement, certain obligations will continue to apply: Does the manufacturer have to return all fabrics and labels? What consideration will still be owed to the agent for his past services? Does the distributor have the right to sell stock? How long will your name remain on the window of the franchised shop?

RECOMMENDED

Bentley, L., Davis, J., Ginsburg, J.C. (2011) *Trade Marks and Brands. An Interdisciplinary Critique*. Cambridge: Cambridge University Press.

Colston, C. and Galloway, J. (2010) *Modern Intellectual Property Law*. Abingdon: Routledge.

Darcy, J. (2013) Under-Regulated or Under-Enforced: Intellectual Property, the Fashion Industry and Fake Goods. In: *European Intellectual Property Review*, 35 (2), 82-92.

Erstling, J. (2013) *The Practitioner's Guide to the PCT*. Chicago: American Bar Association.

Goldstein, P. and Hugenholtz, B. (2010) *International Copyright, Principles, Law and Practice*. New York: Oxford University Press.

Goldstein, P. and Trimble, M. (2012) *International Intellectual Property Law, Cases and Materials*. New York: Oxford University Press.

Michaels, A. and Norris, A. (2010) *A Practical Approach to Trade Mark Law*. Oxford: Oxford University Press.

Stone, D. (2012) *European Union Design Law, A Practitioner's Guide*. Oxford: Oxford University Press.

Van Keymeulen, E. (2012) Copyrighting Couture or Counterfeit Chic. In: *Journal of Intellectual Property Law and Practice*, 7 (10), 728-737.

case # 5   Elvis Pompilio

When Belgian hat designer Elvis Pompilio opened his first shop in Brussels back in 1987, the mood was optimistic and energetic in local fashion circles. Although nobody was wearing hats then, Elvis Pompilio felt that the times were on his side: the world had started to discover that Belgian fashion did exist and that, like France, Italy, Great Britain and the States, Belgium had incredible fashion talents.

Pompilio was right. His career took off and in nearly two decades he built a "hat imperium": after Brussels, he opened boutiques in Antwerp, Paris and London. His collection was also sold in prestigious American department stores and high fashion boutiques in Japan. Madonna, Harrison Ford, Axelle Red and half of Europe's royal families were clients. Forty people worked in his studio, making 30,000 hats a year, all by hand.

In 2002, he made the radical decision to close his boutiques and take a break. Still, he continued designing hats for fashion shows and collections of the likes of Véronique Leroy, Ann Demeulemeester and Veronique Branquinho. In 2010, he went back to basics with the opening of a boutique-workshop in Brussels.

Interview by Trui Moerkerke

After you opened your first boutique in 1987 your brand grew at a rapid pace. How did you manage the business side of things?

In the early days, I was on my own. But, very quickly, I developed a good network of lawyers and people with a business background. It helped that I had a clear vision; I knew in which direction I was heading. And I didn't start overnight. In the years before I opened my boutique, I had a day job and took lessons in the evening to become a milliner. My art background – I studied visual arts – was an advantage too. I had the skill to make my own hat moulds, I created my own logo, I did the boutique decor. I could work very independently. I don't regret not going to a fashion school. This made it easier for me to break the rules. I don't like rules. I studied all the classic milliner techniques just to make them my own and then use them in a completely different way.

"I don't like rules"

FASHION MANAGEMENT

"Very quickly, I developed a good network of lawyers and people with a business background"

At the height of your career you decided to take a break and you closed your shops and points of sale. Why?

I just wasn't happy with my job anymore. People assumed that I had gone bankrupt or that I was ill. It's totally not done to stop when your business is a success. But I felt like a creation machine and above all I had to be a full-time manager. That wasn't what I dreamed of when I started. When your business reaches a certain level, you have to make up your mind: either you sell a part of the company to someone who can run it for you – this implicates that you're giving up at least part of your freedom – or you scale down and continue on your own. For me, freedom is not negotiable. To be free and independent was my drive in choosing this profession in the first place. Of course, stopping wasn't an easy decision. It took me a while. I talked to friends and consulted other fashion professionals. We had long discussions, but eventually they understood my point of view. And even though I closed the shops, I could go on and do interesting projects. I created hats for couture houses and fashion designers. I was able to pursue my passion.

I didn't enter this business for money. Yes, you need money to live and yes, I like a luxurious lifestyle, but the greatest luxury on earth is doing what you like.

What are your plans for the future?

It has been nearly four years since I reopened a shop in Brussels. It's a lovely boutique and I've been there three days a week. After my break, I really enjoyed this renewed interaction with clients. But I knew in advance that I wouldn't do this for another 10 years. Apart from freedom, I also like change. So in 2014 I will close my shop again. I will set up an online shop. I will also open a showroom on appointment only and of course I continue to work for fashion designers. The latter gives me the opportunity to meet incredibly talented and interesting people.

Elvis Pompilio

FINANCIAL DECISION-MAKING IN FASHION MANAGEMENT

Raf Vermeiren

"Don't be afraid!"

We sometimes read about it in the media: great designers who don't make it because of financial difficulties. Fashion design is certainly not the easiest sector in the industry in which to start up a successful business.

By nature, most creative people prefer to focus their energy on their creative endeavours rather than on finance and figures. Financial matters tend also to be explained in a way that makes everything sound very complex, making it easy to get lost in an overload of information and numbers. Nonetheless, in the complex fashion business, finance should be high on everyone's agenda.

For those of you in a panic by now, relax: in this chapter are some tools that will help you manage your budgets, even if finance isn't your core business. This doesn't have to be a doom and gloom story. Not every creative entrepreneur has to become a tough manager. You just have to focus on *four key drivers* within financial decision-making. The hands-on tools presented in this chapter will help you to stay on top of your finances. These tools will give you the knowledge to steer your business; they will be your guide to a better-structured company.

The secret to successful financial management lies in understanding each aspect of your business, in understanding the impact of specific fashion-related timings on an organisational level and thereby on a financial level.

Use your creativity, your biggest talent, for this part of the job, too! You may even begin to enjoy knowing how your business is doing and managing its finances.

A VERY SPECIFIC BUSINESS MODEL

The fashion business is fast and competitive and fashion entrepreneurs are confronted with a very specific business model. The way the fashion market is organized has a substantial impact on your operational planning as well as on your finances.

Traditionally, for independent labels there are two sales opportunities ("seasons") a year. Whether you sell your collection or not largely depends on that limited time period when potential buyers come to your showroom. There are no second chances; be prepared. You will need to approach potential buyers and make appointments with them well ahead of the date, as well as ensure that fully completed prototypes of your new collection, with different fabric options, are ready to be presented at this moment.

If you have your own store(s), you can expect a longer time frame in which to sell your collection. You will take in a larger range within your collection to show more combinations and you will have a larger overall view (in comparison to buyers who will always be more selective). This larger range and larger numbers of pieces means a larger risk when the sale to the end consumer won't take off as hoped. The risk of excessive stock due to an unsuccessful season is also larger. Owning your own shop(s) will also leave you with fixed costs such as rent and sales employees, which have to be paid each month no matter the sales figures.

Today larger brands, mostly luxury fashion companies or retail companies, try increasingly to extend the traditionally short sales period with pre-collections, capsule collections, new arrivals, and other marketing innovations. Smaller brands, like those of independent designers on the other hand, are experimenting with pop-up shops, online shops, Facebook events... all methods to consider in enlarging your sales potential. These brands try to increase their turnover and longevity. This is where your creativity can make a difference, both in the perception of your collections and in your finances.

The fashion industry differs from (for example) electronics stores, which make sales and cash transactions on a daily basis, or from Starbucks, which operates more or less every minute of the day. The fashion entrepreneur, however, will need to maximize sales at key moments. As discussed earlier, this means your collection has to be ready in time, but it also means that pre-finance of the design of your collection, sales costs and its production will have to be found in advance.

The tenability of your collection lasts a maximum of six months. The collection you have put so much energy into is no longer marketable at the end of the season. To overcome this problem, some brands try to supplement their collections with basics that can be sold over a longer period of time.

There are myriad other creative ways to sustain your business. However, to be financially viable, these techniques need to take into account the very particular business model(s) of the fashion brand.

THE FOUR KEY DRIVERS

These four key drivers will help you focus on the essential factors to staying on top of your finances:

- ⋯ timing/deadlines
- ⋯ impact of timing/deadlines on cash
- ⋯ profit and margin
- ⋯ structural finance

Timing is the key word in the fashion industry – not only the timing of your collection, but also the timing of all your operational activities. While people in the streets are still buying this season's fashion, you are already producing a new collection and researching and designing for the season thereafter. In between, you may be organizing a way to control your excess stock from previous seasons.

You will need a clear *plan* to organise these different overlapping activities. It's important to manage your time in order to jump on board the high-speed train of fashion.

And of course, amongst all this planning you have to provide enough *funding* for all this. You will need sufficient initial funding on a long-term basis. Every designer has to look further than his/her first or even first 4 collections. He/she has to put in place sufficient finance on a long-term basis: with a duration of at least 5 to 7 years. To survive and grow, cash and profit are equally important. Cash and profit are different ways of looking financially at your company. *Cash* is the money on your bank account at a certain moment. A *cash flow plan* shows you the money you need over a period of time to pay your bills; it shows how long you can work with that amount of cash until cash of customers is coming in.

Profit is the money you have earned at one point in time, taking into account all expenses. Keep in mind that what begins with your first sketches on paper must always result in profit. We put it black/white like this, to emphasize that on average the majority of the sketches have to be commercially viable. Thus, although there is still room for experiment, your business needs to be commercially viable from the beginning to be able to grow.

The difference between cash and profit can be confusing. The cheque you receive after delivering a range to a buyer is unfortunately not all profit. You cannot just book a trip to the Seychelles with all that hard-earned money. You need cash to pay your bills, buy fabrics, do research… but it isn't always there at the moment(s) you need it. There is a big time delay between cash-out and cash-in. In the fashion business, cash flow problems often occur because of long pre-financing terms. You will need money to pre-finance your collection for the following season long before it appears in the shops and long before shop owners will pay you for it. Because a lot of payments are delayed, the necessary pre-financing remains increasing. When you deliver to new clients or clients in difficult markets as Russia, you only deliver after payments, but to returning customers a lot of designers (have to) give customer credits.

Some of the necessary activities for the creation of the following collection will have to be prefinanced for almost a year prior to receiving income from it. For example, you may be buying fabric samples in February for the creation of your summer collection for later this year, only to receive a cheque for it in the beginning of the following year – sometimes even later, if payments are delayed. Needless to say you need a cash flow plan to monitor all this outgoing and incoming money.

TIMING

To explore how to organise your cash flow, it is important to first understand "timing" in a fashion year. The key is to start with a *creative overview*. Draw a timeline with a calendar of months (for the next two years) on the horizontal axis and the seasons (spring/summer and autumn/winter) on the vertical axis (see Figure 1). Put it on a wall in the centre of your workspace. Next, determine which steps of which collection you need to show on your timeline. Focus only on timing at this stage; we will take the financial impacts into consideration later.

Every key process in the fashion year – from buying sample fabrics, designing, ordering fabrics, making and adjusting prototypes to marketing, contacting buyers, show, showroom, production and logistics to cash-in from customers – must be clearly marked on your timeline. Make sure each step in the process of the different seasons is clearly marked. This timeline enables you to visualise all your activities, big and small, and shows clearly which activities of which season will overlap. Allow enough time for each activity; be realistic as some of them are immensely time-consuming. Of course, your timeline will be specific to your situation and may differ from the example below.

Figure 1. | Timeline of one collection.

FS   fabric samples
PS   pre-sales
F   fabrics
D   deposits

The next step is to add the upcoming seasons to your timeline (see Figure 2). This figure is just an example: you have to create your own timeline, specific to your situation that can be a bit different. Even though this looks already very complex, you have to realize that in reality, different seasons will overlap. To keep an overview. it's important to add the next seasons to your timeline.

For example, it's possible that in April you may be in the middle of monitoring the production of autumn/winter of that year *and* designing and developing spring/summer of the following year. In August you will just have finished dispatching your orders for autumn/winter of that year and be collecting payment for it while simultaneously starting presales of spring/summer of the following year.

As you can see, it is essential for the success of your business to be absolutely sure what's coming next; to plan ahead; and to know which activities will overlap, and how this will affect your time management.

Another crucial aspect of timing is to have your production ready *at delivery time*. A disruption in delivery can start a financial snowball effect with huge and damaging consequences. Shops have to present the new collection to their customers at the beginning of the season; they will miss out on sales if products are not delivered on time. This may sound simple, but in reality it is far more difficult than it sounds, largely due to the limited amount of time you have for each step. Your timing in the beginning of the process in particular has to be spot on. If you miss these early deadlines, you will almost never be able to catch up or deliver on time.

Your prototypes should also be ready in time, meaning they have to fit and look the way you want them to and be made in the right fabric. This back and forth always takes a lot longer than expected, so start early and plan well.

If your clothes are delivered to your buyers on time, you will gain their confidence, which will lead to a sustainable relationship. They will be more likely to buy your products next season, buy bigger amounts and pay their bills on time. This asks for strict managing of your production, logistics and quality control. If you have small production numbers, factories will try to push back your range to a later date. You will have to anticipate this to ensure your delivery can still be on time.

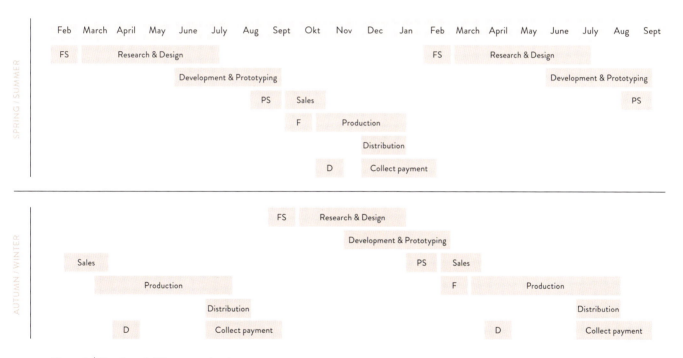

Figure 2. | Timeline of different overlapping seasons.

FS fabric samples
PS pre-sales
F   fabrics
D   deposits

Now comes the moment to take your timeline to the next level: to integrate (financial) figures into your timeline, to combine the organisation of your activities with your financial needs. It's crucial to know when and how much money is required. Adding this to your timeline will give you clear insight into your cash needs.

IMPACT OF TIMING/DEADLINES ON CASH

As mentioned earlier, cash flow problems are often the main cause of failure in the fashion business. Even profitable, fast growing companies can go bankrupt if their cash isn't coming in on time and as required. *You have to know what money comes in and what money goes out.* Be sure to understand every step in the process and in what (outgoing) expenses and (incoming) cash each step will result. There will be periods with virtually no income in which you will nonetheless need lots of money for expensive materials or productions.

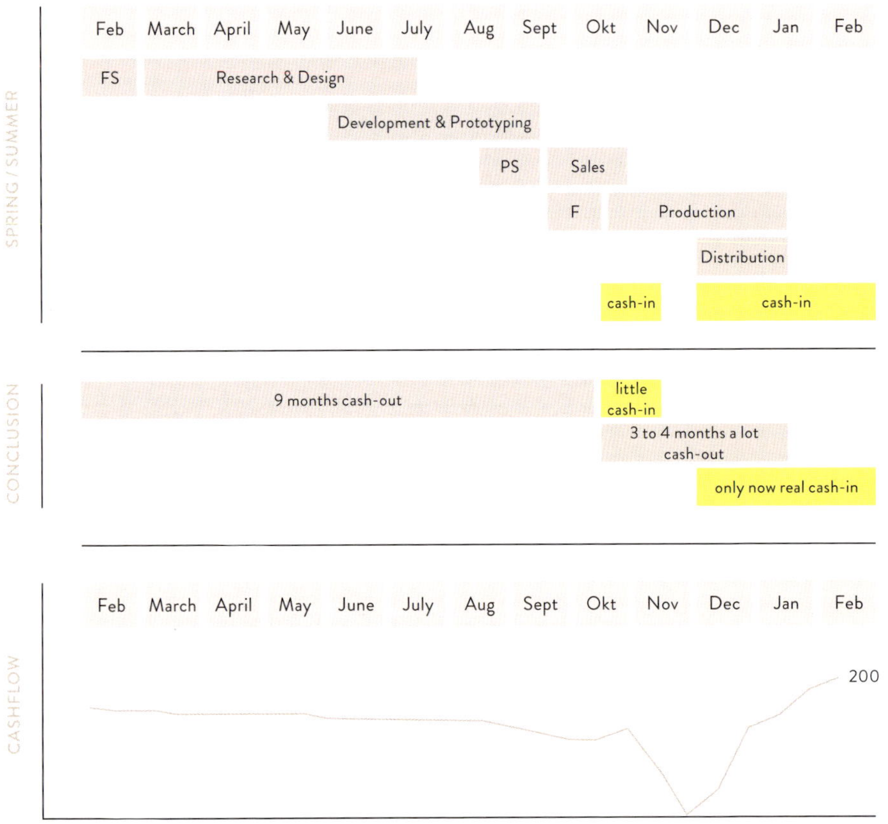

Figure 3.
Translation of your timeline to cash-outs & cash-ins of one season. Line going down and up = evolution of your cash flow.

FS	fabric samples
PS	pre-sales
F	fabrics

As you can see it will take a long time before income arrives for the season you are busy creating.

A cash *flow plan* is a perfect tool to constantly monitor your "cash-in" and "cash-out". An honest cash flow plan – that is realistic about deadlines – will give a clear picture of actual and forthcoming financing needs and periods. To make a valuable cash flow plan, you will need an understanding of market dynamics and supplier and customer deadlines. To fully understand the impact of producing a collection season after season, create a cash flow plan for the next two years. Of course you have to take into consideration that, just as well as the creation of the different seasons overlap, so will overlap the cash-in and cash-out of the different seasons.

Start with your *cash-out*. Work out the budget needed to finance each activity on your timeline. Whether small or big, every budgetary requirement must be taken into account. You will now have a clear idea of how much money you will need, and when. Again, be realistic about the financial costs. Underestimating the numbers will only make your life difficult at some later stage

To convert your timeline to a cash flow plan, capture your cash-out figures in a table as a starting point.

Keep in mind : Cash the moment the money disappears of your bank account

cash-outs	Sept	Okt	Nov	....
Research & prototyping				
Research				
Development				
Fabric Samples				
Partners prototyping				
Production				
Fabrics				
Garments & accesories				
Packing material				
Partners production				
Dispatching				
Sales				
Own sales people				
Freelance sales people				
Agents				
Show				
Showroom				
PR				
Lookbook				
Office				
Rent				
Electricity & heating				
Mobile & internet				
Accountant				
Consultant				
Other fixed costs				
Consultant				
Financial costs				
Consultant				

Figure 4. | A working table to create part 1 of your cashflow plan = the cash-outs.

The next step is to figure out your **cash-in**; i.e. to forecast how much money will be coming in and when. This will depend on the nature of your business. Do you have a mix of different sources of income? Is your collection only sold B2B (business to business) or do you have your own shop(s)? Will there be online sales? Are you planning a (temporary) pop-up shop? Do you earn additional income from projects other than your collection (like exhibitions or teaching) or from designing for a commercial label?

Divide your income into different categories (see table as an example).

Keep in mind : Cash the moment the money appears on your bank account

cash-ins	Sept	Okt	Nov	....
B2B Business to Business				
Sales local				
Sales Europe				
Sales Asia				
Sales US				
B2C Business to Consumer				
Online sales				
Pop-up shops				
Own retailshops				
Projects				
Designfees commercial brand				
Exhibitions				
Teaching				

Figure 5. | A working table to create part 2 of your cashflow plan = the cash-ins.

When forecasting cash-in, it is important to also take into account the influence of payment terms and seasonal market effects. It is not realistic to expect that you will sell all products and that all customers will make their payments in time. Monitoring your cash flow will reveal potential future difficulties; these are always easier to overcome if allowed an early stage. *Knowledge* gives you the opportunity to successfully *manage* your cash flow.

The art of managing your cash flow successfully will lie in attracting customers as soon as possible (and insisting on deposits), as well as gaining the confidence of suppliers so they will grant credit with longer terms.

| Feb | March | April | May | June | July | Aug | Sept | Okt | Nov | Dec | Jan | Feb | March | April | May | June | July | Aug | Sept |

SS1 9 months cash-out

little cash-in

3-4 months a lot cash-out

only now real cash-in

AW1 cash-out

little cash-in

AW2 9 months cash-out

little cash-in

only now real cash-in

only now real cash-in

SS2 9 months cash-out

Highest financial needs   Highest financial needs   Highest financial needs

Figure 6.
Seasonal financial needs.

Figure 6 reveals when exactly are the most critical financial needs and when the cash is coming in. This tells you two things: first whether the costs incurred for the creation, production and distribution of your collection will be (at least) balanced by the possible incomes for the collection (and any other income sources) and, second, when extra (outside) funding will be required.

Adding these numbers on your timeline (cash going out and cash coming in) does not yet tell us whether your business will be *profitable* or not. To determine this, we need to look at *profit and margin*. This viewpoint will help you to forecast whether your business will break even, make a profit or run at a loss in the next couple of years.

PROFIT AND MARGIN

Everybody has to make profit. You have to make profit to pay your costs, to honour the people that work hard for you, to pay back investors, to have extra cash for other creative projects, and so on. Keep in mind that what begins with a fantastic creative process must always end in profit. Parents, friends, banks and investors can only help to bridge that period until the cash is coming back in. You have to make profit to re-invest and to grow both your collections and financially.

Let's start off simply, first by looking at costs and then at profitability. All costs can be divided into two groups: variable costs and fixed costs. Variable costs are those costs that will increase by the volume sold (for example: fabrics and production costs). As an independent designer it's customary to also include costs for the making of your prototypes. Fixed costs are all other costs used for sales, employees, office requirements and rental, financial costs, You will have to pay these costs month after month, even if you only sell four items from your collection.

When talking about profitability, we refer to margin – sales minus variable costs – and profit – sales minus variable costs minus fixed costs. Figure 7 summarises the various factors involved in calculating *margin* and *profit*.

Also key to profitability is "mark-up", whereby, piece by piece, you multiply your variable costs by an appropriate factor to establish the sales price for your products. A "mark-up" is a valuable tool if it includes the right ingredients! Only if you try to understand these ingredients better, collection by collection, and learn to adjust them you will keep your collection profitable.

After working day and night on your designs, samples, and adjusting of samples, your prototypes are ready to be shipped to the showroom. It is time to set the right price, one that is reasonable enough for customers to buy your pieces, but also sufficient to sustain your company. Your production assistant has long listings with items, numbers, euros that can be used to set a sales price.

At this stage in the process you are probably exhausted; your mind is spinning. Stay attentive: this mark-up exercise is crucial. You only have a short period in which to sell your range and it must make enough profit for the next six months! Don't let this be a last-minute job. Try to finalise your mark-ups for 80 to 90% of your collection at least two weeks before presenting it in the showroom. In the last sprint you will need to decide only on the last 10 to 20% of the collection.

It's even more important to learn from this exercise season after season. We've seen many designers proudly demonstrating their mark-up of 2.3 to 2.4. However, if they were to make a calculation after sales, they would end up with a very different figure in reality. It's necessary to make such a post-season calculation and write down your conclusions for the next season.

The architecture of your collection won't always be a perfect blend. Some items will be very successful and sell in relatively high volumes, whereas you may sell two pieces in red, five in blue and 20 in black of another item. Some sizes will sell well, others won't. If you have your own stores, you will inevitably end up with left-over stock in certain sizes and colours. Even if you sell to stores and only take into production the number of items your customers ordered, factories won't always be prepared to produce small numbers or they may charge you surplus prices for small amounts. Sometimes you may end up with unexpected stock due to a cancellation or a store going out of business. Overstocks will have a huge impact on your profitability: a lot

Sales

minus Production costs
= Margin after production

minus Prototyping
= Margin after prod & proto

minus sales costs
minus office costs
minus other fixed costs

minus employees
minus depreciation
investments

Operational profit

minus financial costs

Profit

Figure 7.
From Sales to Margin to Profit.

Mark-up

= multiple on protoyping
taking into account fabrics
+ garments
+ productioncosts

but also take into account
+ transportation costs
+ commission fees for agents
+ medium loss on stocks

Figure 8.
Ingredients of your mark-up.

of euros are stuck in your stock and, if not sold this season, your collection will be practically worthless. Note that almost everybody is confronted with overstocks.

In deciding on your mark-up it's therefore healthy to include a *medium loss in stock*. Ask a slightly higher price for all your items to end up with a good average mark-up. If you don't, your post-season calculation may show an actual mark-up of 1.9, or even 1.7, and not your "theoretical" 2.3! This small shift doesn't seem all that bad, but, as Figure 9 shows, it can have an enormous impact on the margin left to cover your fixed costs.

Production costs	Mark-up 2.3 / sales	Mark-up 1.9 / sales
100.000	230.000	190.000
Sales minus production costs	130.000	90.000
		-40.000
		less margin to cover your fixed costs

Figure 9. | High impact of too low mark-up.

It's clear charging a mark-up well above 2.3 for some items is more realistic. For items that will almost certainly be successful, use a mark-up of 2.5 or 2.6 (for example) to compensate for those items whose actual mark-up is likely to be lower than 2.3.

Furthermore, make sure that your "ingredients" are right by including all variable costs (see Figure 10). Then make sure you have a mix of high mark-ups and less-high mark-ups – this is as important as a good blend in your collection architecture.

As mentioned earlier, profit is sales minus variable costs minus fixed costs. Whether you sell 400 pieces or 400,000 pieces, you will always have fixed costs (see Figure 10) to pay month after month. For this reason you will have to go to a higher financial level to achieve real profit.

Fixed costs

• Employees
• Office
• Office supplies
• Communication
• Salespeople
• Salesagents
• PR
• Showroom
• Financial costs
• ...

Variable costs

• Fabrics
• Garments
• Prototyping
• Productioncosts
• ...

Figure 10.
Details of Fixed and
Variable costs.

STRUCTURAL AND SEASONAL FINANCE

After drawing your timeline and including the cash-ins and cash-outs, it becomes clear that a designer needs a lot of cash in certain periods. Even profitable companies need sufficient cash to bridge costs for prototyping, sales and production until the moment of distribution and cash-in.

Your cash flow plan shows that twice a year, for eight to ten weeks each, you need deeper pockets. Of course cash is not required only in these two periods. *Besides seasonal finance* (= finance on short term, only in place during a couple of months) every business needs *structural long-term finance* (= finance on long term, in place during at least five to seven years). Whether you are in design, music or theatre or in coffee or in electronics, it is only with sufficient structural finance you will have the capacity to act when necessary – and quickly.

We already showed Figure 11 (see Figure 6), but its good to repeat that you have to put in place structural finance over several years combined with recurring seasonal finance in the yellow periods with higher financial needs.

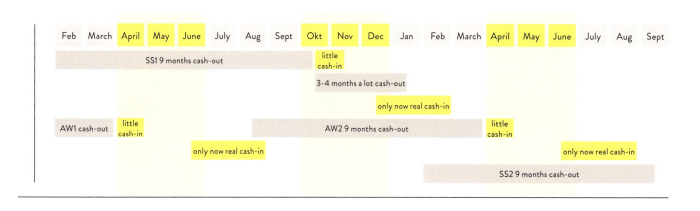

Figure 11. | Seasonal financial needs.

In designer fashion, the necessity for sufficient structural finance is high because of the long pre-finance periods and therefore high risks. What then are the sources of seasonal and structural finance?

For *structural long-term finance* you can rely on:
- ⋯ Own capital
- ⋯ 3F: "friends, family and fools"
- ⋯ Business angels
- ⋯ Investors in terms of shares
- ⋯ Investors in terms of subordinated loans
- ⋯ Investment loans of banks

For *seasonal finance* you can rely on:
- ⋯ Commercial loans of banks
- ⋯ Crowdfunding
- ⋯ Payment terms of suppliers

Structural long-term finance is money that will be engaged in your business for at least 5 to 10 years. Generally, structural finance can be divided in two groups: equity and debt. *Equity* is money put at risk as a shareholder. Debt is money put at risk as loans, mostly by banks but sometimes also by investors. *Debt* has to be paid back over *the loan period*, while equity has to be paid back only at *the end of collaboration*.

DIFFERENT TYPES OF EQUITY

Before you ask other people to go into business with you, you will have to put at risk your *own money*. Only when you show financial engagement, will investors and/or banks be prepared to join you in the business risk. If you don't have a big budget, you can at least try to convince others of your engagement by working on other income (such as design fees or temporary project fees) in your company.

Business angels and investors may also be prepared to take on risk for your business. *Business angels* are (former) entrepreneurs who want to invest, not only financially but also their management expertise, market experience and network. As they decide their own budgets, they can make quick investment decisions. Other investors mostly work within a fund structure and have to convince a board of directors of their investment proposal.

DIFFERENT TYPES OF LONG-TERM DEBT

In general, long-term loans can best be compared with a loan for buying a house: you get 200,000 euro (for example) and for the next 20 years you pay back every month, partly in capital repayments and partly in interest payments.

The so-called *3Fs* (friends, family and fools) are a possible source of long-term debt (finance). People in your direct entourage, people who believe in your enthusiasm, may want to help you financially. These "soft loans" (i.e. not based on commercial arguments) can help you to start up and overcome your cash flow problems in the early stages. However, their total investment usually won't be sufficient in the long run, so it will be essential to get in long-term finance from other parties, too.

Another type of long-term debt is an *investor* loan. Besides investing in shares, some investors may also want to put in place "subordinated loans", which means you won't have to grant extra guarantees, like your private home. Subordinated loans will also show repayment in capital and interest payments. Because these type of loans don't have guarantees, the risks of losing all this money are higher for the investor, so you will have to pay an extra risk premium within your interest rate (in comparison: loans that are fully guaranteed will show rates of 4 to 5% while rates for subordinated loans will be 12 to 15% (as at 2014)).

Finally, you have the option to approach *financial institutions*. You often hear "banks don't take risks anymore". Financial institutions are not allowed to take risks. They are obliged to have sufficient guarantees to balance the loans outstanding. However, you still can convince banks to finance your activities once you can show sufficient sales, your activities are profitable, you've put enough equity at risk and when you can deliver guarantees. That's a long list of conditions to fulfil! Banks will also only bridge a financial need over a certain period of time. Financial institutions want to see your cash flow plan to make sure at what moment sufficient cash will be coming in to make capital repayments and interest payments.

SEASONAL FINANCE

Seasonal finance is finance you use only at certain short periods in a year. The most important sources for this are *commercial loans of banks*. These commercial loans are mostly offered in a credit line you can use ("get into the red" for a couple of days/weeks). Interest rates are very high (up to 9 to 11%), but you only pay on the amount you use for the period you use it. Figure 12 shows the biggest difference between a commercial loan and an investment loan.

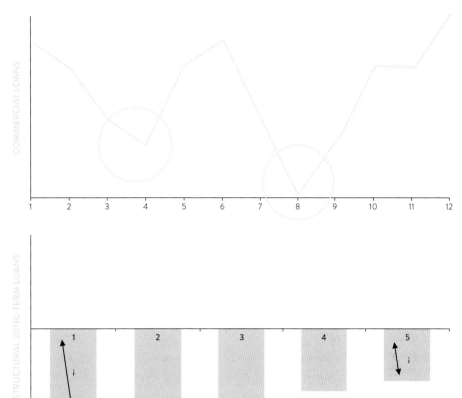

when a customer pays = less use of line
when you pay a supplier = more use
Interest only on part in use

as loan an a house: every month
you repay a bit every month
interest on total of outstanding

Figure 12.
Comparison of commercial
loans and long-term loans.

Another "source" of short-term finance is to gain more confidence from your *suppliers* so they grant your company longer payment terms. This takes time though... at least 2 to 3 years of "good behaviour".

Crowdfunding is also becoming a popular form of short-term finance (or rather "project finance"). Online platforms have arisen whereby project creators pitch their creative and entrepreneurial projects to members (or the online public) and raise money "in the cloud". If people like a project, they can pledge money to make it happen. Be warned: from experience, this tends to be *short-term* project finance, because often it is destined for one collection only. An interesting advantage of crowdfunding is that you can leverage your fan base as proof of your market acceptance to other investors.

AIM FOR A MIX OF FINANCING

It is as important to have a good blend of financial sources as it is to have a good mix within your collection architecture. On the one hand you need a mix of equity versus debt. On the other hand you need both sufficient long-term as well as seasonal finance.

The ideal combination is both time and situation dependent; there is no "abracadabra" formula. In general, at start-up stage you will need relatively more equity or investor loans before you can convince a bank to take a chance with you. When your turnover is really growing after a couple of good sales, the banks will be more eager to finance your order confirmations with seasonal finance.

But even when you've been on the market for 5 or 10 years, when your company is growing fast and you want to realize big investments (for example opening a flagship store), it's possible that you may first need extra equity before financial institutions will follow. It's important to understand that long-term finance is not a question of this or that partner, but rather of this and that and that partner... It's the mix that is crucial to be prepared and to be sustainable.

Be sure you put enough structural finance in place to bridge at least four to five seasons! We've seen designers take off enthusiastically, rely a lot on seasonal finance. But they get stuck in the race of fast-growing seasonal needs where banks cannot keep up because the equity part or long-term part of the company does not follow the growth. In the beginning of their growth, banks keep up by delivering more seasonal finance in accordance with growing turnover. But banks not only look at growth in turnover, they permanently evaluate the growth of total debts in comparison with the growth of equity. At those moments where your equity is not growing at the same pace as your debts, it will be very hard to convince investors or banks. So put in place enough structural finance in the beginning.

BUSINESS PLAN

A well-constructed and well-written business plan is vital to obtaining structural financing from banks and other financial institutions. Don't be afraid to start writing it; it is not an exact science (see also CHAPTER SEVEN).

Making a good business plan is very much like telling a story. You have to capture your audience's attention, take them by the hand and lead them into your plot. Make them want to listen until the end. A business plan is an interesting tool to use in communication not only to banks and other investors but also in your communication to suppliers and large clients. From another perspective, it is also useful to write down your ambitions, your goals and how to get there.

We could write 200 pages on business planning. You can find two million hits on the Internet on the subject. But we have experienced the power of keeping it *simple*. Use the guidelines below to develop your content, keep it focused and discuss the plan with different colleagues, potential clients, suppliers, etc. This will make the process far more rewarding.

Your business plan should cover the following:
- ··· What is your background?
- ··· What goals have you realized thus far?
- ··· Describe your activities and unique position
- ··· Is there a specific market for your product?
- ··· What are the specific sales efforts in your go-to-market plan?
- ··· Which channels do you want to use to sell your products?
- ··· What are your income sources?
- ··· What are your basic fixed costs and what are your variable costs?

Some tips for crafting your business plan include:
- ··· Keep it relevant. Mentioning that you love dogs (for example) is only relevant if you're designing a dog fashion collection!
- ··· Pay particular attention to the going-to-market aspect. Don't lose yourself in detail or theories; keep it pragmatic and practical. It is also far more convincing to explain your focus in the first six months.
  - ··· Will you be using your own salespeople?
  - ··· Part-time freelancers to contact buyers?
  - ··· Scouting of 200 buyers resulting in 40 appointments?
  - ··· Private showroom or multi-brand store?

When you talk about a big order, is this 20,000 euro or 12,000 euro? When you talk about small orders of 6,000 euro or 5,000 euro on average?

What will be your focus/growth in the next six months?

··· The answers to these questions are far more effective than calculating that your market share is "0,75% and within three years it will grow to 6%..."

··· Dare to ask what (or how much) you need. Many entrepreneurs leave this open, as if the bank and/or investor can make a guess. This is not the professional way to handle the situation. Explain on the one hand the reasons for your financial needs and explain on the other hand where your funding will come from. Elaborate on how much of your own money you will put into the business and how much outside funding you already have in place versus need to find. Finally, state how much you want the bank (or investor) to contribute.

SUMMARY

The main message of this chapter is to focus on the *four key* pillars of a successful fashion business:

··· Pay attention to the *timing* of your various activities, keeping in mind the overlapping of different activities and different seasons.

··· Make sure you know how much *cash* you need and when you will need it..

··· Never forget that every business needs *profit* to survive. Make sure you adopt a healthy *mark-up* and do not leave this decision till the last minute.

··· Put in place sufficient *structural long-term finance*. Profit is the only way you can obtain structural finance, which you need to grow.

In creating a well-structured business, you will have the freedom to focus on what is most important to you: the creative process of designing your collection.

REFERENCES

Online resources

About timelines and visual planning: http://www.youtube.com/
watch?v=80c-LRRJ0W8&feature=player_detailpage

Building blocks of a business plan: http://www.youtube.com/watch
?v=NPZSEj2yaH8&feature=BFa&list=PLB59B4751EC90DE8B

http://www.youtube.com/watch?v=2FumwkBMhLo

Tools from the Flanders Fashion Institute

Business plan: http://www.ffi.be/sites/default/files/
downloads/2013/01/bp_template_eng_sept2011.pdf

Starter's guide: http://www.ffi.be/sites/default/files/
downloads/2013/06/ffi_start-up_guide_june13_lr_0.pdf

RECOMMENDED

Drury, C. (2011) *Cost and Management Accounting. An
Introduction.* Seventh edition, Australia: South Western Cengage
Learning.

Ehrhardt, B. (2010) *Financial Management. Theory and Practice.*
South Western Cengage Learning.

Jackson , T. & Shaw, D. (2006) *The Fashion Handbook.* Abingdon
NY: Routledge.

Jeffrey, M. & Evans, N. (2011) *Costing for the Fashion Industry.*
Oxford: Berg.

Reamy, Donna W. & Arrington, Deidra W. (2012) *Fashionomics.
The Fashion Industry from a Business Perspective.* Prentice Hall
PTR.

Towse, R. (ed.) (1997) *Baumol's Cost Disease. The Arts and other
Victims.* Cheltenham: Edward Elgar Publishing.

Tennent, J. (2008) *Guide to Financial Management.* John Wiley
& Sons.

case # 6   Essentiel

SS 14

"Our goal is to conquer the international market"

It all started with a basic collection of T-shirts in 1999. Esfan Eghtessadi (son of Belgian fashion designer Nicole Cadine) and the charismatic Inge Onsea, partners in life and in business, called their collection Essentiel. Their apartment served as a showroom.

Interview by
Trui Moerkerke

Today Essentiel, a fashion brand with a fun and glamorous touch and mid-range prices, has 27 own stores, 135 collaborators and is sold in more than 500 multi-brand stores. Eghtessadi and Onsea still own and run the company, while Tom Depoortere is art-director. He explains the philosophy of the brand.

"Since we worked on having a clear identity, we have gained international attention"

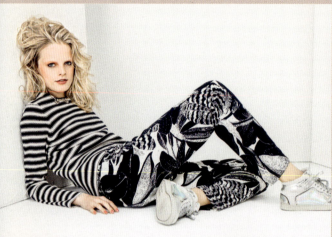

SS 14

FASHION MANAGEMENT

"We believe that in these difficult times, people still want to dream"

The story of Essentiel is impressive: in a short period of time the brand became a household name in Belgium. What do you consider the main factors of this success?

Passion, hard work, a portion of good luck and especially holding on to our own identity and story, even if that was not always the easy way. We kept on questioning ourselves. And we were not afraid of experimenting and searching for new directions. You have to stay ahead of your competitors.

In 2012 Essentiel reduced the collection in order to focus. Why did you do that? And was this a radical modification?

Yes, the changes we made were very thorough. At some point we had more than 20 agents and everyone of them gave us their unseasoned opinion. The problem was that we wanted to please everyone. We didn't know which way to go anymore; neither did our clients and agents. Along the way we lost ourselves. It was necessary to recharge our batteries and secure our identity. That, of course, caused a lot of stress and uncertainty, but eventually it helped us to move forward.

Essentiel opened flagship stores early on. Why did you do that?

We find it very important to give people the Essentiel image as we see it. We want to immerse customers in our universe. The best way to do so is by having your own stores. Shopping is an emotional experience. It's far more difficult to create the same Essentiel emotion in a multi-brand store. That is why the choice of opening our own stores was made very quickly. Now we try to do the same thing with our webshop. Even online, it is very important to give customers the complete Essentiel experience.

Recently, Essentiel started to expand abroad. Why do you want to go international?

In Belgium, the market for our business is saturated. We have stores in almost every large city in Belgium and we also sell in all the decent multi-brand boutiques. That's why we eventually had to look for other and different markets. Our company is ready. We feel strong enough to explore other markets abroad. Some international clients have asked for us. Since we worked on having a clear identity, we have gained international attention.

Where do you see Essentiel five years from now?

We definitely want to open more stores abroad, in all the important fashion cities. This way, we can reinforce our international fame. We also want to expand our webshop – at the moment we only sell online to Benelux and French clients. Our goal is to conquer the international market. We would like Essentiel to be an established international fashion brand.

What did Essentiel do differently? The economic crisis created a difficult environment for mid-range brands, but Essentiel has shown very good results.

We stayed true to ourselves. Even in times of economic crisis we never chose to take the "safe" or "easy" way. On the contrary, our collections have become more audacious. We went bolder and even more "out there"! We believe that in these difficult times, people still want to dream. They still want to discover new collections.

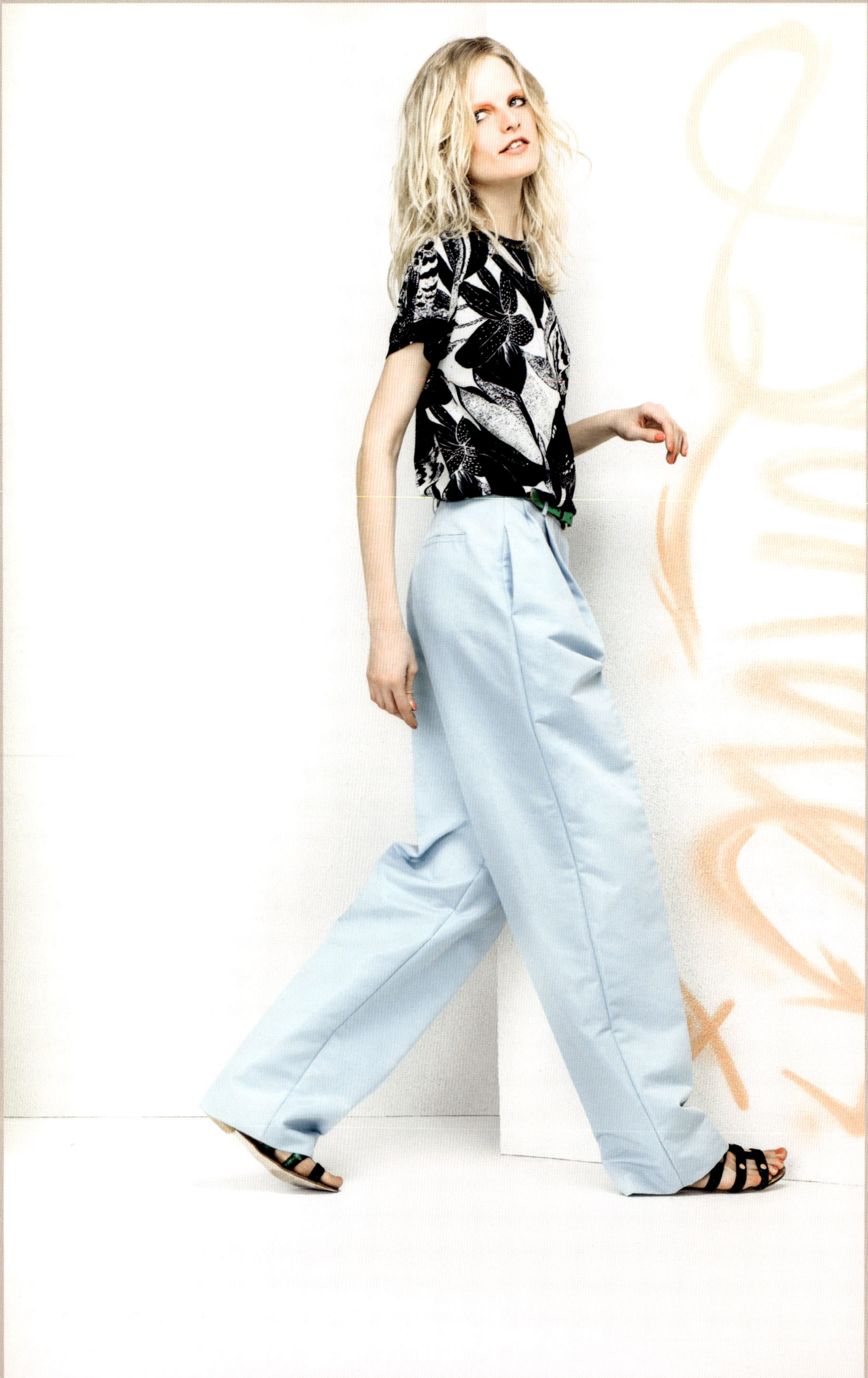

Essentiel
SS 14

7

THE NUTS AND BOLTS OF STARTING AN INDEPENDENT FASHION LABEL

Marie Delbeke

This chapter will focus on the practical means to starting a fashion label. It is the result of a balanced interpretation between the day-to-day reality of starting designers, business readings about the fashion industry and many conversations with people within the Belgian and international fashion industry.

It is actually a simplified approach of the reality of this complex industry and a superfluous reading for everyone already surviving for years in this business. But for an *"outsider"* not all rules and standards of the industry are evident and therefore this contribution takes you through the basics. It's a creative and emotional sector, but in the first place, a business reality where hard work is the only road to possible success.

We will focus from the outset on the competitiveness of *independent fashion labels* (see **CHAPTER ONE**: Unraveling the Fashion Industry). Because this sector characterizes the Belgian fashion industry and has made it known (and count) on an international level.

The golden thread throughout this article is the advice to start your fashion adventure well prepared. Of course, you can never be fully prepared, but reading this book is a great starting point. Being well prepared involves understanding how the industry works, defining the "dominant logic" behind it, keeping track of the forces influencing the sector, and defining a strategy and plan to enter the market.

This deals with the different aspects of the "dominant logic" this segment follows. As understanding it, allows you to potentially break out of it and achieve a competitive advantage (Van Andel, Jacobs & Schramme 2012).

"Fashion is not an art,

but it needs an artist to exist"

Pierre Bergé

The penultimate section will highlight some of the more recent changes of this fast-paced industry. This should trigger you to stay informed about new tendencies and evolutions to allow you to detect future opportunities and tackle difficulties – at an early stage.

We finish off this chapter with a summary (in the form of some tips and tricks) that will come in handy when launching your fashion business.

Before we start though, it is important to highlight the difference between a *business to business* (B2B) environment, in which you sell your collection to a customer and he/she re-sells it to the end-consumer, and a *business to consumer* (B2C) environment, in which you sell directly to your end-consumer.

The focus of most independent fashion labels will be B2B, meaning they will sell to (online or offline) multi-label shops, boutiques and department stores (mainly referred to in this as buyers or customers). Therefore, note the difference between *customers* and *end-consumers*.

THE COMPETITIVE INDUSTRY OF INDEPENDENT FASHION LABELS

The Five Forces analysis of Michael E. Porter is an economic model that is frequently used to define the level of competition in a particular industry (Porter 1979). Porter's model is based on five factors influencing an industry, namely *bargaining power* of both *customers* and *suppliers* and the threat of *new entrants*, *substitute products* and *competitors*. The level of competition in an industry is then a combination of these factors, from which conclusions about the attractiveness and profitability of the sector can be drawn. Applying this model to independent fashion labels suggests that this sector is *saturated* and *extremely competitive*:

THREAT OF NEW ENTRANTS

It is fairly easy to start a fashion label and barriers to enter this sector are rather low. New labels are popping up everywhere and competition from this side has become steep especially due to new designer labels from emerging markets. We can conclude that the threat of new independent fashion labels entering the market is severe.

BARGAINING POWER OF CUSTOMERS

Buyers (in a B2B environment) are very powerful in this niche segment. Only a limited number of end-consumers are able to pay its high prices and not everyone appreciates the high level of creativity of the designs. Therefore the amount of shops and boutiques offering these high-end niche collections to end-consumers are also limited. They in turn target loyal end-consumers and, to limit their risk, mainly offer brands and labels that their consumers know, like and buy.

Buying from a *new* independent fashion label presents a risk to the buyer, who cannot be sure your collection will sell well, that you will be able to maintain the same level of creativity and aesthetics in the future or that the quality (fitting, materials and production) will be as promised.

Buyers also increasingly keep a close eye on their own purchasing budget. Their drive to be profitable makes it difficult for starting designers to sell to these buyers. In practice this means that buyers will often follow a designer for one to three seasons before they will place a (modest) order. If the first season sells well, the buyer might place a bigger order the following season.

BARGAINING POWER OF SUPPLIERS

There is no specific indication that suppliers have significant bargaining power, putting pressure on the market from the suppliers' side. However, as the fashion industry is a time-intensive sector, a reliable production partner is a true asset enabling you to meet quality standards and strict delivery deadlines.

THREAT OF SUBSTITUTE PRODUCTS

Indirect competition exists in the form of retail chains (such as Zara and H&M), luxury brands that advertise aggressively and more commercial labels balancing between commerciality and creativity. Money spent by consumers at the latter is money that cannot be invested in your designer item implying that the market is offering many substitute products.

The increasing offer of the entertainment industry and the many choices consumers have these days are, in a sense, also a "threat" to the consumption of your label. Personal budgets are limited and money spent on interiors, or city trips, or a house, is budget that cannot be invested in designer clothing.

THREAT OF COMPETITORS

Direct competition includes other young fashion labels, but also many established fashion labels that have already built a (loyal) customer and consumer base and have the expertise and sales volume to continue competing. As the amount of consumers of highly creative prêt-à-porter collections is limited, competition for starting fashion labels is high and on a worldwide scale.

The above factors show that a young independent fashion label is likely to face fierce competition. Many designers nevertheless launch fashion labels. Remaining in business for longer than three years, and scaling the business to become competitive in the longer term, however, seems to be more difficult.

You will need a combination of talent, creative skills, business and commercial insight (whether on your part or a partner's), a gift for entrepreneurship, great networking skills and a fair amount of luck to launch and sustain an independent fashion label.

LAUNCHING AN INDEPENDENT FASHION LABEL

To significantly improve your chances of success, it is essential to prepare the launch of your fashion label, firstly, by getting informed about the environment in which you will be operating (as discussed above) and, secondly, by developing a (business) plan as to how you will enter the market.

Many new designers are not excited to be writing business plans, yet it is a crucial phase of any start-up. Take it step by step and consider the plan as a guideline of what needs to be ready before you launch.

Start by defining your mission – the "raison d'être" of your label – , your vision – where/what you want to be in five years – and set a *measurable goal*. Your business plan will then include the steps required to achieve this goal.

Don't see a business plan as something "static" that serves only to help you find a (business or financial) partner in the beginning. A business plan is in fact a valuable tool for doing business in the long run, too. It pushes you to develop a vision for the long term and helps you focus and define which opportunities and decisions you should take along the road and which ones you should let pass. Be sure to adjust your business plan on a regular basis and in response to changes in the environment, but always keeping in mind your initial goal.

You may want to be the next independent fashion designer presenting your collection at international fashion weeks, or you may want to create a small collection that you sell to a limited customer base while you collaborate on creative projects with partners from other industries. Each person's road to success will differ, depending on his goal. Comparing the career of the Belgian high-end designer Dries van Noten to that of Walter van Beirendonck clearly illustrates your vision will influence how you define success. Dries van Noten has an established company; his collection can be found in the most important department stores worldwide and flagship stores have been opened in the most important fashion cities, whereas Walter van Beirendonck creates niche collections targeted to very specific markets. He focuses on creative collaborations and combines his job as a creative designer with his function as the head of the Fashion Department of the Royal Academy of Fine Arts in Antwerp.

Next, some key elements that need to be considered when launching a fashion label are listed. Making decisions around each aspect illuminates how you will reach your vision and goal – taking the constraints and conditions you face into account. These elements are all necessary building blocks for your business plan.

STRATEGY

A *business plan* plots your road to success and takes the reader through the set-up of the company; from the company structure and history, to the vision and goal you want to achieve and the strategy you will use to reach it.

A strategy is first defined in more abstract terms, but then breaks into more concrete planning about the position you want to take in the market, the competition you will face, the way you will communicate, and last but not least the financial side and how you will finance these plans.

As you are entering an already saturated market, you will need a focused, proactive and smart strategy to ensure you remain in business for a while. Because having a highly creative and unique collection is not a guarantee of success.

Every successful company has a *Unique Selling Proposition (USP)*: something that makes the company unique and competitive. What makes your label unique in this market? What sets it apart from the extremely creative and luxury collections, as well as from affordable high-street chains offering new collections every few weeks?

Often it helps to identify your (direct and indirect) competitors and examine their strengths and weaknesses. Research not only the brand or label's collection, but also how it communicates, where it sells, at what prices, and so on. This will help you to further define your USP and strategy.

PLANNING

The fashion industry is a time-intensive industry, which makes planning essential. Deadlines are so tight that, often, you are already delayed at the time you do your planning! Independent fashion labels generally work according to a two-season structure, which implies working and spending money on (at least) three seasons at the same time: designing one collection, presenting/selling another collection, and delivering still another collection.

Therefore you need to plan continuously *and* be prepared for unexpected delays. Retro planning is a useful tool in this regard: start from your deadline and calculate backwards what you need to do to meet it.

An *operational* plan lists your day-to-day operations. In the fashion industry your most important deadlines will be the presentation of your sample collection to buyers and press during fashion weeks and delivery of the collection to stores. Everything needs to be planned with these deadlines in mind.

Next, align a *communication* plan to your operational plan. Every interesting project or event is a potential media story. Plan when and how you will try to connect with the press and use retro planning to ascertain what's required i.e. work from your deadline backwards to the current day.

Executing your plan also requires and implies budgets. Make a *financial plan* and tie budgets to your operational and communication plans. The fashion industry is characterized by long pre-financing periods; as *cash on delivery policies* are in place, designers receive (the bulk of) the payment after their investments in the sample collection and the production. Therefore, keep in mind that the more you sell, the more budget you will need to pre-finance the production.

Working with two seasons a year (spring/summer and autumn/winter) also implies only two sales periods a year (during the fashion weeks) to cover 12 months of expenses. The most important part of your financial plan will therefore be a *cash flow plan*. This is a tool to plan your monthly finances and it gives an overview of when money is coming into your business and when money is going out. Remember that this has nothing to do with receiving or sending invoices, but with the moment of payment. A cash flow plan will help you to calculate how much money you need to bridge the investments into your sample collection and pre-finance its production, but also how you will allocate the earned money in the following months (see CHAPTER SIX: Financial Decision-Making in Fashion Management).

COMPANY AND TEAM

Thinking about the strategy of your company requires thinking about the team you will put together to set up and run your business. Many designers start a company by themselves, but launching it within a partnership with someone who has complementary skills significantly increases the success rate of start-up fashion labels. In this scenario the designer can focus on the creative part, while the partner takes on organizational and business matters.

To grow a solid business relationship, it is important that you have a good understanding, that you both respect the other's work and talent and understand the mutual responsibilities. Make sure you agree on the vision of the company and that you share the same idea about how you will realize this. Talk this through at the start because if you have different ideas about how to grow the company, this will be detrimental to the company at some point.

Your core team will remain rather small in the first years, as hiring staff is an expensive (and therefore risky) business. In contrast, you will work with a lot of suppliers, customer, freelancers, and other partners. Given the intensity of the industry nowadays (and its pace is only increasing), you will need to have an efficient "team" around you in order to meet deadlines. A delay in one part of the chain can cause cancelled orders and therefore unsold stock – and no budget for the creation and sampling of a new collection. It is therefore advisable to build long-term relationships with the different partners and do PR around the clock.

Make sure you know your strengths and weaknesses (and those of your partner, if applicable). Define your gaps in competences and surround yourself with people who have these skills as well as those who like to do aspects you don't enjoy.

BRAND COMMUNICATION STRATEGY

Brand communication is important in a business as creative and emotional as fashion. Communication happens every time someone is confronted with your label: its name, the designs or the collection itself, but also how you act, dress and behave as a designer will affect how people interpret your brand or label.

A starting point for a communication strategy is defining a *brand identity*, which can be expressed in words (for example, the name of the label, a baseline, an introductory text on a website), but also visually (through images, typography, colours).

Pinpoint what makes your label unique in the market and figure out a communication strategy that expresses this.
Note that a brand identity is stable over time, whereas a collection needs to be new and surprising every season. Your brand identity is therefore the coherent story you tell throughout your collections.

PR and communication are all about storytelling; building an interesting story about your brand (identity) in line with the way you want to appear in the press, both in print magazines and on blogs, social media, etc. As an independent start-up label, attracting press attention at the beginning will be fairly easy. People love to read about new creative and entrepreneurial talent. Keeping the story interesting will be more of a challenge.

To define what a good story is, identify "your consumer" or in short, *the person you design for*. This will be the basis (and audience) for both your communication strategy and your sales strategy. Don't define your consumer merely by demographic and/or geographical elements. Picture how and where your consumer lives, shops and goes out, what keeps her interest, and which magazines, blogs and other media he/she reads. Knowing and understanding your consumer will allow you to build a story that genuinely appeals to him/her, using the right media to reach him/her.

You can either reach out to the press yourself or work with a *press agency* to tell your story and build a relationship with the press on your behalf. Although the latter involves a monthly (fixed) cost, a good press agency will have an excellent network and understands which stories different media outlets like to feature. Don't think that a press agency will take care of all your communication difficulties though: you still have to give them interesting material to work with. Although a press agency saves you time (and limits the effort of daily follow-ups), you will still need to invest time and money to bring your story to the world.

Print media is increasingly under pressure as large companies have both cut communication budgets (as a result of the economic downturn) and allocated their budgets to new ways of communication. The pressure on print media to please any remaining advertisers has increased and editorial teams are getting smaller. Therefore, it is advisable to make it as easy as possible for the press to work with you: make sure you have good pictures and interesting pieces for shoots; answer your emails and phone quickly; and come up with interesting stories.

Explore the possibilities that *social media* hold. There are numerous (free) initiatives and possibilities to spread the story of your brand and/or build and inform your community. These channels give you the opportunity to be creative about reaching out to "your consumer" without the need for advertising budgets or press agencies.

You could, for example, conclude to combine different strategies by taking care of social media internally, while requesting the expertise of a press agency to reach out to print media, or for specific projects or areas (see **CHAPTER THREE**: Communicating Fashion in the New Era: Understanding Social Media and Corporate Social Responsibility).

Good communication also implies that your team, as well as your many (business) partners know and understand the company's values, vision and strategy. Clearly demarcate responsibilities and be sure to conduct your business in a manner coherent with your brand identity and communication. Transparent and open communication at all levels will help you reach your goal as efficiently as possible.

DEFINING THE MARKET

An entrepreneur will look for a gap in the market and launch the relevant business, but a fashion designer essentially wants to create beautiful collections and will need to go after his market. Knowing (the life of) your consumer (as discussed earlier) will enable you to reach him/her, but it will also define your market and help you research what competitors are already be offering to this market.

Everything starts, however, with *price*. Deciding on the prices for your pieces is one of the toughest but most important decisions you will make.

First calculate the *production price* for each piece in the collection and factor in an (average) mark-up – usually a minimum of 50% if you are running an independent fashion label. This is known as the *wholesale price*. At first, you might only calculate materials and manufacturing cost, but a true production price should also include a percentage of your sample collection and overhead costs, transport and (direct) sales costs.

Next, calculate the price your end-consumer will pay for your piece in the store by multiplying the wholesale price by 2.7, (See also **CHAPTER SIX**: Financial Decision-making in Fashion Management: 171) which is the average industry margin for shops and boutiques offering prêt-à-porter collections. Compare this recommended retail price with the price your consumer is willing to pay; i.e. based on what competitors are offering in the market. If your prices don't align, look into ways of lowering your production price.

Generally speaking, every detail you add that raises your production price by €10 will mean an increase of €54 in the final store price. When you design, ask yourself if your consumer cares so much about this detail that he/she is willing to pay €54 more for the item. Prices are also important because they partly define your image, the segment you are working in and how you will communicate about the label.

Ignoring these margins at the very start – for example to convince customers and consumers with more affordable prices – will not only cause financial difficulties covering your expenses, but also pricing and perception problems with the (loyal) customer base you have already built.

Every fashion label will have to seek its own place, balancing creativity and commerciality. Although many designers claim the contrary in the beginning, it is almost impossible to run a fashion label without considering some commercial trade-off. One solution to this is to create a sub-line offering more affordable pieces, based on a more production-friendly collection, to service a wider audience. The high-end line can then continue to serve as an outlet for the creativity of a designer and the communication of the label's essence.

SALES STRATEGY

The basis of a good sales strategy is knowing and understanding your end-consumers, your customers and the market. Key to this is setting the right prices for your products (as discussed above) and creating a sound *collection architecture*; i.e. planning the range of your collection, making it appeal to as many consumers in your target market as possible. Your collection will then include more extravagant pieces to communicate to the press, more difficult and more basic pieces being built up in a balanced and coherent manner.

Mapping out each collection in a matrix – a *range plan* – will enable you to communicate your creative vision about the collection to your (sales) team, customers and the press.

The choice of *distribution channel* will depend on your target consumer. As mentioned earlier, you can either work in a *business-to-consumer* (B2C) environment or in a *business-to-business* (B2B) environment. Most independent fashion labels operate according to the latter at first, but add a B2C component when their business grows.

In a B2B environment you will present your (sampling) collection to press and buyers during the *international fashion weeks*, among which Paris, London, New York and Milan remain the most important. Big brands and fashion houses tend to organize fashion shows for their collection to appear in the press. A show is the most important communication tool in fashion, and for highly creative companies, it replaces the investment of advertising. The shows will present the most extravagant pieces of the collection, but more wearable pieces will be sold at the showrooms where buyers place orders during these weeks. After order confirmation, the production process can start and delivery in the store will be foreseen a couple of months later.

As the financial means tend to be limited for starting designers, they usually opt for an own showroom – to which they invite press and buyers – but skip the investment for a show. The most important customers, from all over the world, attend these fashion weeks, seeking new talent. As the market in Belgium for designer clothing is (too) small, designers are obliged to operate internationally from the start. Depending on the strategy and vision, some designers also take a stand at (international) fairs organized during these fashion weeks, which mainly target more commercial brands operating in a two-season structure.
The real challenge is to attract the right customers to come and view your showroom collection. Before participating in fashion weeks, do extensive research into which stores fit your image and which customers might be interested in your collection. Invite broadly, but pay special attention to those stores whose attention you really seek. Don't focus only on reference stores

(the list of the 20 stores every designer wants to be in); rather focus on building long-lasting relationships with your customers.

Buyers receive numerous invitations to shows, showrooms and events, so it is important to attract their attention by doing something new, exciting, or inspiring. You want to make them curious about your collection so that they come and discover your collection in real life. This may increase the possibility of them investing in your collection, although (as mentioned earlier) buyers rarely invest in new talent due to the (financial) risks involved.

Working in a B2B environment does not mean you have to hire a sales team operating globally. You could opt instead to operate via a "middleman" i.e. by working with an *agent and/or distributor*, who will represent your brand and (re)sell your collection to retailers. An agent works in a defined geographic area and on a commission basis, whereas a *distributor* buys your collection and takes on the full risk of re-selling it.

A good agent or distributor should have a comprehensive *customer network*. If there is a good match between its network and your collection, this could significantly increase your sales. A disadvantage, however, is an increased distance between your brand or label and the end-consumers; your control over how your label is presented in stores also diminishes.

Carefully consider the pros and cons of working with a middleman. At all times, keep in mind that an agent or distributor is not the silver bullet for struggling sales... it all starts with a good collection, collections architecture, and price-quality relationship.

If you decide instead to follow the B2C route, you will open stores and hire a sales team (if you don't work with licensing contracts – which will be explained later on). In this scenario you have full control over how your brand or label is presented in the store and the store itself becomes a communication tool. It also allows you to analyze buying habits of end-consumers and to then adapt a future collection appropriately. These are also the reasons why labels applying a B2B approach open flagship stores in key markets, offering the full collection directly to end-consumers.

Don't overestimate the margins (see the above discussion about pricing) you will earn by running your own fashion boutique. You will need the budget to cover expenses such as sales staff, rent and (more importantly) investment in stock. The choice to open a store should be driven only by the desire to build an image and a loyal consumer basis.

Of course, the *Internet* also hosts a wealth of opportunities for independent fashion labels. Although it may appear easier to sell online, it really depends on how you work. One option is to sell your collection to an *online retailer* who then re-sells it online. He takes the full risk and behaves much like an "off-line buyer", which contrasts to many webshops of high-end designers, rather functioning as creative platforms or online showrooms. The latter implies that, once an item has been sold through the platform, you will need to take care of its packaging, shipping and delivery. The webshop will take care of attracting an audience, but you will take the investment risk in relation to returns, follow-up and investing in stock.

Launching your own webshop is also dependent on your strategy and could be interesting if you work in a B2C environment, already investing in stock and communication with end-consumers in mind.

In short, in an online environment, you should always bear in mind that there is a difference between people liking your product on social media and buying it online, not to mention managing back office activities like return policies, shipping and the investment of stock. Stock is worth almost nothing at the end of the fashion season and returns are significant in the fashion industry given the many body sizes and shapes. Accessories such as shoes and bags, as well as children's clothing, are therefore often more successful online. As a new high-end fashion label, it is also hard to demonstrate good fit and quality online, which reduces the likelihood of selling expensive pieces in this way.

FINANCING

Your financial plan – and in particular your cash flow plan – will unmask your financing needs by listing and forecasting income and expenses necessary to achieve your goal. Be sure to realistically forecast the amount you need to bridge in order to grow your business.

Apart from financing the fixed costs to run your business, you will also have to pre-finance important expenses, such as sampling costs and production costs. When you start, sampling costs will, proportionally speaking, be a large cost to take and to break even out with your sales. When your business starts to grow, the difficulty will be pre-financing an increasing larger production volume and taking on board personnel. Observing many start-ups in fashion, we could conclude that you will need a budget for at least 10 seasons to build your brand or label. Financing need often reaches a maximum after five or six seasons, which is an important reason for many labels to drop out.

When you know how much money you will need to grow your label, it is advisable to look for a good financing mix to fund your activities.

Entrepreneurs in general often start up their businesses with their own financial means or that of their "believers", otherwise known as "friends, fools and family".

When your company has developed, you will need more financial means to grow and a bank may be an appropriate financial partner. At this stage you will have built up a (hopefully good) track record and might be able to offer the guarantees a bank requests. In a fashion company operating B2B, the need for cash will reach its most critical point when the production of the collection needs to be pre-financed (after the sales period has closed and orders are confirmed). These confirmed orders might act as a guarantee, enabling you to get a bank loan (to finance the production).

When you need more substantial means, or if your business is perceived as too risky for a bank, you may wish to approach a (private) investor. A traditional investor is out to earn a good return on his investment, which is not a good fit with the time- and finance-intensive process of growing an independent fashion label. A good investor in this business is therefore more interested in the process of growing a creative business and being part of its network rather than in earning huge amounts of money on a short term.

Designers often make decisions that may appear irrational from the point of view of the investor, but these kinds of decisions can make the creative business successful. The right investor should therefore be open to a creative process that is at times difficult to grasp. A designer, on the other hand, should also be respectful of the knowledge and experience an investor can bring to the company.

An open-minded attitude from both parties, as well as a shared vision and strategy, are crucial to a successful collaboration. Do not be seduced by a large (potential) upfront investment; talk everything through before making any decisions.

The Belgian fashion industry is internationally known and especially appreciated for striving to stay independent rather than being sold to a luxury group. This limits the quick returns on investments and can make the venture more risky, but it also makes it a more interesting business in which to invest from a creative point of view.

Fashion is not a cultural activity in Belgium, but it is in some parts of Europe. Depending on your situation and where your business is located, you will find different forms of government support. In recent years, the attention for the support of creative industries in Europe has increased, positively affecting this sector.

The Flemish and federal government of Belgium for example do not offer grants to fashion designers, but have implemented some measures to help entrepreneurs, and creative entrepreneurs in particular, to get better access to financing. Apart from some general measures to support start-ups and entrepreneurs in an early stage or to expand their business internationally, an important initiative for creative industries is "CultuurInvest", an investment fund for entrepreneurs in the creative industry[37].

As mentioned earlier, a *financing mix* is advisable i.e. employing a combination of the different measures listed above. It is essential to do thorough budget calculations upfront (see **CHAPTER SIX**: Financial Decision-Making in Fashion Management) and to look for financial partners while you are at a healthy stage of the company's development. It will be difficult to convince potential partners to invest in an indigent company.

LICENSING

A *licensing agreement* grants a third party the right to use your intellectual property right – your creative collection – in exchange for which you receive a royalty or fee. Fashion companies use licensing in a variety of ways, but the key motivation is to balance out the peaks and dips in cash flow and spread or lower the risk. Licensing agreements in the fashion industry are used to extend the variety of products in a company – brand extension – and/or to *conquer a new market*.

Licensing is used especially by luxury groups, who collaborate with manufacturers of cosmetics, fragrances, eyewear so as to rely on the specialty of another company and avoid the investment of research to produce a good product. These additional products are often an important source of income for luxury brands, as they tend to be more affordable products appealing to a wider audience. These products create the idea with consumers of being part of a luxury world.
Independent fashion labels also use licensing agreements for brand extension, but the licensed products will often be communicated as collaborations and therefore be co-branded. Belgian companies are fond of these collaborations. Examples include the limited edition of lingerie Veronique Branquinho designed for Van de Velde, the Eastpak creations of Raf Simons for Eastpak and the designs of Tim van Steenbergen (amongst others) for

Ambiorix and Deltalight. This is a smart way to earn extra cash, but also to raise brand awareness in another part of the market – and usually these are good stories for the press.

Designers may also sign a licensing agreement with a clothing manufacturer. In this case the designer draws the collection and the manufacturer takes it from there. The designer will then get a commission based on sales. As the latter especially implies a very intensive partnership, we stress again the importance of an open attitude of both parties and sharing the same ideas about the vision and strategy of the company to grow a successful business.

As mentioned earlier, licensing is also used to *conquer new markets*. A designer will grant the right to a sales agent or a distributor to use the intellectual property rights of the company to sell the collection in exchange for a commission. These "middle men" will mainly be brought in markets that are more difficult to access due to cultural differences and language issues.

Franchising contracts are another example of licensing, although these will mainly be used for larger companies extending their network of own shops in a new market.

LEGAL PROTECTION

Intellectual property is the main creator of value and money in a creative business. A designer builds the basis of value creation within the company by designing the collection and making it stand out from the other collections in the market. The designer or company can grant someone the right to use this intellectual property, asking a fee or commission in return.

Although protection of intellectual property and other legal issues of running a fashion company has been discussed more in detail (see CHAPTER FIVE: Fashion Law) we would like to stress here that it is important to protect this property in order to earn the money you are entitled to earn, as well as to prevent and to react on infringements.

FORCES INFLUENCING
THE INDUSTRY

Thus far we have explored ways to start your own fashion label using techniques employed by hundreds of designers today and in ways designers have been operating since prêt-à-porter was invented. You should be aware of this "industry recipe" so that you can reflect upon it, know your position and do business in a creative and innovative way. This will help you turn some of the threats into opportunities. Just look to how iTunes has changed the music industry and how bloggers have found their way to the front row and you should be encouraged to try something new.

In the following section, some of the major transitions influencing the fashion industry are briefly discussed.

The *Internet* opens up a lot of possibilities in which large fashion labels can invest, such as developing applications, new visuals to sell the collection online and extended reality in shops. However, labels also face an increased challenge in terms of protecting intellectual property rights. Some of the advantages you can enjoy as a small fashion label are the enlargement of your market to the world, e-commerce opportunities and free ways of communication and creating an engaged community. The Internet may create global competition, but it also enables you to reach out to a niche market on the other side of the world.

A real challenge for smaller labels is the *pace of the industry*, which has rapidly increased since Zara entered the market, radically changing the dominant logic of the industry at that time and democratizing fashion. In parallel our (consumer) society demands more products and more variety, resulting in commercial labels and luxury brands presenting collections in between the traditional autumn/winter and spring/summer seasons.

Offering more than two collections per year can be a useful tool if you have the capacity and structure to exploit it (planning and managing a two-season structure is already challenging). This is especially true for businesses operating in a B2C environment, as it allows you to react to what consumers desire and buy, and cash flow extremes are less severe as a result of income spread over time and production scheduled throughout the year.

Generally speaking, specialized independent multi-brand boutiques are more investing in young designer talent than department stores. The last ones are using more strict conditions and offer mostly well-established

FASHION MANAGEMENT

fashion and luxury labels, that are able to produce and deliver large orders and merchandising. Unfortunately, these independent boutiques – especially in Western countries – are increasingly under pressure due to the *stagnating economy*. Meanwhile the end-consumers have a lot of alternatives and can go to a wide variety of fashion retailers. These threats result in *less risky purchasing behaviour* and makes the independent multi-brand boutiques less keen to invest in starting designer labels.

An additional difficulty in this sense for high-end fashion labels is the *perception of consumers about the cost* of an honest and qualitative piece of clothing. The fashion industry is a very labour-intensive industry. Companies focusing on a highly creative and qualitative product manufacture small quantities, implying elevated production prices and thus retail (store) prices. Keep the cost of one hour of labour in mind to get a good grasp of what would be the true manufacturing cost for one piece.

The high prices of design labels contrast with the incredibly low prices of the pieces offered by high-street fashion chains. The unlimited offer of these products make people forget that these ranges are only possible for mass marketed standardized products produced in low wage countries and for companies controlling a large part of the value chain.

And one last important trend to mention here is that *functions and roles in this sector are shifting* and the borders between them are increasingly fuzzy. We observed fashion journalists leaving the media sector to apply their experience to fashion retail and bloggers collaborating with (mainly high-street) fashion brands to design capsule collections. Fashion shows have already evolved from an industry-only event into one to which bloggers are invited, while consumers can watch the show simultaneously via live streaming.

This *democratization* shifts the importance of the fashion show and makes it more difficult to communicate directly with the end-consumers as the collections will only be for sale in the store six months later. Fashion chains will have picked up new trends by then and have designed, produced and delivered collections based on the creations of high-end fashion labels.

The forces mentioned above are only a few of the things that makes one wonder if the current way of selling prêt-à-porter collections during international fashion weeks is sustainable.

The advantage for labels in their start-up phase is that it is no longer necessary to go to international fashion weeks and put large budgets on the table. Internet, new technologies and cheap travel opportunities have generated *new ways to interact* with customers and consumers. In this sense, smaller initiatives with a personal approach appear to be on the rise.

The bottom line is that you also need to *be creative in the way you are doing business* by applying other rules, using different business models or changing the relationships within your network. React to the changing environment and keep track of trends and possibilities. As a small start-up, one of your biggest advantages is that you are flexible to experiment with new ways of communicating, selling, and interacting with your audience. Intensified competition may make it more difficult to conquer your spot on the market, but it will also stimulated opportunities for creatives.

TIPS & TRICKS

Starting up a fashion business with a partner who has complementary skills and interests will significantly increase your success rate. Make sure you share the same goal and ideas about the mission/vision and strategy of the company.

Do not rush the process; give yourself time for proper preparation and grow steadily. Building an independent fashion label takes time (and money).

Write down or capture all relevant aspects of the business (financial, logistic, organizational) before you start; this functions as a good reality check of what's required to launch and sustain your business.

A successful business starts with a vision and strategy, a coherent identity and fair prices. Balance your price between the cost of production, the level of quality you want to achieve, and what people in your market are willing to pay. Make sure this is aligned with the story you bring to the press.

Be clear about the market (segment or niche) in which you will be doing business. Read about the industry and stay abreast of changes influencing it.

Nobody is waiting for a new fashion label, so pro-actively reach out to your market; being a good (or great!) designer is not enough to make it in this business. Adding a creative and innovative way of doing business will increase your chances to success.

Don't take on unnecessary costs such as building a stock before you have sold anything, hiring staff before you have made (any) money, working with a press agency without having a sellable collection, presenting during fashion weeks without informing and inviting press and buyers...

Everybody lacks time in this industry, and so will you. Nevertheless, get out there to be inspired (by other industries), to meet interesting people, and to build a network and long-lasting relationships with partners.

Stay true to yourself and to the goal you want to achieve when you start working with a (financial) partner, when you try out new creative or commercial collaborations, when you start working with a licensee, when you create a subline, and so on.

(Fashion) media might suggest that fashion is all about glitter and glamour, but in reality, it is all about hard work and persisting. Know what you start with and only proceed with your plan if you are truly passionate about it.

REFERENCES

This chapter is mainly written from the experience of guiding designers starting up an independent fashion label and based on the many conversations with people within the (inter)national fashion industry.

Other sources include:

Meadows, T. (2009) *How to Set up and Run a Fashion Label*. London: Laurence King Publishing Ltd.

Porter, E.M. (1980) *Competitive Strategy. Techniques for Analyzing Industries and Competitors*. New York: The Free Press.

Schrauwen, J. & Schramme, A. (2013) *De mode-industrie in Vlaanderen gesegmenteerd*. Antwerp Management School/ University of Antwerp.

Website of *Business of Fashion for daily* fashion (news) readings.

Women's Wear Daily website for breaking news in the fashion industry, business coverage and trends in fashion, beauty and retail.

Fashion Talks – Get inspired in Antwerp 2013, international fashion conference 10th of October 2013, Flanders Fashion Institute.

Summer School Fashion Management (2012, 2013), Antwerp Management School/University of Antwerp in collaboration with Flanders Fashion Institute.

RECOMMENDED

Books

Hinssen, P. (2010) *The New Normal*. Ghent: Mach Media NV.

Breuer, S. (2009) *Blue is the new black: The 10 Step Guide to Developing and Producing a Fashion Collection*. Amsterdam: Bis Publishers.

Gehlhar, M. (2008) *The Fashion Designer Survival Guide, Revised and Expanded Edition; Start and Run your Own fashion Business*. New York: Kaplan Publishing.

Osterwalder, A. & Pigneur, Y. (2010) *Business Model Generation*. New Jersey: Wiley.

Websites & blogs

Business of Fashion – a blog with a focus on the business side of fashion written in a very comprehensive way, while not losing sight of the creative forces driving this industry.

Women's Wear Daily – an important source with (breaking) news from the fashion industry.

Advice to keep track of what important (international) journalists – amongst others – *Suzy Menkes, Tim Blanks, Cathy Horyn, Vanessa Freedman*, ... write and share (also via social media).

case #7   Jean-Paul Knott

SS 14

FASHION   MANAGEMENT

"You have to find a way to survive"

Interview by
Trui Moerkerke

His fashion resume is impressive. Belgian born, but growing up "everywhere except Belgium", Jean-Paul Knott studied in New York and worked for a large part of his career in Paris. Fresh from school, he started working as an assistant at Yves Saint Laurent, and he stayed at this iconic fashion house for more than a decade. In 1996 he became the designer of the Yves Saint Laurent Rive Gauche collection and assisted Mr. Saint Laurent with his haute couture collections. In 2000, Jean-Paul Knott started his own company, describing his collections as "basic chic pieces with light shapes and precise volumes".

Apart from his own collection, Knott took on consecutive and prestigious fashion jobs, working as creative director for Krizia and later for Louis Feraud and Cerruti. He also designed for the Swiss Bejart Ballet and collaborated with DIM, 3 Suisses, and La Redoute. In 2005 he embarked on his first gallery concept, followed by a stint as interior designer for a Brussels hotel. Since 2006, Knott has worked with Japanese clothing company Tomorrowland. His Jean-Paul Knott Made in Belgium collection, meanwhile, is managed by the Gysemans Clothing Group (GCP), who handle manufacturing, distribution and international sales. On March 20th of 2001, the respected fashion critic Suzy Menkes writes a great review of his work. "Jean-Paul Knott showed that there are more ways of doing femininity than strewing frocks with roses. Knott is a cutter but one who slices into soft fabrics, making drapes and shapes across the body... and with draped dresses a strong trend, these were modern and some of the best we have seen in four fashion capitals this season."

Your fashion career is an eclectic one. You like to work with artists and you run an art gallery in Brussels. Do you consider yourself a fashion designer or a designer/artist?

Tough question. I suppose I think of myself as a designer. I don't want to limit myself to the concept of fashion design. I have an outspoken vision on making clothes and making fashion. I believe in making clothes, that's my job. But that's only the start. On top of that I believe in bringing my clothes in "a fashion". The French expression "à la mode" captures it perfectly: it's about a group of people having the same sensibility at a precise moment and place. It all stems from there. I bring my clothes into contemporary fashion by collaborating with people who create an aesthetic context.

Your vision seems very different from the fast fashion cycle and global e-commerce. What do you think of the recent changes in the fashion world?

I don't have any problems with those changes. I think it's kind of cool. It makes people think in other ways. I worked for La Redoute and 3 Suisses, big distributors with a fast fashion cycle. For my women's collection in Japan, we deliver once a month. But it still fits into my concept of working on clothes. I work on the design, on the concept and then I put them into the fashion cycle. For Jean-Paul Knott Made in Belgium, we have four collections a year – pre-collections and main collections – as well as a menswear collection. I have never worked any other way. Even 20 years ago, when I was at Saint Laurent, there was always a collection to work on. In a way, this is easier. When you do smaller collections, the workload is more balanced, but you have to find a way to survive. There is no ultimate answer. Fashion shows, yes or no? Advertising, yes or no? All are options, but whether you do it or not depends on how relevant it is for your product and your image.

Do you like the management part of your job?

I don't have to manage that much. I have always collaborated with people who took care of the money side; I am really lucky with that. It's a choice. I don't want my company to be too big. I know how things are in big companies. I've worked for investment groups at Saint Laurent. I know what it means, I know the reality of it, the stress.

I prefer to work on different projects. I have an amazing collaboration with Tomorrowland, while in Belgium I have been working with Marc Gysemans (GCG) for 15 years, first at Feraud and Cerruti and now for my own label. It's extremely convenient to go to Rotselaar, the place where Marc Gysemans is located, and have meetings and fittings there.

You studied at the Fashion Institute of Technology in New York. Is the approach there different to that of Belgian fashion schools?

I don't know. New York was the school I could afford. There was no La Cambre, the fashion school in Brussels, at that time, only the Antwerp fashion school, where the language instruction was Dutch. I didn't, as I grew up everywhere except in Belgium.

I don't think where you study is that important. What you take with you when you finish art school depends on who you are and how you feel. You have to take whatever you can. I was lucky, somehow. I studied in New York in the mid-eighties, amazing times, and I had amazing teachers.

Looking back, are you happy with the way your career has evolved?

I should be very happy, but it depends on how you interpret this question. On a personal level, I am much happier than I was 20 years ago. Am I happy with the way fashion has evolved? No, generally spoken I am not. Maybe I've been in the industry for too long. The excitement for fashion lasts a while then later on you go into other circles and meet other people and you do it for other reasons. If I had to give a piece of advice to young fashion designers, maybe I would say: don't even think about it. But I understand the appeal of working in fashion. It's one of the most amazing jobs because it has everything to do with emotions, good and sometimes a bit stupid. But that makes it so exciting.

"I don't want to limit myself to the concept of fashion design"

SS 14

case # 7   Jean-Paul Knott

Jean-Paul Knott
SS 14

THE INDEPENDENT STATE OF BELGIAN FASHION: DAVID VERSUS GOLIATH?

Veerle Windels

Over the past two decades, Belgian fashion designers have become regulars on the international fashion scene. Coming from a country that hardly claims to have a fashion tradition, most of them have ventured to Paris, only to find recognition and applause. But not every designer was able to turn the first success into a fully-fledged fashion brand. What's more? Most of them weren't even interested in doing so.

HOW IT ALL BEGAN

It all started at the beginning of the eighties, when a bunch of students of the fashion department at the Antwerp Academy of Fine Arts graduated. They didn't venture out to Paris immediately, **where fashion had been thriving for decades already**, but learned the trade in Belgian-established fashion houses, designing commercial labels like Scapa, Olivier Strelli and Bartsons. By the end of the eighties, they rented a van together and made their way to the other side of the Channel, to London Fashion Week, where they presented their work for the first time. A day later, the newspapers were full of their ground-breaking designs, not mentioning all of their names – far too difficult to spell – but coining them as "the Antwerp Six". A season later, the Six took off for Paris's Semaine de la Mode (Fashion Week). There again, *les Six d'Anvers"* became an instant hit, sharing a "salon" at the Saint James and Albany hotel. It took foreigners still a bit longer to correctly pronounce the names of Dries Van Noten, Walter Van Beirendonck, Dirk Van Saene, Dirk Bikkembergs, Marina Yee and Ann Demeulemeester. There is a seventh designer in this story: Martin Margiela, who decided against staying in Belgium after graduation. Instead he immediately took the train to Paris and became first assistant to Jean Paul Gaultier, at that time the most avant-garde designer of the Paris fashion scene. We can say the real adventure started there and then for all of them. But there was no such thing as a plan, let alone a business strategy.

However, Willy Claes, the left-wing minister of economic affairs of Belgium at the time, had had a plan for a while. His so-called Textile Plan started on January 1st 1981 and was in full bloom when the Antwerp Six did their first try-outs in London and Paris. The plan was meant to offer financial and economic stimuli to the Belgian textile companies, who at that time were losing impact and even more money. It also involved a communication strategy based on the slogan *"Mode. Dit is Belgisch"* ("Fashion. This is Belgian").

Tags with these words were attached to all fashion designs made in Belgium, in order to raise awareness about the fact that the pair of trousers, the dress or even the underwear you were wearing did not necessarily come from Italy or France, countries that for ages had been regarded the only places in the world where fashion could have originated. The Textile Plan was the pivotal reason of being of the Institute of Textile and Confection in Belgium (ITCB) and also involved a new fashion magazine (called *Mode. Dit is Belgisch*, which was later sold to Roularta's *Weekend Knack*) and a fashion contest (called *De Gouden Spoel*; The Golden Spindle). Even though the Institute was full of political heads (who hardly knew anything about fashion), there was one woman who made all the difference: Helena Ravijst. She would prove to be the guardian angel of many young designers of that age. Moreover, she understood quite early on that Belgian fashion should try and look beyond the Belgian borders. Ravijst took her designers abroad, even to Japan (a trip that Van Beirendonck among others still recalls as "incredible") but also opted for an international jury at the Golden Spindle, bringing Jean Paul Gaultier and Romeo Gigli (among others) to Brussels. The winners of the contest? Ann Demeulemeester (in 1982), Dirk Van Saene (1983), Dirk Bikkembergs (1985), Pieter Coene (1987) and Veronique Leroy (1989). With Leroy, a graduate from Studio Berçot in Paris, the contest came to an end. In the meantime, Belgium had become a federal state (since the St. Michael agreements of 1993) and the Institute had no money left. It was a pity that the Textile Plan died with only a whisper. Even though most designers keep repeating that they had never actually received any money from the government, the plan had its advantages, especially for the industry. And it made people in the streets aware of the existence of Belgian fashion.

THE BELGIAN WAVE

What made these Belgian designers so interesting? What triggered the interest of international buyers and fashion press? Was it their conceptual vision of fashion, their new way of defining glamour? Was it their unrelenting gusto for work? Or their newness? The newness-factor was definitely a plus. At that time, Belgian designers were often compared to the Japanese designers who had come to Paris just before them. Rei Kawakubo and Yohji Yamamoto shocked the fashion crowd with their completely different take on glamour. The holes inside Kawakubo's sweaters were regarded shameful, but the in-crowd was enchanted by such a modern (sometimes political) view on clothes. Don't forget: at the time Montana and Mugler ruled the fashion world, exuding a glamour on stilettos and making waves with fashion shows that were spectacular in their own right. What you saw on the catwalk did not necessarily end up in the stores though. That was different with the Japanese, and with the Belgians. What you saw (on the catwalk) was what you got (in the showroom).

But there's more to explaining the success of the first Belgian fashion generation. They clearly did not share the same vision of fashion (unlike, say, the Surrealists, they were not part of the same movement, so to speak), but all of them were eager to take their chances. All had a distinct concept. As the philosopher Kant once said: "Intuition without concepts is blind. Concepts without intuition are empty." And that concept went far beyond the clothes. It had to do with the way they organised fashion shows, how they chose their own stores, how they communicated with the outside world, how they lived their lives. Few critics mention that most of them still live fairly normal lives in Antwerp, even today. They stick to the city where they studied, far away from the glam in Paris or New York. An exception is Martin Margiela, who, as we mentioned earlier, left Belgium to live in Paris early on in his career. Compared to the Antwerp Six, he was the only one to show his collection through a fashion show, and thus started the Belgian wave: a completely different vision on models, on staging, on receiving an audience, and, of course, on fashion. Together with Van Beirendonck, Demeulemeester and Dries Van Noten, Margiela completely changed the fashion system. As all of them were outsiders, coming from a country with little fashion heritage, they did everything their own way. Lacking big bucks, the five-star hotel lounge, where most fashion houses organized their fashion shows at the time, was replaced by a far more interesting show venue: a forgotten metro station, a derelict garage, a closed-down factory, an open-air food market, an old supermarket. Dries Van Noten was especially keen on giving his audience an off the beaten track tour of Paris: he invited press and buyers to places that immediately put the collection in the right context. His women's collection for the summer of 1996 was shown in an empty swimming pool, whereas his menswear collection of spring 1994 was shown in Passage Brady, home to a strong Indian community (among others). The collection was inspired by India and the venue was well chosen: Van Noten even had fake money printed, to be spent that same afternoon in the Passage. Another incredible moment? His show for winter 1996 on an open market off Boulevard Rochechouart. It was January, freezing cold (at the end of the show it even started snowing). Upon entering the venue, guests received warm blankets and were taken to their seats – all of them front row.

Margiela would also pick unusual show venues, such as a forgotten metro station, and he was the first one to question the notion of supermodels. At a time when the supermodel Linda Evangelista declared she wouldn't get out of bed for less than $25,000, Margiela organized castings in the streets of Paris. Today, this type of casting has become commonplace, but then people like Gianni Versace ended up booking all of the supermodels for one of his shows, a statement about power and money, and about how he saw fashion at that time. The Belgians, and certainly Margiela, went far in rethinking the position and importance of the model; Margiela even blindfolded them at one of his shows. Van Beirendonck has done the same with masks. And Raf Simons (much later) did it with helmets. The message was clear: it's never about the models. And please, look at the clothes...

TURNING FASHION ON ITS HEAD

Especially in the beginning of their careers, they didn't care for hierarchy. Whereas front-row guests traditionally sat, well, front-row, at a Dries Van Noten show there was only one row, and it got filled on a first come, first served basis. Of course, over the years, he had to change that, but he none-theless made every member of his audience feel welcome, whether they were from French *Elle* or from the local newspaper, *Gazet Van Antwerpen*. Lots of journalists have applauded his way of treating every one to a good beer, to French fries, to sweets, upon entering the venue. He even had his team bring sandwiches to the photographers, that bunch of hardworking people that often is forgotten when catering is involved. Of course this is just a small anecdote, but in a way it says a lot about human behaviour.

What also set the Belgian designers apart was that they were all willing to grow slowly. Read any interview with Van Noten, Van Beirendonck or Demeulemeester of those first years and you will find they all agreed on this: don't sell your soul, but keep going in that one direction you chose, even though it will take time. Today, most young designers step out on their own and very quickly end up being bought by a big group. Sometimes they become creative director of a big label, sometimes they even lose the right to use their own name. The Antwerp Six weren't at all eager to do that. Some were asked to become creative director of big couture houses in Paris, but refused, saying the focus was on their own brand only. Margiela joined Hermès as creative director at one point, but he kept his own brand alive and kicking too, and when he was replaced, no damage had been done. Van Beirendonck joined the German jeans brand Mustang to launch a special collection called Wild & Lethal Trash (W&LT) and was able to organize spectacular shows in Paris. But when, after a few years, a large part of the collection was being designed by another design team, Walter quit out of principle. He was urged to lay off part of his own team (and on a personal level he lost a lot of money), because he had no more income to pay them on a monthly basis.

Another possible reason for the success and impact of the Belgian Six was their artistic approach. Long before art and fashion were married in zillions of projects, the Antwerp designers collaborated with artists, photographers, graphic designers and video artists to make their concept clear. To put it bluntly: a young American fashion designer with hardly four collections behind him would talk about the roll-out of boutiques or the instalment of an accessories collection, whereas his Belgian colleague would talk about the creative process behind yet another small ready-to-wear collection. Walter Van Beirendonck worked together with visual artists like Orlan and Erwin Wurm, and produced the stage outfits of the music group U2 and the Paris Opera dance company. His first exhibition was hosted at the Boijmans Van Beuningen Museum in Rotterdam; in 2012, his work and the world he wanted to create were shown at museums in Dallas and in Melbourne. Margiela worked with video long before the fashion scene got involved in fashion cinema. His first exhibition in Rotterdam's Boijmans Van Beuningen was all about infusing bacteria into clothes, making them contaminated – which of course was a compelling metaphor for the essence of fashion: that it always becomes outdated. He wanted to show the essence of fashion: that after one season it's out and the scene longs for something new

FINDING CREATIVE SYNERGY

In retrospect we might say all of this *must* have been written down somewhere by a strategy guru, but this is not how they worked. Who took decisions then? A CEO? A marketing director? Nope. The main thing that they had in common was that each designer kept an overview of design, of marketing, of sales, of communication. There were also not that many people working for them at the start... Dries Van Noten started his company and worked hand in hand with the late Christine Matthys and Linda Loppa, the director of the Fashion Departement at that moment, and Margiela teamed up with Jenny Meirens (who formerly owned a boutique in Brussels) to start his company (she would prove to be his soul mate and his link to the outside world). Growing their businesses meant going slowly and steadily, and keeping their independence. A roll-out of stores? Forget it. Even Van Noten, who is arguably the most successful of them, will only open stores if he finds the right spot. He has to "feel" the area, the place itself, and the interior design must be adapted to the building and to the city or quarter where

"An iconic image for the cover of 20 years of *Mode, dit is Belgisch (Fashion, this is Belgian)*, with all the most important Belgian designers of the moment, including the Antwerp Six" (*Knack Weekend*, 10 September 2003). **Top, from left to right:** Walter Van Beirendonck, Marina Yee, Erik Verdonck, Dirk Bikkenbergs, Dries Van Noten, Haider Ackermann, Veronique Branquinho and Xavier Delcour. **Middle:** Dirk Van Saene, Tim Van Steenbergen, An Vandevorst, Filip Arickx, Ann Demeulemeester, Sami Tillouche and Véronique Leroy. **Bottom:** Bernhard Willhelm, Jean-Paul Knott, José Enrique Oña Selfa and Bruno Pieters.

the store is opened. Van Noten opened his first store, Het Modepaleis in Antwerp, in an old architectural gem, that stood out in the Sint-Andries Quarter, a few minutes from the Meir, the main shopping street in Antwerp, where most chain stores were situated. Demeulemeester, Van Saene and Van Beirendonck followed suit. They opted for spaces that underlined their fashion vision. Demeulemeester's store opened just between the Royal Museum of Fine Arts and the Flemish Museum of Contemporary Arts (MuHKA), Van Saene and Van Beirendonck's "Walter" store sat in a derelict garage, off the beaten track. All of them would only open stores if they were ready for it, and if they found the right partners (in the case of the Far East). Needless to say, some of the Six have since found their Pierre Bergé (Bergé being the man who let Yves Saint Laurent design, and made sure the bills were paid). Demeulemeester met Anne Chapelle and she would prove to be the right woman at the right place – not just as an investor, but also as a strategic thinker. Bikkembergs was able to build his brand on an even larger scale, bringing in Serge Dewilde as CEO (but only much later on, when his name was already established outside fashion circles).

THE SIX TODAY

From the first season onwards, The Antwerp Six sold their collections to international buyers. Soon their names were being uttered by clients in New York, London, Sydney, Milan, Los Angeles and Tokyo (Japan immediately embraced their vision). Their communication with buyers and press was predominantly clear during fashion week: the fashion show being the only tool of marketing. Not one designer except Bikkembergs, has taken publicity pages in fashion magazines. They claim they don't have the money (even today), but the truth is that they were able to break this unspoken law, too: fashion magazines talked about Belgian designers not because they had a large publicity budget, but because they loved their work. It's true that Anna Wintour, editor in chief of US *Vogue*, had never seen a Dries Van Noten show until his fiftieth show (in 2004, and in which the catwalk was a long dining table). She's been a regular ever since and talks about him and his work frequently in the magazine. Van Noten's company, NV Andries Van Noten, is still completely independent and has an outstanding reputation.

For Ann Demeulemeester, business has had its ups and downs. Demeulemeester was lucky to come across Anne Chapelle in the mid-nineties. After meeting at their children's school's gate, Demeulemeester invited Chapelle to her company, to have a look at the numbers, and the latter never left. Chapelle has since put money into Demeulemeester's business and let it grow slowly, opening stores only when the time is right, and again, only with the right people. Recently, Ann Demeulemeester announced her withdrawal from the business and the fashion scene all together. She feels her label is in good hands, with a team that can hold on to the vision she installed all these years. By the year 2000, Dirk Bikkembergs had become a household name in the sportswear world (at one point he was the owner of the Italian Fossombrone football team), but he sold his company to Zeis Excelsa group in 2011, staying on as creative consultant. Walter Van Beirendonck kept his menswear collection going after the Mustang debacle, and combined this with working for commercial lines (such as his ZuluPapuwa children's collection for the Belgian commercial chain JBC and his artistic directorship of the Belgian commercial label Scapa Sports) and teaching at the fashion department of the Antwerp academy – which he has been at the helm of for several years. Dirk Van Saene opted for a low profile, and brings out a small collection whenever he feels like it. He also teaches at the academy, has a flair for ceramics (which he exhibits) and runs the DVS-store in Antwerp (where, among others, the Van Beirendonck and Van Saene lines are sold). Marina Yee teaches at the fashion department of the Ghent academy, but also regularly creates costumes for opera and theatre or other artistic projects. Probably the biggest player in the field of that first generation is the least visible: Martin Margiela. In 2002, he sold his company to Only The Brave, the holding of Renzo Rosso, who also owns Diesel. Margiela quit fashion altogether and is said to be painting somewhere between Paris and Tuscany.

BEYOND THE ANTWERP SIX

We shouldn't forget the designers that came after the Antwerp Six. Several generations of designers have studied fashion in Antwerp and made their mark in Paris. They tend to be referred to as "Belgian fashion designers", but in a number of cases, their passports will not agree. For example, Stephan Schneider and Bernhard Willhelm are German and Izumi Van Hongo is Japanese. "Belgian" therefore refers to them coming from a Belgian fashion school or "being part of the Belgian fashion wave".

After the Six, most graduates tried their luck in Paris immediately, barely stopping to design for other commercial lines. They saw that the road was paved, that Belgian fashion was well respected and took a train to Paris to try their luck. Of course, press and buyers compared them to the Six, weighing up their vision on fashion and their possible success. But, as with the first Belgians, success is relative. Organizing a show in Paris didn't imply the best buyers or journalists sitting front-row. It's never mathematics. You need an exclusive network and a good spot on the show calendar. Moreover, organizing shows is really expensive so some stayed away from it, in the beginning at least. Veronique Branquinho hired a few models to show her first collection in a Paris gallery and immediately sold to important buyers. So did Jurgi Persoons, who organised fashion events at night, on the Quai de Paris. Stefaan Schneider kept to a showroom (and still does today). AF Vandevorst and Willhelm stayed out of the gallery circuit and organized a fashion show immediately, getting international attention from day one. Soon 10 to 15 Belgian fashion designers were present on the Paris Fashion Week, showing their collection on and off schedule. Some of them had to quit, because fashion is an expensive business and talent is not enough to succeed. Jurgi Persoons shut down his business after a couple of years, and so did Branquinho. Fortunately, she reinstated her label, cutting a deal with Gibo – the famous Italian manufacturer makes it possible for her to focus only on design. Anna Heylen organized some shows at the beginning of her career but decided to keep her business solely in Belgium, opening up a "Maison" in Antwerp and upgrading her collection to a luxury version of ready-to-wear. Tim Van Steenbergen conquered Paris in his own way: first by organizing shows, later on by inviting buyers to his Paris showroom. Cutting the expenses of the show, he had more money to put in elsewhere. And that worked!

BUILDING BELGIAN TALENT

Over the years, more and more people began to look at the fashion department of the Antwerp Academy of Fine Arts as an exceptional cradle of talent. The department was founded in 1963 by Mary Prijot, and has always been part of an academy that was founded in 1663 by David Teniers the Younger, painter to the Archduke Leopold and Don Juan of Austria. Teniers wanted "to encourage the arts and raise their esteem"; as an example he cited the famous schools of Rome and Paris. The Six graduated here in 1980 and 1981 (they were not in the same class). Since then, the aura of the department has grown tremendously and increasingly attracted students from abroad. Each year over 200 applicants try their luck at the entry exam; only about 30 get in. What would be quite impossible in other fashion schools is quite normal in Antwerp: every year, some students fail. The bar is kept high, even for students in the last year of their bachelor studies. The highlight of the year is in June, when more than 6,000 people come and see the department's show.

What's rare about this show is that even first-year students are allowed to show their work (making for a long show indeed). For most of the audience, it's more than a show though. It's an event that brings them into a different world: that of creativity, of talent, of daring. Several awards are up for grabs: awards given by shops, magazines or businesses related to fashion, based in Antwerp or Brussels. Sometimes the award involves money, sometimes a trip to New York, or a job... It's an exceptional way for the students to get in touch with the real fashion world. Because the Fashion Department of the Academy of Fine Arts in Antwerp until now opts for a complete immersion into one's own world of creativity and heralds a totally artistic fashion program. Although this approach contributes to their strong image and reputation, it can be a weakness for the students, once they have finished their studies and are confronted with the hard business reality of the fashion world.

After graduation, upcoming designers are not on their own. In the mid-nineties, a few people in Antwerp had a dream: they wanted Antwerp citizens to witness the international emanation of Belgian fashion and to create a fashion platform which all kinds of players could call their own. The not-for-profit association Mode Antwerpen was created in 1997, before changing its name to Flanders Fashion Institute (FFI). From the start, the FFI wanted to promote Belgian fashion, in and outside of Belgium. It seemed logical to search for a location that could host FFI and the fashion department of the academy, as well as a completely new fashion museum, MoMu. Thanks to a funding collaboration between the city and province of Antwerp, Flemish community, Textile Flanders and others, ModeNatie opened its doors in 2002 in the centre of the city, just a stone's throw away from Dries Van Noten's Modepaleis. The building has a fashion tradition: in the nineteenth century, the ground floor was rented to New England, a renowned Belgian fashion house at the time. For the Belgian (and international) audience that likes to come to Antwerp, the ModeNatie has become part of their lifestyle – dynamic, interesting, open minded. MoMu in particular attracts a lot of attention, with exhibitions as diverse as international names (Yamamoto, Madame Grès) to Belgian talents (Veronique Branquinho, Walter Van Beirendonck, Bernhard Willhelm) to more eclectic installations (Black in Fashion, Unravel, Knitwear in Fashion). The FFI became part of the not-for-profit Flanders District of Creativity in 2010 and has continued to help hundreds of start-ups with business plans, mentors, key strategies for international business, job opportunities, etc. What started out as a dream has become a reality. And it doesn't end here. Right now, all players are discussing the possible opening of a House of Fashion.

SUMMARY

It's quite impossible to name everyone that has been involved in Belgian fashion. The truth is that the Belgian fashion business is much more than a bunch of fashion designers. Around Ghent, Antwerp and Brussels, an entire creative ecosystem has emerged, with many fashion graduates moving on to become photographers, make-up artists, journalists, stylists, event organizers and so on. All of them know that becoming "the new Dries Van Noten" does not happen overnight. But they should understand that craftsmanship is important, that staying focused makes all the difference, even in a globalized market with lots of (very big) players. Most of them have one thing in common though: they work like crazy, keeping up the vision and the initial pride that comes with working in this creative business. In a way, that's linked with how the Six started it all. Working their butts off and keeping on track. Never deviating. Never out of control.

REFERENCES

Windels, V. (2001) *Young Belgian Fashion*. Antwerpen: Ludion Publishers.

Windels, V. (2010) *Act(e) on Tim Van Steenbergen*. Antwerpen: Ludion Publishers.

RECOMMENDED

Van Godtsenhoven, K. (2013) De wonderjaren van de Antwerpse 6+1. In: *Mode Antwerpen Academie 50*, Tielt: Lannoo, 65-125.

Heynssens, S. (2013) Tussen Avant-Garde & Traditie. In: *Mode Antwerpen Academie 50*, Tielt: Lannoo, 13-41.

Menkes, S. (2013) De identiteit van de Antwerpse mode. In: *Mode Antwerpen Academie 50*, Tielt: Lannoo, 41-49.

case # 8   Anne Chapelle

Ann Demeulemeester

FASHION MANAGEMENT

"Managing a fashion or creative company often amounts to finding the right balance between emotion and reason"

When fashion designer Ann Demeulemeester announced in late 2013 her departure from the label bearing her name, in an email with a beautiful letter, written by hand, the national and international fashion press went into overdrive. Demeulemeester is one of the famous Antwerp Six and she gained worldwide recognition for her gothic-inspired yet Bohemian style, often in black and white.

Interview by
Trui Moerkerke

Anne Chapelle is the CEO of bvba 32, the company behind Demeulemeester. Via a separate holding companies, Chapelle also has a controlling interest in the company of Haider Ackerman. She also backs Brussels based fashion and costume designer Jean-Paul l'Espagnard. She runs a team of 90 people at bvba 32.

You have built up a reputation as a successful fashion manager. Is there a difference between doing business in fashion and being an entrepreneur in more traditional economic sectors?

If there is any difference at all, it has to be the emotional factor. Fashion is about emotions. Designing is "bringing a human expression into a form"; in our case, clothes. Managing a fashion or creative company often amounts to finding the right balance between emotion and reason. You absolutely have to find that balance to keep your company healthy and to let it grow.

Both Ann Demeulemeester and Haider Ackermann are established names. How would you describe your role in these success stories?

I've always been and had to be the reasonable and social part of the story. This role is not everyone's favourite. But it keeps the company on track.

"Learn to judge the difference between risk and opportunity"

In the mid-nineties, you left your job as an executive in the chemical industry to work with Demeulemeester, who needed someone with business experience. What was going wrong?

It was the usual story of a weak cash flow position. It's a well-known problem. Lots of young companies face this challenge when they start to grow. A weak cash flow position is dangerous for a growing business.

We needed to set up a structure even though the company was very small back then. Once we had found that structure and once we had calculated the budgets without any concessions regarding the quality of our products, the company could make a new start and grow successfully.

What does Demeulemeester's announcement in 2013 mean for the company?

It hasn't changed our way of working. Our principles of quality and sustainable entrepreneurship are still the same. It's a generous act of trust from Ann towards the younger generation in our company. Ann really worked hard to teach them and to pass on her vision. For the younger designers, it's an opportunity to prove themselves. Besides, Ann may have left the company, but it's still bearing her name. (She will definitely follow her pupils with interest.)

We don't think a designer should die before someone can take over. We are all confident about the future, Ann and her husband, too. We believe our fashion house is a solid one worth keeping alive. I am proud of the beautiful story we could write. And I am sure this is not the last chapter. This isn't the end; I see an interesting future ahead.

Why did you create a new company for Haider Ackermann?

When your daughter is ready for the big world, you have to be able to let her go. Also, emotionally Haider's story differs from ADM's story, which implies another approach. Haider works with different people, who look at fashion with a different set of eyes and from a different perspective. All of this warranted a separate company. Once they achieve enough financial independence the sky is the limit for further growth.

You are also supporting Jean-Paul L'Espagnard and have been described as a "Style Angel". What exactly is your role and what are you trying to achieve?

I love being a mentor for up-and-coming talent. I want to help talented people find their strengths and weaknesses, so they reach a state where they know what they want and have the skills and the strength to strive to achieve that.

What would be your advice for young beginners?

Don't rush into an independent position. Work for an established company for a while, observe, learn how the business and management side of things work before you start your own business.

Learn to judge the difference between risk and opportunity. Develop a realistic plan of action and once you have such a plan, reassess your ideals. Do you still want to get into this tough and unforbidding game? If you can't translate your dream into a realistic business plan, you probably shouldn't get into the fashion business.

What is the importance of pre-collections?

You have to accept that they are a commercial reality. They are the answer to a market that wants to offer new products at an ever increasing rate. Often they do not reflect any new visions or ideas: they are market-driven, not creativity-driven.

Ann Demeulemeester
SS 13

Ann Demeulemeester
FW 87-98

Haider Ackermann
SS 14

case # 8   Anne Chapelle

NOTES

1   The term *haute couture* is protected by French law and by the *Chambre Syndicale de la Couture Parisienne*. For this reason, the term "couture" is often used to identify collections that have emerged in a manner similar to that of the *haute couture* collections, but that have not been recognised by the Chambre Syndicale. The rules of the *Chambre Syndicale* concerning couture houses are as follows: the house must present a collection of at least 35 pieces, consisting of day and evening wear, twice each year, one for spring/summer (January) and one for autumn/winter (August). The collections must include designs tailored for private customers who receive one or more fittings, and the house must have a studio located in Paris with at least 15 full-time equivalent employees (Sterlacci & Arbuckle 2009).

2   In contrast to such customisation, the terms *ready-to-wear* and *prêt-à-porter* refer to garments that are designed for sale through *department stores*, online or through other retail channels. Other terms that are commonly used include "off-the-rack" and "off-the-peg" (Sterlacci & Arbuckle 2009). Over the years, there has been a significant narrowing of meaning, whereby the term "ready-to-wear" is used primarily in the higher price segments.

3   The concepts of "weak" and "strong" ties find their origin in sociology (network theory). Weak ties are relationships that require little interaction, affection and time. Strong ties are relationships with friends and family, where interaction, attention and time are important. The more varied and heterogeneous a network is, the "weaker" the ties are and the more information is available within the network. In networks with "strong ties", the members share a certain social and cultural background, making it harder for the network to access various sources of information and various forms of support.

4   oami.europa.eu/eSearch

5   E.C.J., 16 September 2004, C-404/92, *Nichols plc v Registrar of Trade Marks*, § 30 and 34 (www.curia.eu).

6   E.C.J., 30 March 2006, C-259/04, *Elizabeth Florence Emanual v Continental Shelf 128 Ltd.* (www.curia.eu).

7   www.wipo.int/romarin

8   oami.europa.eu/eSearch

9   www.uspto.gov

10 United States Court of Appeals for the Second Circuit, 5 September 2012, Docket No. 11-3303-cv, *Christian Louboutin S.A., Christian Louboutin L.L.C. and Christian Louboutin v Yves Saint Lautent America Holding Inc., Yves Saint Laurent S.A.S. and Yves Saint Laurent America Inc.*

11 oami.europe.eu/ohimportal/en

12 oami.europe.eu/ohimportal/en/route-to-registration

13 www.wipo.int/classifications/nice/en

14 www.wipo.int

15 www.wipo.int/madrid/en

16 Art. 10 of Directive 2008/95/EC of the European Parliament and of the Council of 22 October 2008 to approximate the laws of the Member States relating to trade marks and Art. 15 of Council Regulation (EC) No 207/2009 on the Community trade mark.

17 www.icann.org

18 See, for example: www.wipo.int/amc/en/domains

19 For more information on the background of these cases, check: www.wipo.int/amc/en/domains/search/legalindex.jsp

20 Berne Convention for the Protection of Literary and Artistic Works of 9 September 1886 (www.wipo.int/treaties/en/ip/berne/)

21 Art. 7 of the Berne Convention.

22 Gerechtshof 's Gravenhage, 19 april 2011, Case 200.048.312/01, *H&M Hennes & Mauritz AB and H&M Hennes & Mauritz Netherlands B.V. v G-Star International B.V.* (uitspraken.rechtspraak.nl/inziendocument?id=ECLI:NL:GH SGR:2011:BQ2113)

23 www.boip.int/wps/portal/site/trademarks/search

24 www.boip.int/wps/portal/site/trademarks/search

25 oami.europa.eu/eSearch

26 oami.europa.eu/eSearch

27 oami.europe.eu/ohimportal/en/rcd-route-to-registration

28 www.wipo.int/classifications/nivilo/locarno

29 Art. 11 of Council Regulation (EC) No 6/2002 of 12 December 2001 on Community designs.

30 Regulation (EU) No 1257/2012 of the European Parliament and of the Council of 17 December 2012 implementing enhanced cooperation in the area of the creation of unitary patent protection and Council Regulation (EU) No 1260/ 2012 of 17 December 2012 implementing enhanced cooperation in the area of the creation of unitary patent protection with regard to the applicable translation arrangements.

31 www.epo.org

32 www.wipo.int/pct/en

33 www.ilo.org

34 www.iccwbo.org

35 Art. 17 of Council Directive 86/653/EEC of 18 December 1986 on the coordination of the laws of the Member States relating to self-employed commercial agents.

36 See, for example: Directive 2000/31/EC of the European Parliament and of the Council of 8 June 2000 on certain legal aspects of information society services, in particular electronic commerce, in the Internal Market.

37 CultuurInvest is part of PMV nv and invests in creative businesses through subordinated loans and/or participations in the capital http://www.pmv.eu/en/services/cultuurinvest.

INDEX

INDEX

AUTHORS

JENNIFER CRAIK | Jennifer Craik is Research Professor in the School of Fashion and Textiles at RMIT University, Melbourne; and Commissioning Editor of the Australia New Zealand School of Government ANU E-Press series, Canberra, Australia. Research interests include interdisciplinary approaches to the study of fashion and dress, contemporary culture, cultural and media policy, cultural tourism, and arts funding. Publications include *The Face of Fashion* (1993), *Uniforms Exposed* (2005), and *Fashion. The Key Concepts* (2009).

MARIE DELBEKE | After a bachelor in Science of Education, a Fashion Marketing and Communication degree at Instituto Europeo di Design in Barcelona and a Master degree in Business Economics at the University of Louvain, Marie Delbeke started her career as project manager for the creative industries at Flanders District of Creativity. Later, as a project manager for Flanders Fashion Institute, she advised fashion designers launching their business, while setting up numerous projects aiming to create opportunities for designer as to increase their chance to be successful in the business. At this moment she is employed at PMV/CultuurInvest, a Flemish invesment fund – amongst other sector – investing in the creative industries.

MARLIES DEMOL | Marlies Demol holds a master's degree in Literature and Linguistics (UA & UvA) and Cultural Management (UA). She works as a researcher at the Competence Center Creative Industries where she mainly works on research projects for Flanders District of Creativity. Her research topics include the internationalization of fashion brands and the economic impact of the creative industries.

DIETER GEERNAERT | Dieter Geernaert is a lawyer and partner at the Belgian law firm Praetica (www.praetica.com). He focuses on intellectual property law, commercial law and unfair commercial practices, often for clients in the creative industry. Dieter Geernaert has been appointed as arbitrator to rule on ".be" domain name disputes. He is a member of the Benelux Association for Trade mark and Design Law (BMM) and the Belgian National Association for the Protection of Industrial Property (BNVBIE). He was also a guest lecturer in copyright and media law at the VLEKHO Business School (Brussels).

TRUI MOERKERKE | Trui Moerkerke has a BA Law, MSc Communication. Was a journalist, fashion editor and later editor in chief of Knack Weekend, the leading weekly on fashion and lifestyle in Flanders, Belgium. She is currently the communication manager of Flanders DC, the Flemish organisation for entrepreneurial creativity. Flanders Fashion Institute is a part of Flanders DC.

KARINNA NOBBS | Karinna Nobbs has a passion for the aesthetic aspects of fashion brand management and was a visual merchandiser by trade before entering academia in 2001. She has industrial experience with a variety of international brands at differing levels of the market place including United Colours of Benetton, Kookai, House of Fraser and Ralph Lauren. Karinna has operated in the fields of fashion retail, visual merchandising and PR. In her lecturing career she teaches fashion marketing and retail brand strategy at both undergraduate and postgraduate level and she has also delivered Executive Education Courses in the same areas. Furthermore, Karinna has an extensive conference publication record with appearances at over 60 global academic and industry events. Whilst in academia Karinna has also developed her role as a consultant through advising SME fashion brands on their marketing and communication strategies, with a specific attention for visual merchandising and social media.

FRANCESCA ROMANA RINALDI | Francesca Romana Rinaldi is Director of the Master in Retail and Brand Experience Management of Milano Fashion Institute (consortium of Bocconi University, Cattolica University and Politecnico di Milano), she teaches fashion management at Bocconi University and MAFED at SDA Bocconi School of Management. Her main research and executive consulting focus is on fashion brand management, management of sustainable fashion and digital strategies in fashion. She has published articles in international magazines such as: "Getting the E-Shopping experience right: Tips and Traps in multi-channel distribution", Detail on Retail, June 2012. In 2013 she wrote a book on management of Corporate Social Responsibility in fashion: "L'impresa moda responsabile" ("The responsible fashion company", Egea). She is also journalist and creator of the blog Bio-Fashion on sustainable fashion and lifestyle (http://bio-fashion.blogspot.com).

ANNICK SCHRAMME | Annick Schramme is full professor and academic coordinator of the master in Cultural Management at the University of Antwerp and the Competence Center Management, Culture & Policy (Faculty of Applied Economics). She is also Academic Director of the Competence Center Creative Industries at the Antwerp Management School in cooperation with Flanders DC. Over the last years she published about Fashion Management, arts policy, international cultural policy, heritage management, creative industries and cultural entrepreneurship. From 2004 until 2013 she was also advisor-expert of the Vice-Mayor for Culture and Tourism of the City of Antwerp. Finally she is member of several boards of cultural organizations and advisory committees in Flanders and the Netherlands. In 2013 she became the president of ENCATC, the European Network on Cultural Management education.

JOKE SCHRAUWEN | Joke Schrauwen holds a Master degrees in Art Sciences (2005, Ghent University) and Cultural Management (2010, University of Antwerp). Since August 2010, she has been working as a researcher at the University of Antwerp/Antwerp Management School. She has completed several studies on a wide variety of topics in creative and cultural field, including the fashion industry.

WALTER VAN ANDEL | Walter van Andel is a researcher on entrepreneurship and creativity at Antwerp Management School, Belgium. His research focuses on management practices, innovation, business models, and entrepreneurial growth at small and medium-sized creative enterprises. In 2012 he co-authored the book "Creative Jumpers" in which business models for fast growing companies in creative industries are examined. Before joining Antwerp Management School, Walter worked as researcher and consultant in the Netherlands, Mexico and the United States.

RAF VERMEIREN | Raf Vermeiren has 17 years of experience in coaching and investing in Entrepreneurs, with a special interest in Creative Entrepreneurs. The first 6 years of his career he was financial consultant, the past 11 years he was an investor. Today he is financial director of Sputnik Media, a fast growing tv-production company with diversification to web & mobile. Before that he was co-developer and fund manager of CultuurInvest, a pioneering investment fund in the creative industries. He worked closely with music labels, fashion designers, product designers, tv producers, theatre-producers, book publishers, PR-agencies, ... The past years he screened more than 120 business plans and coached aprox. 20 companies regarding Business Plan, Cash flow Plan, Creative financial reporting, Investor relations, ...

VEERLE WINDELS | Veerle Windels is a freelance fashion journalist based in Belgium, where her opinion pieces can regularly be read in the daily newspaper *De Standaard*. She published *Young Belgian Fashion* (featuring 10 young fashion designers: 2001), *Werken met woorden* (bringing together her best interviews) and *Act(e)*, a monograph on Tim Van Steenbergen. She also teaches costume history at the fashion department of the Ghent Academy.

AUTHORS

D/2014/45/388 – ISBN 978 94 014 1238 4 – NUR 801

Book design: Lodewijk Joye | www.lodewijkjoye.be

Photo credits | P 12: © Ann Demeulemeester / P 24: © Hidemi Iizuka / P 46, 49, 50 © Etienne Tordoir / P 70: © Natan
P 72, 74: © Etienne Tordoir / P 92, 99, 100: © Shoji Fujii / P 120: © Tomas Vandecasteele / P 123: © Tomas Vandecasteele,
upper right: © Koen Broos, lower right: © Diego Franssens / P 124: Tomas Vandecasteele / P 154, 156, 158 © Cici Olsen
P 180, 182, 184: © Essentiel / P 208, 211, 212: © Hidemi Iizuka / P 219: © Roger Dyckmans / P 226: © Ann Demeulemeester
P229: © Ann Demeulemeester, upper right: © Haider Ackermann

Lannoo Campus Publishers
Erasme Ruelensvest 179, box 101
3001 Leuven
Belgium

WWW.LANNOOCAMPUS.BE